The Great Wall of China

Margaret Clyne and Rachel Griffiths

CELEBRATION PRESS
Pearson Learning Group

Map of the World

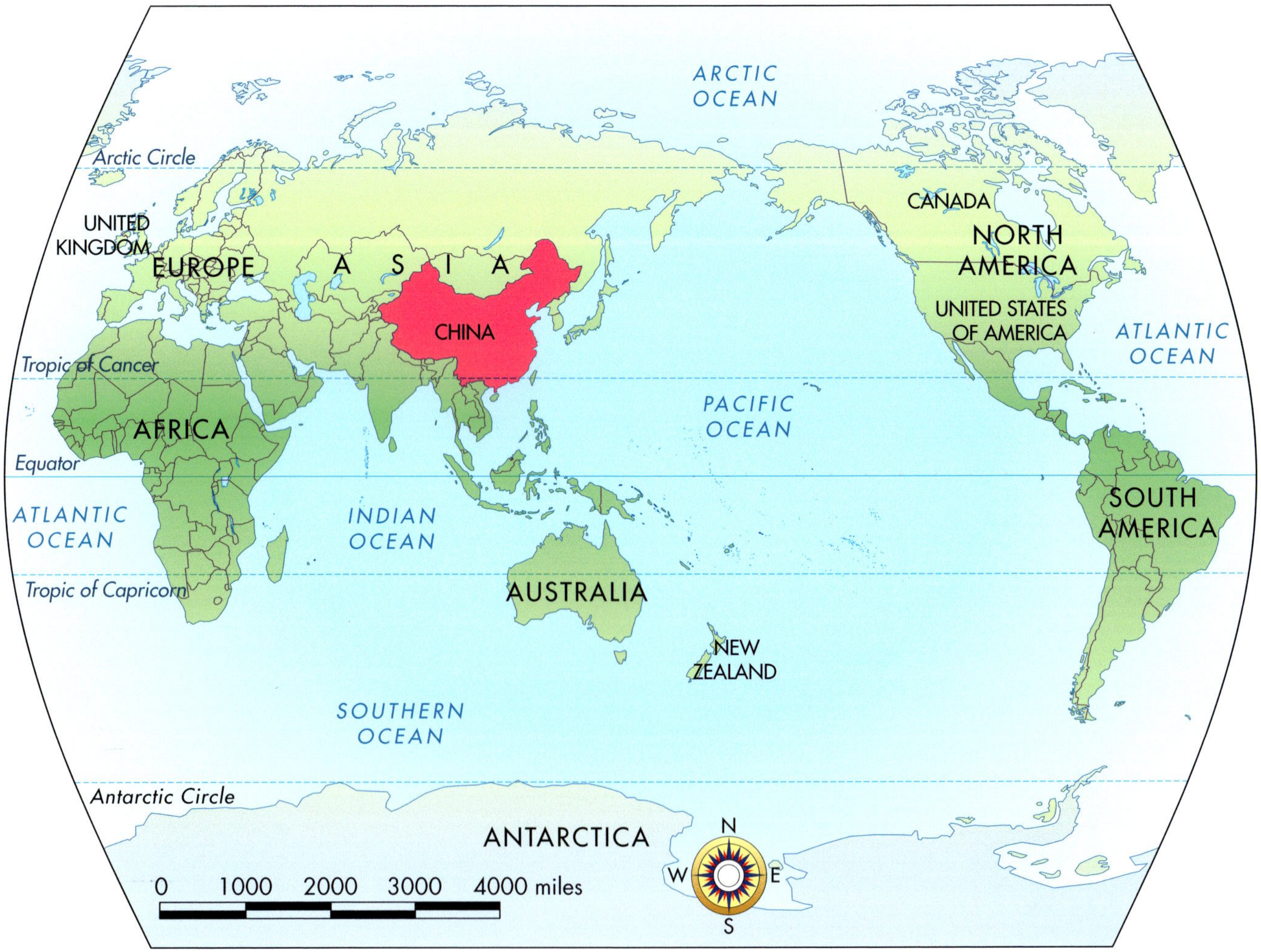

Contents

An Ancient Wonder of the World

The Great Wall

The Great Wall of China is one of the ancient wonders of the world. Its original name is the Long Wall. Its **immense** size and length and its long history make it very interesting. Seen from the air, it looks like a giant roller coaster, as it winds its way through deserts, grasslands and valleys, and over mountains.

The Great Wall stretches from Shanhaiguan **Pass**, in the east of China, to Jiayuguan Pass in the west. It is approximately 4,500 miles long.

The Great Wall varies in height and width from place to place. It stands approximately 23 to 43 feet high, and is 13 to 43 feet wide.

Shanhaiguan Pass, at the eastern end of the Great Wall

Jiayuguan Pass, at the western end of the Great Wall

Why Was the Long Wall Built?

Invaders from Mongolia, in the North

In ancient times, the people who lived in the northern parts of China were often raided by fierce groups coming from farther north. The northern Chinese people wanted to protect themselves from such attacks. Small walls and protective mounds were **erected** in around the 600s B.C. to keep out the attackers.

These small protective walls and mounds erected by the northern Chinese were in fact the beginnings of what we now call the Great Wall.

The majestic Great Wall grew out of a number of mounds and protective walls.

Emperor Shi Huangdi's Great Idea

Emperor Qin Shi Huangdi

More than 2,200 years ago in around 220 B.C., Shi Huangdi, the first emperor of the Qin **dynasty**, decided to connect the protective mounds and small walls that were already standing. He wanted to create one huge, solid wall that would protect northern Chinese borders from further invasion.

What is a Dynasty?

A long time ago, China was ruled by royal families. Each ruling family was called a dynasty. The head of a dynasty is the emperor.

At the time the Great Wall of China was built, China was ruled by the Qin dynasty. The king of the Qin dynasty took the name *Shi Huangdi*, which means "first emperor".

China, at this time, was made up of many states. Shi Huangdi conquered these states and unified China. However, the Qin dynasty ruled China for only fifteen years.

The imperial palace, in the grand Forbidden City in Beijing, was built in the early 1400s by Yong Le, the third emperor of the Ming dynasty, and has more than 900 rooms.

Chinese Peasants Build the Long Wall

Emperor Shi Huangdi forced thousands of peasants to build the wall. More than half a million Chinese peasants marched north to do this unpaid, harsh labor. They built the whole wall entirely by hand. During this time, the wall was still called the Long Wall.

The Long Graveyard

The Emperor's armies defended the northern boundaries of China. They also watched the workers to ensure that they kept working. Those who did not work hard enough were punished. Those who ran away were caught and punished also. The Great Wall has been called the "Long Graveyard" because many people died while building it.

The Long Wall was built of rock, earth, bricks, wood, and lime. The workers formed a human chain, passing the building materials from one person to the next. Sometimes, handcarts, goats, and donkeys were used to move the materials. The workers built watchtowers, gates, gatehouses, and arrow towers.

Chinese workers building the wall

Guards at the Long Wall

Soldiers were **stationed** as guards along the Long Wall to keep watch for northern invaders. The watchtowers, which looked something like **turrets** on a castle, were 43 feet high and 330–655 feet apart.

There were two types of watchtowers: one type was the *qiangtai* (wall towers), which were built in the wall, or jutted out of its side. The other was the *ditai* (enemy towers), which contained the living quarters and storage for army equipment.

Each watchtower was built so that the guards could see the watchtower on either side of them. Soldiers wore armor and helmets, and they had crossbows.

A guard at a watchtower, with a crossbow

Watchtower on the Great Wall

View from a watchtower at Simitai

The arrangement of the watchtowers allowed the guards to see invaders approaching from a distance. Each guard had a flag or torch to use for signaling. The guards would immediately send warnings, such as smoke signals, as soon as they saw an enemy. This system made it very difficult for invaders to carry out a surprise attack.

Life on the Long Wall

The interior of a watch tower, showing the soldiers' living quarters

Though the Great Wall is world famous, the fact that people once lived on and in it is not well known. On the lower level of the watchtowers, there were rooms for the soldiers as well as stables, sheep pens, and storage areas for food and other provisions.

Food, water, and supplies were brought to the Long Wall over the mountains and along narrow paths. To bring the supplies to the top of the Long Wall, there were tall posts erected on the Chinese side of the wall. Ropes were slung over these posts, and baskets filled with supplies were hauled up by hand.

Supplies being hauled to the top of the wall

What Makes a Great Wall?

This section of the wall is made from bricks and paved with stone.

The Long Wall was made of building materials, such as stone and earth, and natural structures, such as mountains, were also used.

The materials that were used depended on what was available nearby. Some parts of the wall were made from earth, twigs, and stones that were packed very tightly inside wooden frames. The earth, twigs, and stones were pounded down until they were solid.

Sundried bricks, called adobe, as well as rocks were used. In the western deserts, where it is very hot and dry, adobe and tightly packed earth were commonly used on the wall.

Some parts of the wall used part of the natural landscape, such as cliffs, gorges, and mountains. Sometimes, river dikes that were already in place took the place of a section of the wall.

The mountains sometimes became a part of the Long Wall.

Preserving the Great Wall

Today, not much of Emperor Shi Huangdi's original wall exists. Most of his wall fell to ruins. The Han dynasty (206 B.C.–A.D. 220) continued building the Great Wall. Under this dynasty, the wall reached a total length of around 6,200 miles.

The Great Wall as it stands now was mainly built by China's Ming dynasty between the years 1368 and 1644. Again it was built for protection from the northern groups, and the building involved strengthening and adding to some existing walls that had fallen into disrepair. The wall built during the Ming dynasty, however, followed a different route from the original wall. By the sixteenth century, stone was the main material used to build the wall.

Creators of the Great Wall

The Long Wall, or Great Wall as it is now known, is the work of three dynasties—the Qin, the Han, and the Ming.

Emperor Hong Wu was the founder of the Ming dynasty.

Restoration work on the Great Wall

The Great Wall is recognized as one of the great wonders of the world. However, that recognition has not protected it from damage. Roadways have been cut through, at several points, and many parts have been neglected over many hundreds of years.

In the 1950s, some **restoration** of the wall took place. Later, between about 1966 and 1976, many parts of the wall were torn down. At this time, the Chinese government wanted to destroy anything linked to traditional culture. Then, in the 1980s, people began to restore the Great Wall to its earlier condition. By the 1990s, the eastern section of the wall around Shanhaiguan Pass had been rebuilt. Today, **preservation** of the Great Wall is important.

The Great Wall Today

Tourists on the Great Wall

The Great Wall today is no longer a continuous stretch of wall. It has become a series of walls that has big gaps between its sections. Many parts of the wall are in ruins. It is a **tremendous** tourist attraction.

The section of The Great Wall at Badaling, in Nankou, has become a popular tourist attraction, drawing people from all over the world. This part of the wall is about 50 miles north of Beijing. There is a special train service from Beijing to Badaling, which runs daily in the summer months.

The eastern end and the western end of the wall are also very popular.

The Great Wall extends beyond Shanhaiguan Pass and meets the sea at a place called Dragon's Head.

Facts About the Great Wall of China

- The Great Wall of China is the longest structure ever built and one of China's greatest tourist attractions.
- The Great Wall was built by hand.
- The Great Wall is as long as the distance between the North Pole and Miami, Florida, in the United States.
- Three dynasties were responsible for erecting the Great Wall, spanning a period of almost 2,000 years.
- Many of the original enemy towers of the Great Wall still exist in the northern part of Hebei Province, 170 miles southwest of Beijing.

- The Long Wall was an important and safe route for the caravans that traveled the Silk Road. These caravans carried goods for trading.
- The Great Wall was listed as a World Heritage site in 1987 by UNESCO (the United Nations Educational Scientific and Cultural Organization).

Glossary

dynasty	a series of rulers who are from the same family
erected	built
immense	very big
pass	a road cutting through mountains
preservation	keep something in a good condition
restoration	repair something to bring it back to its original condition
stationed	under orders to work in a place for a period of time
tremendous	very large; great
turrets	small towers at the top of a building

Index

Enjoying Cichlids

ENJOYING CICHLIDS

Ad Konings (Editor)

with contributions
by:
Kaj Andersen
Mary Bailey
Kjell Fohrman
Lasse Forsberg
Charley Grimes
Willem Heijns
Ad Konings
Gary Kratochvil
Dirk Ottlik
Ole Seehausen
Christian Simon
Frank Warzel

CICHLID PRESS

Photo cover: *Labidochromis caeruleus* at Mbowe Island, Lake Malawi;
frontispiece: a pair of *Microgeophagus ramirezi* guarding their fry;
title page: a male *Neolamprologus leleupi* from Lake Tanganyika;
facing page: a breeding pair of *Nandopsis* sp. "Labridens White" in their natural environment in Río Puente de Dios, Mexico.

ISBN 3-928457-17-9

Printed in Germany

Contents

Introduction

After more than 20 years of keeping cichlids in aquaria and after visiting many different cichlid habitats in Africa as well as in Central America, I have acquired the knowledge of how cichlids live in the wild and also how we aquarists can imitate that natural environment in our homes. This approach has proved to be successful in keeping and breeding cichlids. Additionally, visits to experienced cichlid enthusiasts in more than 15 different countries have yielded a large number of little tricks which can be used to make cichlid keeping more enjoyable. Over the years I have tested many different techniques and procedures and have selected those which I use myself and which I know will be applicable under all different circumstances encountered in keeping cichlids.

The field of cichlid keeping is so large and the species are so many that it is almost impossible to be specialised in all the different areas. My specialisation is limited to Malawi and Tanganyika cichlids and for this reason I will discuss only the cichlids from these regions. Other specialists, who have much experience with other groups like American and West African cichlids, will inform you about their knowledge of keeping cichlids.

This book is not intended to be a complete reference guide for all the possible filtration systems, all the different types of food one can obtain, or all the types of aquaria one can build; it is a book written by specialists who have long standing experience in keeping their cichlids and who know the natural habitats in which their fishes live. They inform you how **they** keep **their** fishes in an optimal condition and not about all the possible ways you **can** keep cichlids. The information given in this book is thus not the only way you can keep cichlids successfully but how experts have kept their fishes for many years and are still very much enjoying them.

The idea of this book is to provide the aquarist with a way of keeping cichlids successfully. When properly quartered cichlids are not likely to contract diseases. This is the main reason why we will not go into detail about all the various diseases. We will, however, discuss some medical treatments for use in case a fish is wounded or when we want to acclimatise wild caught cichlids to our tanks.

Over the years it has become apparent that most cichlid aquarists direct their attention to a particular group, the one they enjoy most. This is the reason that I have divided the main part of the book into several groups, each one dealing with cichlids from one area. Each group is again subdivided into smaller groups containing species with similar aquarium requirements. For each such group of species useful information is given about their behaviour in the wild and in the aquarium, about their food requirements, and about the best way to breed them.

When the water and habitat requirements of cichlids originating from different areas are similar there is no objection to keeping these cichlids together in the same aquarium; it is a matter of personal taste. It is also important to take into consideration compatibility of temperament and behaviour.

I hope this book will provide its readers with a guide to the essentials of enjoyable cichlid keeping.

Ad Konings

The aquarium

by Ad Konings

Cichlids need their own aquarium, or at least a tank in which they are the dominant fishes. More often than not the size of the aquarium appears to be dependent on the available space in the room it is going to be placed in. When choosing the size of the aquarium it should be considered that the larger the better. A large aquarium is easier to maintain than a small one. The larger volume of water has a much greater buffering capacity so that fluctuations in the water quality and chemistry take place at a slower rate.

The position of the aquarium

It is recommended that the aquarium be placed in the room where you relax after a day's work. A part of the seating could be placed in front of the aquarium where one can relax and watch the fishes. Children are particularly attracted to cichlids, especially to fry guarding pairs. When siting a large aquarium (larger than 600 litres) it is advisable to position it at a comparatively low level (30-50 cm rather than the standard 90 cm). It will then not seem to dominate or shrink the interior of the room. Moreover such aquaria are usually populated with cichlids larger than 8 cm in length, which can be comfortably observed while sitting a metre or so away. Well, and then you can take an even larger aquarium....

The aquarium should not receive direct sunlight, at least not at midday, or the algal growth on the glass may call for a daily clean-up. Daylight falling in through the back of the aquarium should always be prevented (see background, page 13).

Insulation

Conserving water and energy is a responsibility many of us have learned to live with. Aquarists should not be ignorant of this principle. It saves water and electricity and, of course, money in your wallet. Two simple

things should be done to drastically reduce the water and energy consumption of an aquarium. One is to cover the tank with glass plates or with other, clear material. This prevents evaporation. It is not so much the loss of water but more the loss of heat caused by evaporating water. The other thing to do is to insulate the aquarium unless it is placed in a special fish room which is being maintained at a constant temperature. In the latter case the room should be insulated.

Complete insulation is not possible and also not necessary. Dramatic heat conservation can be achieved by placing 4-cm thick Styrofoam plates around the aquarium. First of all the tank is placed on Styrofoam, then the back and the closed end(s) are insulated. Most of the heat, however, dissipates from the top of the aquarium and therefore the canopy should be insulated as well.

Facing page: A well-planted aquarium with Malawi cichlids. Both short sides of the aquarium have been covered in order to give its inhabitants ample hiding places.
Photo top: A small aquarium can be integrated in a book case but care should be taken that possible leakage cannot damage valuables stowed beneath. Furthermore an easy access to the aquarium should be provided.
Photo right: A heated indoor pond can be stocked with cichlids as well. The disadvantage of such a construction is that the pond should be covered every night otherwise the tremendous evaporation may damage the interior of the room.

Custom made aquarium hoods are easily insulated on the inside but most types which are bought with the tank are not.

Light

In aquaria without natural water plants the light is not an important factor. The cichlids show a better colour and probably feel better when the light is somewhat subdued. And as long as we can see what is going on in the aquarium more than one fluorescent tube —any type you wish— is not necessary.

Water plants need more light, especially when the aquarium is deeper than 50 cm. Additional light is mandatory to keep the plants growing. Two to three tubes over the entire length are needed for 50 cm deep aquaria. When a strong light is necessary it is not advisable to have a very light-coloured gravel on the bottom. This is in any case unnatural, but the main reason is that cichlids will not show their best colours when kept in such tanks.

One of the mistakes one can make concerning light in the aquarium is to leave it on day and night. Cichlids need a resting period and under natural circumstances this takes place at night. If the light is left on during the night the fishes are unable to rest and become listless after a while. Most males lose their colour and their interest in females. Cichlids need at least 8 hours of darkness per day in order to keep them healthy. The light can best be controlled via a time switch, so it is not forgotten.

Decoration

Rocks and other heavy materials should be laced on the bottom or on the plates of the dergravel filter before sand or gravel is ed to the aquarium. This prevents a col- caused by cichlids digging the sand out from beneath the rocks. Large rocks are best placed on a thin sheet of Styrofoam to protect the bottom glass. It is not the weight of the rock but a possible concentration of it on a few sand grains that may crack the glass.

To make an aquarium appear bigger large rocks should be used, not fist-size stones. Very large rocks are better made of ceramic —see Gerard Tijsseling's method in *The Cichlids Yearbook* vol. 1— because they are more easily handled. The largest rock can be placed solitary, other rocks are piled to create some caves. Large flowerpots can be hidden by stones and serve as caves into which the cichlids may retreat.

After the background (see page 13) has been fixed and the heavy items have been positioned, the bottom is covered with coarse sand or fine gravel. The substrate should not be white, such as coral sand, nor should it contain peat moss or garden soil. The safest way is to buy the sand in a pet shop. Sand collected at a garden centre or along the road may suffice as well but must be properly cleaned before it can be used in an aquarium. It is rinsed under running water until no dirt is washed from it. Then boiling hot water is used to rinse the sand three times. This is meant to kill off parasites that may infect the aquarium inhabitants at a later stage. It is prudent to wash gravel bought in a pet shop as well. When genuine water plants are introduced into the tank it is recommended that fine gravel be used instead of sand unless only *Ceratophyllum demersum* is used.

Rocks, sand and gravel are easily disinfected by cleaning them in boiling hot water, but wood is different. Bog wood, drift wood and any other types of wood (except petrified wood) need to be soaked and cured before they can be used as decoration in an aquarium. Do not use uncured drift wood collected from a stream. It may contain freshwater parasites which can infect the cichlids in the aquarium. Rinsing such wood with hot water is not sufficient to kill off the parasites hiding in it. The wood should be submerged in a strong sodium carbonate solution (at least 1 kg soda per 50 litres of water) for at least one week. Then the wood is cleaned with a stiff brush and soaked in a few baths of clean water to wash out the soda, which may take another week. The wood should not have a slippery surface when it is placed in the aquarium. Soda is alkaline and such wood should not immediately be used in aquaria with soft, acidic water. In such cases it is better to purchase the wood in a pet shop or use pieces that have been cured a long time ago. Bog wood should be soaked for the same length of time to remove tannins if it is to be used in aquaria with alkaline water. Seashore driftwood should be soaked to remove salt before use with acid-loving cichlids. All wood should be well and truly "dead" as green wood may contain toxins.

Plants

Although water plants are almost a must in an aquarium, in the wild they are rarely seen in most cichlid biotopes. In the East African rift lakes water plants are found only in muddy bays in very shallow water. *Vallisneria* and a few *Potamogeton* species are the main plants found in these lakes. *Ceratophyllum*-like water plants are found in the swamps surrounding these lakes but not in the lakes themselves. None of the rift lake cichlids in captivity has been collected in such swampy areas. In West Africa some streams are completely vegetated but these are an exception. Most waters inhabited by cichlids are rather bare. The same is true for South American streams. Here clear water streams often contain insufficient minerals to support true aquatic plants. Other streams are too muddy to let the light penetrate to their bottoms. Of course there are plenty of water plants but they usually have floating or emerse leaves. In Central America true aquatic plants are restricted to a few species and these —usually water lilies— are found mainly in springs where the water is clear year-round. In most streams and rivers for at least six months of the year the water is too clouded to support submerged plant life. The clear mountain streams, which contain clear water throughout the year, are too cold for cichlids.

A "natural" cichlid aquarium should thus not contain water plants. On the other hand water plants are a very welcome decoration which gives a pleasantly contrasting colour to the aquarium.

Not all cichlids can be housed in a planted aquarium and not all water plants can be kept with cichlids. There are only a few cichlid species that eat the plants in an aquarium, the majority do not regard plants as part of their menu. Several large cichlasomine cichlids from Central America and *Uaru* from South America eat water plants, even those with relatively hard leaves. *Limnotilapia dardennii* and *Oreochromis tanganicae* from Lake Tanganyika, and *Protomelas similis* from Lake Malawi are the only species known from these rift lakes to feed on water plants. Apart from a few tilapias all other cichlids can be housed in a planted aquarium without fear that the plants will be eaten.

Unfortunately it is not only the feeding habits of some cichlids that may influence the use of plants as a decoration in an aquarium, but also their excavating efforts. Many cichlids excavate caves under the rocks and move a considerable amount of sand or gravel. When plants are present in their projected nest they are uprooted and removed. Some plants can be grown on rocks which have a coarse structure (e.g. lava stone, flagstone) and positioned away from the bottom. However, when such plants are used in an aquarium with sand on the bottom, their well-being is again jeopardised by sand-sifting or excavating cichlids who drop sand on the leaves and prevent the light from "feeding" the plant. In the latter case fine gravel, which is not as easily displaced by the tank inhabitants as sand and which falls off more readily, is recommended rather then sand, or else plastic plants should replace the real ones. Plants with soft leaves should be avoided at all times.

Many South American and West African cichlids can be housed with many different water plants but for the East African and Central American cichlids only a few "types" are recommended. These are *Ceratophyllum, Anubias*, *Microsorium pteropus* (Java Fern), and *Vallisneria* species. These water plants are tolerant of different water conditions, grow fast, and are very decorative. *Ceratophyllum* has no roots and therefore should not be planted in the usual way. Several stems are bundled together around a small pebble (the weight) and held with a rubber band. Such bundles can be placed at any site in the aquarium —the rubber band should not be visible, of course. When a small *Anubias* is held to a rock with a rubber band it will attach its roots to the surface of the rock within two weeks. After a month the rubber band can be removed and the rock, with plant, placed at the desired spot.

The roots of the plants growing in the substrate of a cichlid aquarium may need to be protected against the digging activities of the tank's inhabitants. It is not recommended that the roots be put without protection in the bottom of a cichlid aquarium unless it is to contain only species with minimal digging proclivities, e.g. Discus, Angels, soft water dwarfs. If plants are

Vallisneria beds can be protected against uprooting by placing small stones around the group. Although in nature plants are not common in typical cichlid habitats, they are a much used addition to the aquarium decor.

to grow in the bottom, only gravel —a grade of 1 to 3 mm is ideal— can be used with success. Many of the available water plants are grown in small plastic pots with a spongy material in which the roots are anchored. Leave the plants in these small containers and place these in small groups or solitary in the gravel. Small pebbles or larger stones, depending on the size of the tank's inhabitants and that of the plant, are placed around each group to avoid digging and uprooting. These pebbles also hide the plastic pots from view.

It is also a very good idea, if not using pots, to let the plants establish for two to four weeks, or till new growth shows, before adding the fishes.

The background

The most important part of the decoration is the background. Unfortunately too few aquarists realise that there is a tremendous difference between an aquarium with a background and one without. A background is not used just because it looks better than the wallpaper shining through a heavily reflecting rear glass —although this would often be reason enough. It is recommended that at least one of the short sides of the aquarium be covered as well.

Cichlids, in common with many other fishes, see through the glass and see what is happening in the room in which the aquarium is placed. Aquaria are placed —should be placed— at a quiet spot in the house or office. Shadows of people walking by the aquarium more often than not frighten the inhabitants. Their natural reaction is to immediately hide in the darkest cave they can find. When light is not prevented from falling in on all sides of the aquarium, there is no dark shelter in the tank. This means that in such aquaria the fishes have no secure hiding places. Many cichlids inhabiting small pools and streams usually live along the margins, where there is a dark backdrop, often overhung by

Large photo: Sune Holm and Joel Malmström in Sweden made this background using a mould of a section of a rocky mountain. Even close up (small photo) one cannot be convinced that this is an artificial rock. Photos by Vagn PalmHansen.

tree roots and branches, again providing a dark and sheltered habitat.

Males of many different mouthbrooding, rock-dwelling, cichlids have very conspicuous colours. These colours are meant to attract females to the territory and to keep competitors at bay. When conspecifics are able to see the conspicuous colours of the male then predators can as well, and this is the reason why territorial males are much shyer than females; they *know* they are conspicuous. The only reason they can be territorial and have eye-catching coloration is the knowledge that they can retreat into their cave at any moment they choose. In aquaria without dark hide-outs such males are not likely to defend a territory and be able to breed nor will they show their best colours.

Sand-dwelling cichlids, on the other hand, flee to deeper water when they are frightened. In the confines of an aquarium, their natural flight reaction is hampered by the limited size of the tank and this must thus be compensated for by providing them with dark corners where they can recover from stress.

Apart from the water the background is the most important element in the aquarium. Moreover it is also the simplest item to provide. From an aesthetic point of view the glass at the back should reflect as little as possible. This means that we can forget about placing photos (of water plants), Styrofoam plates, and other ornamental constructions behind the aquarium unless such decorations are tightly fixed to the glass and no light can intrude between the glass and the background. Two options are recommended and have proven to be successful and durable. The easiest and cheapest way is to paint the glass, on the outside. Of course the paint should adhere to glass but most importantly it should not be of the glossy type. The dried paint should have a matt finish. The type which is used indoors on wall paper or on bare walls is recommended and can be mixed with colorants. It is usually non-toxic when dry. Any other paint could be used but care must be taken to cure it for at least one week in a warm environment, but not in a room where aquaria are already installed. Also the painting should take place away from live fish. Of course you can paint scenery but in the long run a plain colour is most satisfying. The colour should be medium-dark; green, red-brown or grey are best. When daylight reaches into the tank there still will be some reflection from the painted back glass.

The second and best type of background is placed inside the tank. It must be made of non-toxic, inert, material which lasts, submerged, at least ten years. If using any form of plastic great care must be taken that it is "aquarium grade". Some (usually cheaper) types contain toxins: do not use any plastic which has a taste when licked. "Food quality" plastics are safe to use. Plates of hard polyurethane (PUR) are available in some pet shops or at plant and flower decorating stores. They are very hard, durable and have some colorant included giving a neutral and inconspicuous background. A polyurethane plate can be glued with silicone to the glass.

Silicone, once hardened, cannot be removed completely from the glass; a mark will always remain visible. Sometimes an aquarium is turned around especially when the front glass is all scratched. When this is anticipated the background can be held in place by a thick (at least 6 mm) glass bar glued along the back part of the tank just a little above the water level. (Many types of aquaria already have stabilising glass strips glued at the water line.) On the bottom glass a thick glass strip is glued parallel to the back pane leaving enough room to fit the background between this strip and the back. It is meant to retain the background against the glass, so small strips would be sufficient. The background could also be held in place by placing a heavy rock against it but you must then remember this when rearranging the decor. The PUR plates can be cut with a sharp knife to fit precisely in their position.

Catching cichlids

Catching cichlids out of a decorated aquarium is not simple and in the case of a few species even impossible. Of course, the ultimate method is to take all the decorations out of the aquarium, lower the water level to about 10 cm and catch the fish with a hand net. This method is applied when all others have failed.

The simplest method does not require anything but two hand nets. At night when the light penetrating the aquarium is almost zero —which is a normal circumstance for an aquarium placed in a room or cellar— all cichlids rest on the substrate. It is important that absolutely no light, including from outside, reaches into the aquarium. When we switch on the lights after the fishes have rested for a few hours, they don't wake up immediately. During this period cichlids don't react to light for at least 5 minutes which gives you ample time to catch the desired individual (especially mouthbrooding females). The evening before catching, the canopy and the glass covers should be removed to give immediate access to the aquarium at night. It is possible to check the location of the desired individual with a small flash light without arousing the resting cichlids. When it is found hidden behind the decor you can gently poke with a stick behind the rockwork. Sleeping cichlids are only "activated" (but not woken up) when they are touched, and this normally results in a sudden dash forward. Only rock-dwelling cichlids rest between the rocks at night, and then not always. All other cichlids are usually found on the sand or outside the rockwork.

The best way to catch sleeping cichlids is by holding a net in front of the fish and another behind it. Using the latter the fish is gently pushed into the net held in front. The fish is **slowly** taken out of the water and **slowly** placed in the other tank or bucket. In most cases the fish still sleeps when released in the other tank, but if it is suddenly taken out of the water it may become very agitated and damage itself when placed in the container. It is not advisable to take the fish out of the net when transferring to another tank, but if it has to be, only with wet hands! Handling a sleeping cichlid, however, is very difficult because it becomes very agitated. It is better to place it in a bucket and let it wake up before touching it. If you have bad results removing mouthbrooding females in this way, i.e. they spit out the eggs frequently, you may use a plastic bowl. The fish is caught as above, the net raised to the surface, and the bowl used to scoop the fish and water out of the net.

If the desired fish is not found the first time the lights can be switched off and the same procedure repeated an hour later. It is advised that the cichlid(s) be caught early at night because early in the morning they seem to have had enough rest and wake up much more quickly.

The second method involves the construction of a trap, but catching should take place during the day. The trap described here was developed by Maarten Meerkerk (Netherlands) and consists of a Plexiglass box with two sliding gates. Several different kinds of traps have been constructed but most of them have only one gate. Although some of them do work, the main problem is that fishes don't like to swim into a closed end box. They feel they are trapped and immediately back out of the device. Meerkerk's trap has no closed end and fishes can swim through the trap. This fact greatly enhances catching rates.

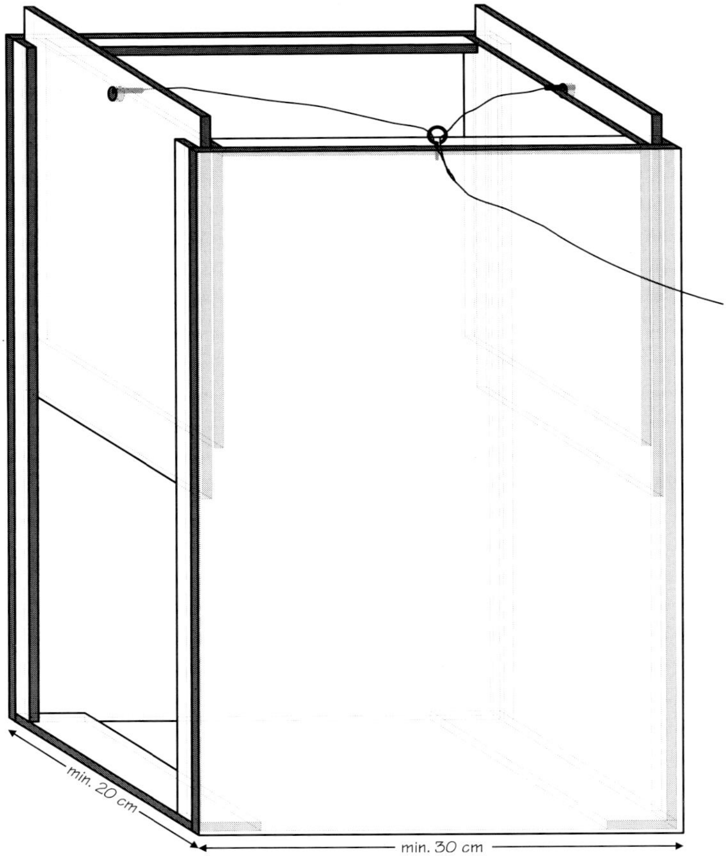

A fish trap designed by M. Meerkerk. Because this trap has two gates there is no dead end in the box which would deter fishes from entering the trap. When the twine is pulled the two gates are disengaged and close the trap. The fishes are taken out of the box with a hand net.

There are of course drawbacks to this catching procedure. Firstly one has to construct the trap and secondly it costs money. It is recommended that Plexiglass or other light and clear material be used to construct the trap. Glass is much too heavy and difficult to handle. The schematic drawing on the left shows how the trap is built. The width of the trap depends on the size of the smallest aquarium it is going to be used in. The height depends on that of the largest aquarium. The trap should stick a few centimetres out of the water when in use. The width and the depth should be as large as possible but such that it can easily be put into the aquarium. The depth depends on the type and amount of decor that has to be removed before the trap can be placed on the gravel in the tank. It is advisable to make it at least 20 cm deep and at least 30 cm wide. The depth is not as important as the width: the wider the better the chance to catch the fish.

The sliding gates are held in the upper (open) position by a pin (a galvanised nail) that is stuck through the hole in the gates and rests on the frame of the box. The two pins are tied to a thin thread (Nylon fishing line would be ideal) which leads through a small eyelet. The other end of the line, which is several metres long, is held in the hand and pulled when the desired fish is in the trap. Although the gates have little weight in the water they quickly drop when the pins are pulled. Since the whole trap is made of clear Plexiglass the fishes in the trap hardly notice when the gates drop.

The efficiency of this trap is remarkable. After it is placed in the aquarium a little food

is deposited in the middle of the trap. Immediately a lot of fishes are in the trap feeding on the unexpected bounty. It takes only a few minutes before the individual we want to catch is found feeding inside the trap. The trap is closed and the fishes can be netted out from the box.

Obviously this method rarely works with sick individuals which are not eating. They are better caught at night.

Large holes in the rockwork may hide even large cichlids such as this female *Nandopsis festae*. Catching cichlids from a decorated aquarium is best done at night, when they are asleep, or with a custom made trap such as the one shown on the previous page.

Introduction of new fishes

Many cichlid species need a certain amount of time to adjust to their new environment after they have been introduced to the aquarium. In the case of many fishes it is not only the aquarium decor but also the other inhabitants that need to be considered. The introduction of a single individual into an established community aquarium may cause additional stress to the new fish. In particular males and females of large substrate brooding cichlids are often impossible to (re-)unite without an adjustment period during which the two fishes are able to see each other but are prevented from any physical contact.

A separator of glass or Plexiglass, or a mesh divider is widely used in breeding tanks but does not really work when introducing new fish to the community. A glass separator divides the aquarium into two smaller compartments such that established territories are likely to be split up as well. This may cause additional problems, especially when the aquarium is overpopulated, as is often the case.

A very satisfying solution was invented by Ulrich Minden (Germany) and has been successfully adapted by many aquarists. The only thing needed is a plastic aquarium with a minimum length of 25 cm (length must relate to size of fish) and a height of 20 cm. This can be obtained from the pet shop at low cost. The types with rounded edges are preferred above the sharp-edged models but the latter work too, although it is advised that the edges be smoothed. About 3 cm from the rim 5 holes with a diameter of 10 mm are drilled in each side. Additionally two such holes are drilled in the bottom at opposite corners. In order to facilitate the placing of the fish inside the plastic container a glass plate is needed which is large enough to cover the container.

The sole requirement for the aquarium, into which the new fish has to be introduced, is an open site on the sand or gravel in which the plastic container can be placed, upside-down. In order to prevent movement of the container a stone is placed on top of it.

The most frequent problem is that of the introduction of a new female to an aggressive male. The best way to proceed is by letting the male sit for two weeks in the plastic container while the new female swims freely around in her new environment. After the male is caught he is put into the container as follows. While the container is held half submerged in the water the male is put in it and prevented from escaping by placing the glass cover over the container. The container, with cover, is inverted and positioned on the bottom. The cover, now between bottom and container, is slowly removed, avoiding any tilting of the container.

The male in the container is fed through the two holes in the top. During the two weeks of acclimatisation the female becomes familiar with the aquarium and with the male, who is not able to harass her. After two weeks, when the fishes are being fed, the container is removed and the pair is closely watched. If necessary the whole procedure can be repeated.

For smaller species a breeding trap can be used. Either to confine a single likely aggressor, or, in the case of Mbuna where all residents are likely to attack a newcomer, the new fish. After a few days the breeding trap is sunk to the bottom. By then the residents "know" they can't get at the newcomer, who, however, soon realises he/she can get out. If chased it will normally retreat to the trap, where it is "safe". After a while it finds a better home and the trap can be removed.

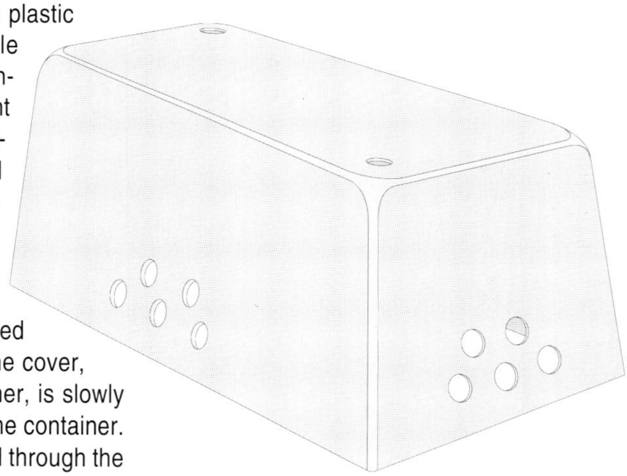

The holes drilled in the sides of the plastic container allow for a sufficient exchange of water. Although the container may seem small to be the living space of a cichlid for two weeks, it never seems to stress them.

The water

by Lasse Forsberg

The chemistry of aquarium water is a complicated issue. In many instances it is not simply a question of providing the perfect water for the species involved but more one of maintaining that quality. The chemistry of water —its pH, hardness, conductivity, etc.— is not stable in a closed environment such as the aquarium. The pH is a measure of the acidity of the water and the correct value (the one encountered in the natural biotope) is very important for the well-being of cichlids. For example, the biological breakdown of organic matter, which is present in all aquaria, will lower the pH if there are not enough buffering substances such as carbonates in the water. To express it more technically: the oxidation (processing) of ammonium (NH_4^+), from the organic breakdown, to nitrite and nitrate (nitrification) utilises bicarbonates and this will enhance the process of lowering the pH. In other words, in water with a low concentration of bicarbonates (soft water) the all-important nitrification process is hampered leading to a build-up of ammonium. As you may realise the water chemistry in an aquarium is first of all a biological problem.

Fresh water

Even if you prepare water with the right chemistry and are able to maintain the values that your fishes demand, you should never forget that fresh water is good for all fishes. We recommend a partial water change of about one third of the volume every week. Tap water, however, usually contains chlorine, and sometimes chloramine, to disinfect it. Unfortunately fishes don't like chlorine and chloramine is lethal to them. A 30% water change with chlorinated tap water is about the limit most cichlids can endure (without adding conditioner), but any amount of water with chloramine is dangerous.

In most areas, however, the tap water is only chlorinated. Often you can avoid this problem by spraying the fresh water into the aquarium, for instance by using a shower head. This drives off the chlorine (a gas) dissolved in the water. Chloramine cannot be removed in this way and should therefore be removed or absorbed by specially developed chemicals, water conditioners. These products are available from your pet shop. Not all water conditioners remove chloramine, so it is necessary to check the instructions on the bottle to be sure of getting the right type. The water can also be cleaned by passing it over activated carbon.

Alkaline water

In aquaria with cichlids that require a high pH, such as rift lake and Central American cichlids, there is often no problem maintaining such levels because one can use limestone and sodium bicarbonate to obtain a high pH. These materials will not only raise the pH but also buffer the water. Even if your tap water has a pH between 7.5 and 9 it can be very poor in carbonates. The carbonate hardness can be measured with test kits which are available in pet shops. In the event of a hardness below 3° you should use limestone and bicarbonate to maintain the pH values between water changes. Malawi and Tanganyika enthusiasts in Scandinavia are plagued by very soft water from the tap. They have to put limestone in the filter or in the aquarium, which brings the pH to about 7.5, and add sodium bicarbonate when the water is changed.

Sodium bicarbonate has many good features. One is that the biological breakdown of ammonium will work well in water rich in bicarbonates. Another advantage is that it is difficult to get excessively high pH values. To get excessively an high value you would have to have added so much bicarbonate that you

would be aware of your mistake. A third feature is that it has a good buffering capacity. Never use sodium hydroxide in order to raise the pH! It has no buffering capability and it is easy to overdose.

The amount of sodium bicarbonate in the aquarium is not very important and is also dependent on the chemistry of the tap water. To start with you should use about 30 grams for each 100 litres of fresh water you add to the aquarium. It is advisable to buy a pH test kit and use it often to start with. First of all you can measure the pH and carbonate hardness of your tap water and learn what amount of bicarbonate is needed to maintain a stable pH of about 8 between the water changes. If the pH has dropped in your aquarium you must change the water before you add the bicarbonate. **Never raise the pH without a partial water change!** The reason is that free ammonium is then suddenly converted to toxic ammonia (NH_3, which is a gas dissolved in water). The bacteria that break down the ammonium need inorganic carbon in order to grow. When the pH of the aquarium has dropped this means that insufficient carbonate is available for the nitrifying

Photo top: Many Tanganyika cichlids need water with an alkaline pH. *Tropheus* sp. "Black" (Bemba) prefers water with a pH between 8 and 9.2.
Photo below: *Anomalochromis thomasi* has been bred for many generations in captivity and does not require the soft and acidic water found in its natural habitat. Though it is recommended that such West African cichlids be kept in water with a pH similar to that found in the wild.
Photo facing page: A male *Aulonocara* cf. *hansbaenschi* shows its best colours when kept in water free from waste products and with a pH between 7 and 8.5.

bacteria and that the waste product ammonium will be built up. A sudden rise of the pH in such aquaria can be catastrophic because free ammonia will be instantly formed. The higher the pH the more ammonia is converted from the built-up ammonium. This is the reason why you should never raise the pH without a previous water change. It should also be stressed that **pH adjustments should be done gradually** because fishes do not appreciate sudden changes in the pH.

Some Malawi and Tanganyika enthusiasts add other salts to the water in order to imitate the natural composition of the lake waters as much as possible. This is unnecessary: I have been unable to observe any differences in the cichlids kept in "bicarbonated" water and those in water with extra minerals added. Moreover, aquarists have not been able to exactly duplicate the composition of rift lake waters.

Acidic water

There is a difference between making acidic water and making water soft. The hardness of the water has not been proven to be of importance for the well-being of cichlids which normally live in very soft water (unless the carbonate hardness is below 3°). The pH, however, is important to those cichlids. When the pH of the tap water is too high for your cichlids it must be lowered artificially. This can be done by an acid. The amount of acid needed depends on the amount of buffering carbonates in the tap water. Although phosphoric acid (H_3PO_4) is not a very strong acid only a little bit is needed to lower the pH of tap water. Do not drop concentrated acid into your aquarium because overdoses may lower the pH to lethal levels. Try it out on a known amount (say 10 litres) of tap water in a plastic

bucket. Before you try anything you need a pH test kit or an electronic pH meter. If one millilitre of your H_3PO_4 solution is too much to bring 10 litres of tap water to the desired pH (usually 6), make a stock solution in which you dilute the concentrated H_3PO_4 four times. When you find out how many millilitres of your H_3PO_4 (stock) solution are needed then calculate how much you need for the fresh water you have added to the aquarium. Dilute this amount in about a litre of water and pour it (distribute it) into the aquarium after you have done the water change.

Phosphoric acid is available from drug stores and is relatively cheap. Once you have determined how much of your stock solution you need to bring the tap water to the desired pH it is a fast and convenient method. After the pH has been adjusted you need to make another carbonate hardness test. If the carbonate hardness is below 3° you should add bicarbonate to compensate for the loss of carbonates caused by adding the acid (see below).

In order to maintain the stability of the pH around 6 to 6.5 you could put peat moss in the filter. However, the buffering capacity of peat moss does not solve the possible problem of deficiency in the carbonates required by the nitrifying bacteria. Normally the amount of carbonates in hard tap water is sufficient for the nitrifying bacteria to do their job properly, but in cases where the tap water is extremely soft bicarbonates should be added in order to support the nitrifying bacteria. In such cases you could use sodium bicarbonate, but remember the goal is not to raise the pH but to supply carbonates for the bacteria. The amount you should add has to be found out by trial and error. Begin with very small amounts, about 1-2 grams per 100 litres. The final aim would be to have a carbonate hardness of around 3°.

Aquaria which are overpopulated, and in which large amounts of food are given, should not have soft water in order to avoid the problem of carbonate depletion followed by the building up of ammonium.

Many aquarists keeping South American or West African cichlids use water which has been made soft by various means. A common method used is reverse osmosis. Another possibility is to remove all (or part of the) minerals in the water by ion-exchange. These are both costly procedures which yield soft water, i.e. water depleted of carbonate. What these cichlids need is a low pH and what the nitrifying bacteria in the aquarium need is carbonates. Neither of these two requirements are provided by soft water. Although it is true that soft water can easily be lowered in pH, this usually brings more problems than it solves.

Oxidation

Hitherto I have discussed the pH and carbonate hardness. Now I shall try to explain the chemical problems fishes cause. In order to keep your fishes alive you have to feed them. In every food there are proteins which contain nitrogen. The fishes break these proteins down into smaller parts which are then used as building blocks for their own proteins. In this controlled process nitrogen is produced which the fish cannot use and must get rid of. Between 30-50% of the nitrogen in the food is excreted, mainly in the form of ammonium. This takes place via the gills. Ammonium, which is not toxic to fishes, can be converted to free ammonia, which is lethal even in low concentrations (0.02 mg/l). Such a conversion occurs more readily at a high pH and is practically absent at a pH below 7 (and impossible below pH 6). Water with a pH below 7 seldom gives concentrations of free ammonia which will kill fish even if the water has a high concentration of ammonium. However, a pH above 7.5 could give concentrations of free ammonia lethal to fishes even with only moderate concentrations of ammonium.

In the nitrification process one type of bacterium produces nitrite from ammonium and another nitrate from nitrite. It takes some time before these bacteria become established in a new aquarium and it seems that those that convert nitrite to nitrate need a longer time to do so. Therefore you will have a build up of nitrite in new aquaria during the first few weeks. Nitrite is toxic and fishes in a new aquarium should be fed very little until a good bacterial flora is established. An alternative is to stock the aquarium with very few fishes the first three to four weeks.

There are some tricks to help start the right bacterial flora in a new tank. The easiest and most successful way is to take some gravel from an established aquarium and put it into the new tank. Another possibility is to purchase freeze-dried cultures of these bacteria and add them to the aquarium water. These preparations are known as filter-starters. Even with such starter cultures it may take two weeks before the bacterial flora in the new tank can cope with the amount of ammonium produced, so feed sparingly.

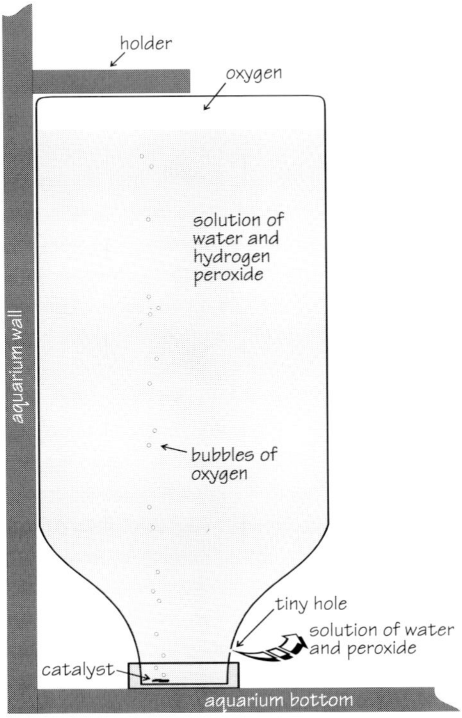

The nitrite blocks the oxygen uptake of the fishes' blood. When the nitrite in the aquarium has reached a toxic level the fishes start to breathe heavily but they will not swim near the surface gulping for air as they would when suffocating. An *acute* nitrite poisoning is best coped with by changing 50% of the water (do not forget water conditioner when changing that much water). We must, however, realise that the water in the aquarium contains many tiny particles carrying nitrifying bacteria. When changing the water in order to dilute the nitrite concentration we also diminish the population of bacteria which can break down the nitrite. For this reason it is recommended that, if the fishes are still breathing heavily after the water change, 1-2 grams of common salt (NaCl without iodine) per litre of water are added and that we refrain from feeding for two days. The salt only lowers the toxicity of nitrite but does not remove it.

Together with a starter culture of bacteria I use an oxidator. This is a unit that contains a weak solution of hydrogen peroxide which slowly leaks into the aquarium water. There are a number of oxidators on the market but these are expensive, whilst they are easy to build yourself. What is needed is a plastic (not glass) bottle of about 250 ml capacity with a screw cap. Pierce a tiny hole in the neck, near the cap, with a hot needle. A small piece of lead or silver thread is needed as a catalyst. It should have a diameter of 1-2 mm and a length of 5-6 mm and is put in the bottle. Make a solution of hydrogen peroxide and distilled water (do not use tap water) with a strength of about 3-6% peroxide and fill the

Photo left: *Aequidens rivulatus* originates from waters with a neutral to slightly acidic pH.
Photo below: It is often not realised that most Central American cichlids —the photo shows *Thorichthys aureus*— are found in hard, alkaline water.

Facing page: The clean water at the waterfalls near Tamasopo, Mexico.

bottle. Close the bottle and put it upside-down in the aquarium. You have to anchor the bottle otherwise it will float after a while. I have glued a triangular piece of glass in the corner of the tank under which the bottle is fitted (see figure).

The lead or silver thread serves as a catalyst in the breakdown of the hydrogen peroxide into water and oxygen radicals. Inside the bottle the radicals form pure oxygen (O_2). This gas rises to the top of the bottle and slowly pushes the solution through the tiny hole into the aquarium water. In the aquarium the peroxide solution slowly disintegrates. The free oxygen radicals formed in the aquarium react with the organic matter in the water including the nitrite, and thereby neutralise its toxicity.

You have to be careful with the concentrations of hydrogen peroxide because an overdose may harm the fishes. The amount of peroxide leaking out of the bottle depends on the concentration of the solution in the bottle, the temperature, and the surface area of the catalyst. In my experience a 250 ml bottle with a 6% peroxide solution empties itself during two weeks at 25° C. If the nitrite concentration cannot be sufficiently reduced (use a nitrite test kit) you should increase the amount of solution leaking into the aquarium water. This can be done by using more or bigger pieces of catalyst. Do not increase the strength of the solution above 6%.

In a 100 litre aquarium I use a 3% solution, one piece of catalyst, and a 250 ml bottle which empties itself in 4-5 weeks with very good results. When using an oxidator the starting up of a new aquarium is made easier. The oxygen level will be perfect and, after about a month, you will end up with a very clean aquarium with no mud or sludge on the gravel. You have to be careful, though, because an overdose can be fatal.

Filtration

by Kjell Fohrman

What is the point of having a filter in the aquarium? How large should it be? Is it really necessary to have a filter? I have seen several aquaria which worked very well without any filter. I have a friend who once had an aquarium of 150 litres with a filter which was built for a 40 litre aquarium. This aquarium worked very well for many years although he never changed the water! He only replaced the water that had evaporated. "Impossible", you might say; not at all. The fishes in the tank —a pair of *Chalinochromis brichardi*— were rarely fed, about once a month. The juveniles born in the aquarium were removed after a while to prevent overpopulation. This is exactly what keeping cichlids is all about: never overload an aquarium.

Unfortunately we normally want more than only one pair of cichlids in a 150 litre aquarium. When there are more fishes in a tank we feed more, resulting in more waste products. Both the food that has been processed by the fishes (faeces) and that which has not been eaten pollute the water. What do you do then? Of course you purchase a bigger filter and hope that it will cope with the increased amount of waste products. But what filter should you chose? If you go to a pet shop without knowing what you require it can become a very expensive visit.

A good filter should fulfil the following functions in an aquarium: ① it should put oxygen into the water, ② mechanically clean the water, ③ biologically clean the water, ④ buffer the water, ⑤ stop the spreading of disease when you have a central filtration system.

The filter types can be divided into two main types: the wet filter and the trickle filter. Of course we should not forget the water change which gives the fastest results. It may be strange to discuss it as a filtration method but fresh water contains a lot of oxygen and has, in theory, no biological waste products —in some areas, however, it may have high nitrate

levels. With every water change we dilute the waste products and add more oxygen to the aquarium. There is, however, a disadvantage in relying on water changes only. It takes time and a lot of heated tap water (and conditioner if it contains chlorine or chloramine). You would have to change water several times a week, depending on the number of fishes in the tank. So, this alternative to filtering the aquarium water is not recommended although water changes are a necessary complement to any filtration system.

In order to obtain stable aquarium water you need a sufficiently large bacterial flora which can process most of the waste products (nitrification). These bacteria are found in a thin film on all objects that come into contact with the oxygen-rich aquarium water. In order to obtain as many bacteria as possible the filter's main purpose is to greatly enlarge the surface area onto which bacterial biofilms can adhere. The nitrifying bacteria need oxygen and carbonate to grow and function properly. The lack of these chemicals completely prevents nitrification. Moreover the presence of processed waste products in the neighbourhood of the bacteria drastically decreases the nitrification rate as well. In other words the water around the nitrifying bacteria should be refreshed as fast as possible.

In a wet filter the filter material is completely submerged and can be placed inside the aquarium. The material of a trickle filter is only sprayed with water and is usually placed outside the aquarium. The filter material, the medium to which the bacteria adhere, can be made of different kinds of plastic, ceramic, gravel, filter wool or carbon. The most important factor here is the total surface area onto which the bacteria can adhere. If you used a stone as a filter the bacteria could adhere to the outside of the stone. If you drilled a hole through the stone you increase the surface area onto which bacteria can adhere but you would not increase the volume of your "filter". Nowadays the construction of filter materials is aimed at the largest possible contact surface area combined with the smallest, but nevertheless efficient, volume.

Wet filter

Power filters which have a small container of filter material are quite often not sufficient to maintain good water quality. The best type of wet filter is the sponge filter. The soft, grey-coloured, and dense plastic foam sponges which are for sale in many pet shops (usually for air lift filters) are too small to work properly in a cichlid aquarium. Their surface area is not large enough to support the bacterial flora needed. After a few days such sponge filters become clogged with dirt which prevents a fast flow of oxygen-rich water through the sponge. This means that only the bacteria on the outside of the filter may process the waste products.

The best material for an inside wet filter is a sponge which has a rather coarse structure (for fast flow), is available in plates, and which is strong enough to be used without support (see photo page 28). You can buy such sponge in different sizes and densities. The density that, in my opinion, works best is ppi 10. The most convenient thickness is 10 cm. How much you need for an aquarium depends on the population density of the fishes present. Many fish-wholesalers use this type of sponge. Their tanks usually have many more fishes than ours, but they find that a sponge volume of 10% of the aquarium volume is sufficient to stabilise the water. For a normal community aquarium a smaller sponge volume is sufficient.

A simple filter for a 400 litre aquarium can be made of a 10 x 10 x 45 cm piece of sponge and a power head with a capacity of about 1200 l/hr. A hole is drilled along the length of

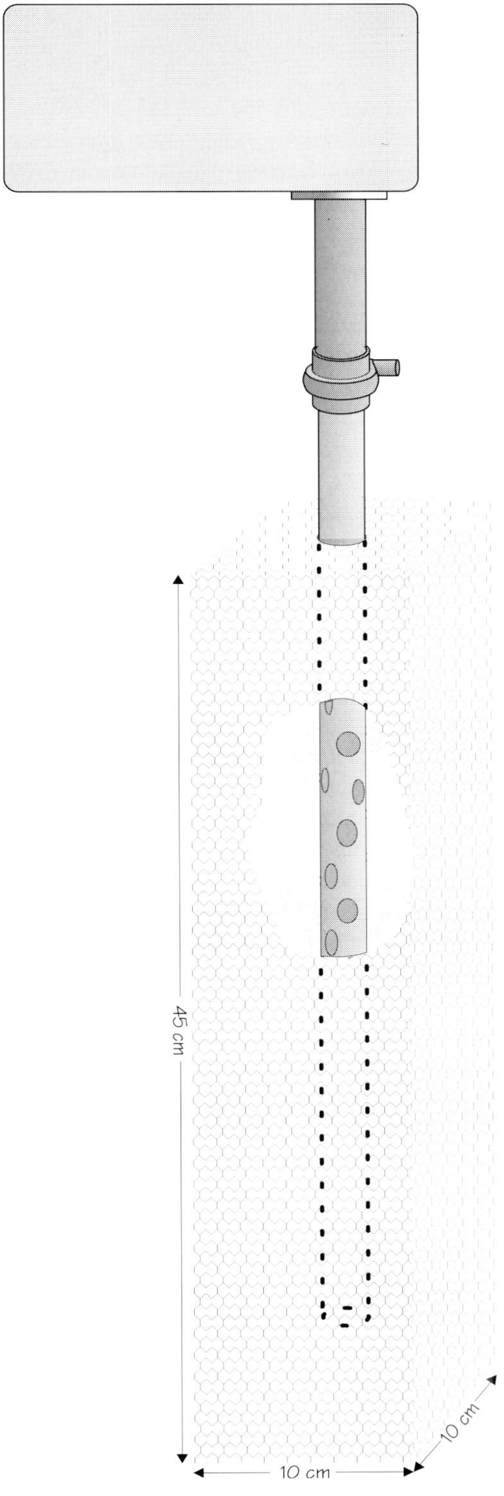

the sponge by pressing and turning a plastic pipe with the same diameter as the connection of the power head (diameter about 16 mm). Into the hole you put a plastic pipe in which many holes have been drilled and which is closed at the bottom end. Depending on the population density in the aquarium such a filter may need to be cleaned only once a year. Of course a weekly water change of about 30% is a prerequisite for the functioning of such filters. Because the filter should be taken out of the tank only once a year, it can easily be hidden inside the aquarium.

For breeding aquaria or for tanks with a high number of fishes a piece of sponge with the size of the short side of the aquarium is cut out. This piece is fitted in the aquarium a few centimetres clear of the short side. Two (when using power heads) to five (when using air lifts) plastic pipes are pierced through the sponge as close to the water surface as possible. These pipes are connected to the power heads or air lifts which draw the water from behind the sponge. The stronger the flow of water (within reason) the better the filter works. Such filters also need to be cleaned once a year.

There are a few points which must be mentioned regarding the use of these sponge filters. The material needs to be rinsed thoroughly many times before it is placed inside the aquarium. Care must be taken that the flow of water through the sponge is fast; stagnant water inside the

The coarse sponge surrounding the perforated suction tube of the power head provides a large area onto which nitrificating bacteria can adhere. The relatively large pores in the sponges facilitate a fast flow of water necessary for the proper functioning of a biological filter. Such sponge filters need to be cleaned once every year.

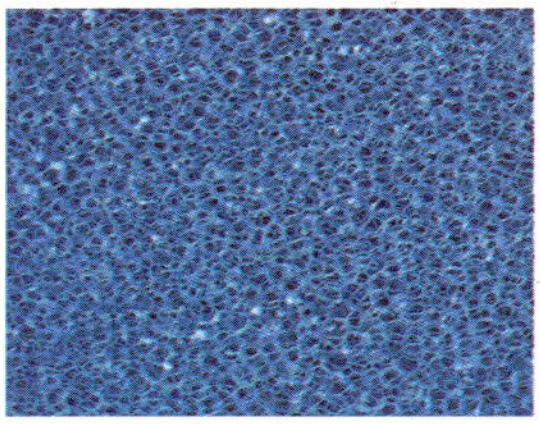

Photo top: In particular aquaria with large cichlids, such as *Cichla ocellaris*, need an excellent filtration system.
Photo left: This is the sponge most frequently used by professional aquarium keepers. Photo by Kjell Fohrman.
Photo below: Even though the substratum is covered with a thick layer of sediment the water in Lake Tanganyika is virtually free of soluble waste products.

sponge may kill off the bacteria, reducing the effectiveness of the filter. Use only sponge material which is meant for use in water. There are other (cheaper) sponges available but they may leach toxic chemicals into the water or be degraded by bacteria because of their cellulose content.

Trickle filter

Recently, the trickle filter has become very popular among cichlid aquarists. Trickle filters have a large capacity in relation to their volume and are therefore recommended to stabilise the water. When an appropriate size filter is installed water does not need to be changed every week. A trickle filter also maximises the oxygen content of the water which will be of benefit to the cichlids' well-being. One can rarely buy a ready-to-use trickle filter and we therefore have to construct one ourselves. Often the filter is placed beneath the aquarium or beside it. This is because it can then be hidden from view. The disadvantage of such a siting is that it becomes more complicated to construct the circulation of the filter. For this reason a better place would be above the aquarium (see later), but then it is difficult to hide.

The function of the material in a trickle filter is to provide a large area onto which bacteria can adhere.

Although all kinds of material can be utilised it is strongly advised to use so-called bioballs or bio-kaskade balls. These are made of

a light plastic and have a very large (in relation to their volume) contact surface area. The structure of some bioballs is such that the water immediately runs off when it is sprayed on. Other balls, bio-kaskade balls, have a complicated construction and are able to slow down the water flow on their surface. The latter type is very effective and one needs only about 2% filter material in relation to the volume of the aquarium. Trickle filters with normal bioballs need to have a volume between 5 and 8% of that of the aquarium in order to function properly. Of course when such filters are used in densely populated aquaria, like those of wholesalers or in fry tanks, their volume should be increased.

Since I published an article in the Scandinavian cichlid magazine about how to make a trickle filter many aquarists have built one themselves. Some of them placed the filter beneath the aquarium but most of them built it on top. In the accompanying figure you will find an example of how to build a trickle filter yourself. You can use a round or a square plastic tube, the length of which is dependent on the size of the aquarium. A large filter can also be made from plastic or glass plates which are glued to form a box. The filter is more efficient when it is much longer than wide. A square tube of 15 x 15 cm diameter and a length of ca. 40 cm is sufficient for an aquarium of 450 litres when you use bio-kaskade balls. It should be at least 100 cm long when regular bioballs are used.

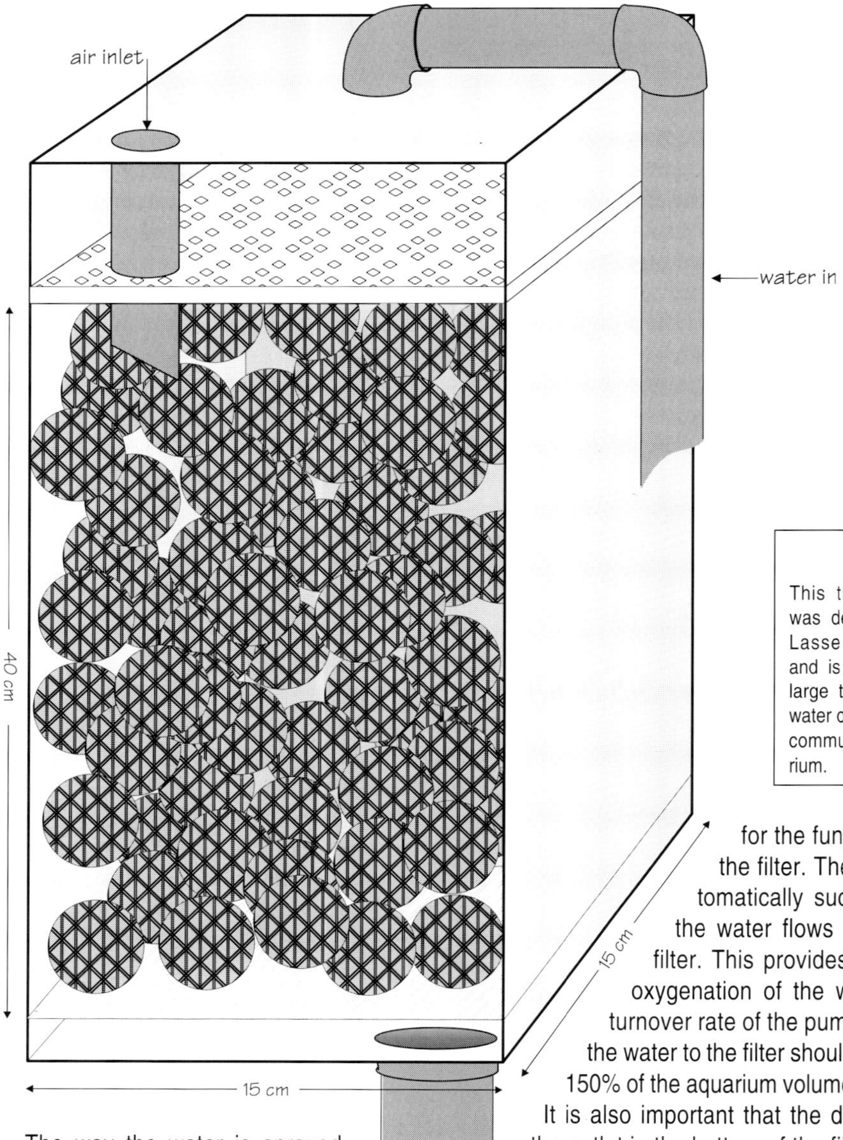

This trickle-filter was designed by Lasse Forsberg and is sufficiently large to filter the water of a 400 litre community aquarium.

The way the water is sprayed into the filter is very important. I use a specially constructed plate (Aqua Medic), but you can easily make a plate yourself. You need a clear plastic plate —the size of the tube— in which numerous holes are drilled. The holes in the centre of the plate should be smaller than those at the edge.

A hole in the top of the filter, above the drip-plate, to let fresh air enter, is important for the functioning of the filter. The air is automatically sucked in as the water flows out of the filter. This provides excellent oxygenation of the water. The turnover rate of the pump bringing the water to the filter should be about 150% of the aquarium volume per hour. It is also important that the diameter of the outlet in the bottom of the filter should at least be double of that of the inlet.

A filter placed on top of the aquarium needs no extra container to collect the water before it is pumped back to the tank. Moreover the aquarium does not need an overflow. A trickle filter under the aquarium is recommended when an overflow is present or when the filter cannot be hidden conveniently above it.

The undergravel filter

by Mary Bailey

When undergravel filters first became available in the 1970's they were extremely popular with cichlid keepers. I have been using them for 20 years for all sorts of cichlids, from *Uaru* to *Apistogramma*s, from densely populated Mbuna tanks to sparse Tanganyikan, and for rearing fry.

An undergravel filter (UG) consists of a filter plate, usually plastic, sometimes a single construct, sometimes made up of smaller plates slotted together to form the desired size/shape. The plates are moulded so that they fit snugly on the bottom glass but have channels through which water is drawn across the underside. Small holes or slots allow water to pass into the area under the plate. All types include one or more uplift tubes which fit onto the plate. Where a "conventional flow" system is used water is drawn up the uplift, using the airlift principle (powered by an airpump), a power head, or even a power filter. At the same time water is drawn down through the gravel to replace that travelling up the tube. Where the system is powered by air it is advisable to have only a single uplift per plate, as otherwise it is almost impossible to "balance" the flow up each tube, so that water may take the course of least resistance down the "weaker" uplift instead of through the gravel, defeating the whole object of the exercise. The suction will be strongest nearest the uplift, so if very large plates are used the remoter areas may have only minimal through-put (if any). This is particularly critical with air-driven UG where flow tends to be limited.

In the first part of this chapter on filtration (p. 25) we have seen how biological filtration is optimised by providing as large a surface area as possible for colonisation by nitrifying bacteria, and how it is vital to maintain aerobic conditions in the filter medium by means of a constant stream of oxygenated water. Exactly the same principle applies with UG. In practice nitrifying bacteria will always colonise the **surface** of the substrate in a healthy tank; UG increases the amount of substrate which can be colonised and optimises oxygen supply to its surface. The oxygenated substrate is the filter medium, and referred to as the "filter bed". For maximum effectiveness the plates, and thus the filter bed, should cover the entire bottom.

Like any filter a UG system needs to be matured before adding fishes; the filter bed can be "seeded" by sprinkling with a handful or two of "dirty" gravel from an established tank, or by a commercial maturing agent. New gravel takes 10-14 days to mature; washed, but previously used, gravel a shorter time. Nitrites should be monitored daily; once they have peaked and reverted to minimal levels the tank can be used. Loading should be light initially (meagre rations), building up **gradually** to the desired level over a period of 1-3 weeks.

Choice and depth of substrate are important. The smaller the grain size the greater the total surface area available; but, a very fine substrate may clog rapidly. UG systems are thus not really suitable for species which require a sandy substrate. A grain size of 2-4 mm is best. The filter bed should be 5-8 cm deep. A very shallow bed may allow unprocessed wastes to be drawn through and spewed out of the uplift, especially if a powerful power head is in use. Too deep a bed may impede water flow too much. The most important thing with any filtration system is to tailor it to a specific tank; the essential criteria being tank size **and** loading. In a tank with a low loading and low turnover rate it will not matter if the filter bed is shallower than my optimum.

Before the advent of power heads aquarists

usually maintained crowded Mbuna tanks using a single air-driven uplift per 30 cm plate, **and** without encountering nitrite problems. Such systems cope equally well with Oscars and *Uaru*. Even with a high metabolic loading the entire tank bottom, whither wastes gravitate naturally, is the filter inlet!

Another mistake that many (most?) aquarists make now is to constantly stir up their substrate or "hoover" it with a gravel cleaner.

Mbuna —the photo shows a male *Pseudotropheus* sp. "Elongatus Chailosi"— can be kept in aquaria with an undergravel filter. They may dig pits and spoil heaps, but a low-turnover UG will cope adequately.

a low to moderate turnover system can cope perfectly adequately. Where power heads score is in Rift Lake tanks, where they supply the turbulence needed to provide well-oxygenated water for the cichlids. They are neither necessary nor desirable for cichlids such as dwarfs and discus which come from slow-moving waters.

Hence rule number one: **Increased turnover does not necessarily mean increased efficiency**. The situation is, of course, different in power filters, where one function of turnover is to stir up mulm and bring it to the filter intake. A great advantage of UG is that

This is highly undesirable. The areas of maximum bacterial activity are at the surface, where there is the highest concentration of wastes and oxygen. Turning over the filter bed almost certainly prevents proper maturation; many bacteria are removed with the "dirt". Tanks subjected to this sort of cleaning often suffer frequent nitrite peaking, while a constant minimal level is the norm with undisturbed filter beds. Of course our cichlids may sift the surface layer, but they are not disturbing it to any depth. They may dig pits and make spoil heaps, but having done so they generally leave well alone, so proper maturation can take place. Even with craters and mountains twice the depth of the original filter bed a low-turnover UG will cope perfectly adequately; this, and exposure of the filter plates, undoubtedly reduces efficiency, but not to the extent that problems arise.

It is normally necessary to interfere with an established UG system only if it can no longer cope, i.e. if there are appreciable amounts of semi-processed mulm (ignore fresh droppings) on the surface. Depending on loading, this may be after 6 months or 2 or more years, when the inert material that remains after bacterial waste processing has filled up the filter bed. Then, and only then, is it worth giving it a good clean, reducing feeding for a week or so while it re-matures. If a gravel tidy is fitted it will not be possible to clean the entire bed, but connecting the water-changing siphon tightly to the uplift will help remove fine debris from the bottom part of the filter.

So, rule two: **Don't interfere with it**.

I often hear the complaint "I don't like UG because the dirt remains in the tank". Although the solids may be removed by a power filter the soluble, invisible, byproducts which actually harm our fishes are still in the tank system! We clean our power filters out when they clog and no longer function properly (and how many who hoover gravel weekly would clean a power filter that often?), not because their contents are polluting the tank. Besides which, solids infiltrate the gravel even if UG is not in use. I prefer to have wastes processed by aerobic bacteria, rather than risk the toxicity which may arise from anaerobic gravel filled with solids. You will never see black polluted gravel in a tank with UG, nor be choked by a dreadful smell of methane when cleaning the tank out. UG is also accused of engulfing fry. Why, I wonder, do I never have this problem, even with the tiniest dwarfs? Perhaps because of my antiquated low-turnover air-driven system? I don't have nitrite problems either. Rule one again!

So far I have discussed only "conventional flow UG"; now a word on "reverse flow" systems. For reasons which escape me, some aquarists use a power filter filled with a medium, to pump water *down* their uplifts, the idea apparently being to remove solids from the water before circulating it through the filter bed. This effectively eliminates all the advantages of UG, the bulk of biological activity taking place in the power filter, where the bulk of the wastes are!

Finally, a word about plants and UG. Plants can be grown very successfully with low to medium turnover UG; it helps, however, if the UG is not set in action until the plants have established their root systems. When they start to show new growth the UG can be turned on, gently at first, then gradually increasing to the desired level. By this time sufficient nitrifying bacteria will have developed **on** the gravel for initial maturation to have taken place, so fishes can be added immediately if fed lightly.

To sum up, UG is cheap (with no repeat outlay on filter media), does not leak, is easy to install, easy to hide, requires minimal maintenance, is cichlid-proof (if the airlifts are siliconed to the plates), and highly efficient. The most important thing to remember about it, or any type of filtration, is to **think** about what you are doing; to understand **how** and **why** it works, because only then will you be able to provide the optimum system for your particular aquarium.

Food and feeding

by Kjell Fohrman

All animals are adapted to some kind of food. This sounds quite obvious to most of us, but some seem to forget this when it concerns our fishes. We all agree that cows should not be fed with meat and that lions would not accept grass as part of their diet. In nature such animals would eat only the food to which they are adapted and most of them refuse to eat other foods in captivity. Unfortunately many cichlids lack this "intelligence" and accept all kinds of food, especially when commercial producers add attractants to it.

Fishes are cold blooded (poikilotherm) animals. They use fat both as an energy resource and as an energy reserve. Therefore they have fat deposits in several parts of the body. Because fishes are cold blooded, which means that their body temperature varies with that of the surrounding water, they specialise in fatty acids with a low melting point. This prevents the fatty deposits from being rigid at low temperatures. Warm blooded animals store fatty acids which have a high melting point. Because fishes cannot assimilate fat from warm blooded animals as well as they can that from cold blooded animals, it is stored in the liver. It has been shown in salmon (in aquaculture) that individuals fed with products from mammals (warm blooded) show a tremendous increase in degeneration of the liver compared to those fed with fish. Beef heart and any other meat from warm blooded animals is therefore extremely bad for your fishes.

Fishes are adapted to the food their environment offers. Apart, perhaps, from piranhas in South America, they are rarely offered minced beef heart, so don't feed your fish with this utterly unnatural "food". Unfortunately fat from warm blooded animals is also present in many types of dry food. It is used as a filler and sometimes as a binder. If you want to do your cichlids a big favour **do not give them food to which (warm blooded) animal fats have been added**. The good quality dry foods use fish or shrimp meal as a filler and vegetable oil as a binder. Most types of commercial dry food declare their ingredients on the package. Look for the right food!

Of course we must try to give our cichlids a type of food that closely resembles their natural diet. An herbivorous cichlid should not be fed an easily digestible, protein-rich food. On the other hand piscivorous cichlids usually refuse to eat spinach or peas. The intestines of herbivorous cichlids are many times longer (relatively seen) than those of piscivores. Piscivores may catch a prey item only once every day. Their food is nutritious and is rapidly digested. Herbivorous cichlids are adapted to continuous feeding. Their food, however, is slowly digested and by no means everything they eat has a nutritional value. If we feed herbivores a very nutritious and easily digested food, even if it is from cold blooded animals, sooner or later it will upset their digestive system. This may easily lead to the so-called bloat (see page 58) and usually has a fatal outcome when left untreated. Still, herbivorous cichlids can be fed with meat, but it should be in the form of **whole** crustaceans (with their chitin shells). The chitin fragments probably have a similar function to the fibre in our diet.

How often to feed?

There is no general rule as to how often you should feed your cichlids. It is a matter of experience. You must be very careful when feeding protein-rich food, such as flake food and pellets. In this case never feed more than once a day as much as can be eaten in two (not five!) minutes. It is better to feed adult cichlids once every other day. Frozen food contains much less protein relative to its weight because most of it consists of water. In this case too never give more per day than can be eaten in two minutes.

Another factor that may lead to upset intestines in your cichlids is a sudden change in the type of food. If you have fed your fishes for a long period with quickly digestible food, such as flake food for instance, and then in the space of a day switch to e.g. *Mysis* (a highly recommended fish food), the fishes may have initial problems and be particular vulnerable to diseases. Even when the new food is much better and closer to the natural food of the cichlids, you must change their diet gradually.

Health food

We all want our cichlids to be as healthy as possible and to show the same beautiful colours in the aquarium that they would in the wild. Quite often the "washed out" appearance of some would-be colourful cichlids (e.g. the Red Zebra) is attributed to inbreeding rather than to the food they have been fed. I think that in 99% of such cases the reason for poor colour is the food.

The Red Zebra from Lake Malawi has not been exported since the early seventies, so all Red Zebras in the hobby are captive raised. Unfortunately these cichlids do not often show their eye-catching red colour but are a rather dull yellow. However, some breeders are able to keep the vibrant red colour in their fishes. In order to know whether this red colour was selected or dependent on diet I made the following experiment many years ago:

300 juvenile Red Zebras were divided into six equal groups each having their own aquarium. The Zebras were intensively fed for a period of five weeks according to the following schedule:

Aquarium 1: Tetra Min; number 2: Tetra Rubin and Hikari Lina; 3: minced whole shrimp; 4: minced whole shrimp with paprika powder; 5: minced whole shrimp with Spirulina powder; 6: minced whole shrimp with Spirulina and paprika powder.

I placed the fishes in white plastic containers and let several aquarists evaluate the results. The Zebras from the first two aquaria were judged as being equal in colour and a difference in colour compared with Red Zebras which had not been included in the test could not be detected. The Zebras in tanks 3 and 4 also showed the same colour as each other, but this was a much deeper red than of those in tanks 1 and 2. The best coloured Zebras were found in the two groups which were fed Spirulina powder together with the shrimps. My conclusion from this small test is that the best food I can give to my cichlids is whole shrimps with Spirulina.

In the mix prepared for all my cichlids (Malawi and Tanganyika cichlids) I include green peas as well as the whole shrimps and Spirulina powder. The binder for this mix is gelatine which is a purified protein from warm blooded animals. There is no fat in gelatine and the amount of gelatine compared to the other ingredients of the mix is low. A binder is necessary otherwise the fine particles in the mixture would pollute the water too much.

The following ingredients are needed for my shrimp-mix:

- 1 kg whole shrimps (the cheapest are also the ones preferred),
- 1 kg green peas, frozen,
- 10 ml Spirulina powder (available in health food stores or from well-assorted pet shops),
- 100 grams gelatin powder,
- 10 drops of concentrated multivitamins (available in pet shops for birds and pets).

Optionally you can add 150 grams of pelleted food —no mammalian fat— if you are going to feed the mix to juveniles.

Put the almost thawed shrimps and peas in

Four stages in the preparation of shrimp mix. See text for details.

a mincer or blender and grind them to a fine mass (photo 2). Then the Spirulina powder, the pellets (when needed), and the multivitamins are mixed in (photo 3). The gelatine is dissolved according to the instructions on the packet. It must be an easily flowing, sticky mass without any lumps. Lumps of gelatine can be dangerous for juveniles. The gelatine is thoroughly blended with the shrimp-mix. The best way to do this is to mix the food scoop by scoop with the hot gelatine preventing it from cooling too quickly (the pan of gelatine is still on a low heat). When ready the mixture is poured onto a flat tray or into plastic boxes and placed in the refrigerator for some hours. The hardened mix is cut into pieces of a convenient size, and frozen in plastic bags (photo 4). After the mix has been placed in the freezer it cannot be cut easily. Because of the high nutritional value of the shrimp mix you should not feed it more than once a day.

Flake food

Only flake food without mammalian fat is considered to be worth feeding to your cichlids. The type of flake food which contains Spirulina is recommended above any other type. Most flake foods have a high protein content and should be fed in small amounts. The ammonium concentration in the aquarium water is in direct relation to the amount of protein processed by the fishes and should be kept as low as possible. When a lot of food is administered it automatically means that water should be changed more often.

Pelleted food

Pellets have the same type of ingredients as flake food. Here too we should be careful to select those which do not contain mammalian fat, because many of them do. Pellets with Spirulina are preferred above other types. Most pellets swell considerably after they have been put into water. When the swelling takes place inside the fish it may explode its stomach. Therefore pellets should be pre-swollen, by soaking, before they are fed.

Granulated food

Granulate is a kind of crushed pellet food. It has a high nutritional value but feeding quantities are more easily measured than for example flake food and it does not seem to pollute the water so much as other dry foods. Granulate is relatively cheap and works well for smaller cichlids and juveniles. It too contains a lot of proteins, which means that you should not feed more than once a day.

Frozen food

Many kinds of deep frozen fish food are available in pet shops. Not all of them are recommended for cichlids (or any other kind of fishes). **Red mosquito larvae**, one of the most popular frozen foods, **are very bad and should not be fed to fishes**. These larvae are found in the mud of stagnant pools and feed from the mud, including when this contains chemicals which are toxic to fishes. Moreover red mosquito larvae induce allergic reactions in about 30% of persons coming into contact with them (Liebers, 1991).

The best kinds of frozen food are *Cyclops* —an excellent colour food—, *Mysis*, and other planktonic crustaceans from clean waters. *Daphnia*, which is not liked by all cichlids, should not be an alternative to *Cyclops* if the latter is available. *Cyclops, Mysis,* krill, and other shrimp-like crustaceans are recommended for all cichlids, including herbivores.

Adult brine shrimp (*Artemia*) should be fed only to predatory cichlids. It could be lethal to some herbivores such as *Tropheus*. In order to prevent a build-up of salinity the *Artemia* should be rinsed in tap water before it is fed to acid water cichlids.

Right: Red Zebras fed exclusively with shrimp mix.
Below: A Red Zebra fed with flake food containing mammalian protein.

Live foods

by Charley Grimes

Please bear with me as I relate a little aquarium history and, of course, personal experiences as an introduction to live foods. Prior to World War II commercially prepared fish foods were not readily available and were of dubious quality. Most competent aquarists collected live foods in nearby ponds and/or cultured foods for their fishes, and supplemented their dietary needs with bothersome homemade formulations which were preserved in some way, compromising the nutritional value.

I can relate this with some authority as I have, over the years, endangered the harmony of my boyhood home as well as my married bliss with the preparation of some evil-smelling concoctions that required either the stove-top or the oven. As the aquarium hobby in general was unaware of the importance of vitamins, minerals, and amino acids in fish food, we thought we were providing the ultimate in care for our highly prized pets.

We now have a better understanding of the vital part such things as vitamins play in the health of fishes, especially in conditioning potential breeders. If we had only known how detrimental the cooking and baking was to the foods we prepared, we would not only have avoided the kitchen confrontations, but could also have done better for our fishes.

Up until the 1950's, most tropical fish stores in the U.S.A. sold a variety of live foods they collected themselves or purchased from professional collectors. Aquarists could purchase a number of different live food cultures for propagation at home. About 1950, due in part to a rapidly expanding population and the resultant spread of urban areas with attendant chemical control of mosquitoes, many of the favourite live food collecting areas disappeared. Another, and even more unfortunate, development was the trend toward "convenience" and prepackaging that invaded every part of our lives, including fish keeping. Basically, only a relatively few die-hards, usually the old timers (who, coincidentally, were also very accomplished aquarists) even bothered with live foods. These old fashioned aquarists were the same ones who were able to keep and breed West African and South American dwarf cichlids and always had a pair or two of breeding Angelfish.

The economy was in good shape, people had more disposable income and they were demanding and getting convenience. They wanted to be able to minimize their time and effort and drop by the fish shop on the way home to buy a box of fish food. No muss, no fuss! Compromising quality didn't seem to be too high a price to pay. Fortunately the tropical fish industry responded with ever better prepared foods, better aquaria and equipment, and a fish farming industry to meet the demand for stock. Relatively speaking the entry level cost of setting up a home aquarium became less and less. It seemed there was a ten gallon aquarium in every home.

Unfortunately, for many people tropical fishes were a disposable novelty item. Tanks were set up for a month or two and then broken down and stored in the attic for six months or a year, after which the cycle was repeated. Eventually, the aquarium ended up in a rummage sale. Gratifyingly this disturbing trend seems to have almost disappeared.

Being in the tropical fish hobby as long as I have gives me the perfect opportunity to apply that time worn old saying, "What goes around, comes around." Almost as if our values had been turned back 40 or 50 years we again see tropical fish elevated to more than just a novelty feature in the family room.

It is not surprising that the tropical fish hobby, and in particular the cichlid hobby, seems to have gone "full circle" so that once again aquarists are wanting to do more than just keep a tank of fishes. Thanks to both professional and hobbyist collectors and professional and hobbyist breeders, a fantastic array of fishes is now available in the cichlid hobby.

As many of these fascinating fishes are rare and/or valuable, it has become important to reproduce them. Now, many cichlid aquarists want more than a tank of healthy fishes, they want fishes that will not only look good but will breed for them. And they want not just to raise fry but to produce a good sized batch of fishes that are as good as or better than the parents, especially in colour and size. Suddenly the secrets of the die-hard old timers of the 1950's are the new secrets of the 1990's —**live foods**!

My introduction to live foods came about when I joined a local aquarium club and got involved in the "Breeders Award Program." Another aquarist and I soon elevated the BAP to an informal and friendly contest to see who could breed and raise the largest number of different species of tropical fishes.

As we were close friends and were in this for fun, we shared breeders, fry, and every discovery we made. Quite logically, it wasn't long before we were using live foods both to bring the breeders into spawning condition and to raise the maximum number of healthy offspring.

I had started keeping fish as a teenager and my first tank was home made. Except for guppies, the first fish I spawned was the Zebra Danio. There must have been well over a hundred fry hatched out and I failed to raise a single one. This was frustrating. Shortly after the Danios, twoAngels (*Pterophyllum scalare*) paired and spawned. Again, I experienced a number of disasters before I was finally able to raise a very few fry. Was it any surprise I was so anxious to embrace live foods when I got serious about spawning fishes and raising fry?

Before long I was culturing over a dozen different live foods and even gained a slight reputation locally for my skills in this line. About the time I thought it couldn't get any better, it did get better: I was introduced to brine shrimp eggs.

Suddenly, I was convinced that I had found the perfect live food: newly hatched brine shrimp nauplii. The eggs were reasonable in price and hatched well. The nauplii were more than adequate from a nutritional viewpoint, the fishes loved them and, most importantly, hatching baby brine shrimp was really convenient.

I, along with aquarists throughout the hobby, fell into some pretty bad practices: feeding the fry baby brine shrimp and the adult fishes commercially prepared foods, mainly flake and frozen brine shrimp. What the heck, it worked and it was convenient.

About 1970, give or take a few years, there was a crisis in the supply of brine shrimp eggs. The supply dropped almost to zero and the quality was even worse.

The shortage in shrimp eggs was a hardship for aquarists but it was a catastrophe for the food fish industry. The brine shrimp crisis had a life of only about eight or ten years and, not typically, had two happy endings as far as I am concerned. Firstly, as I was so deeply hooked on raising fishes, I had to scramble to find a way to circumvent the unavailability of brine shrimp eggs. It wasn't long before I looked to my successes prior to using brine shrimp and rediscovered the advantages of other live foods.

The little extra work involved in culturing live foods was offset by the money I saved by not buying brine shrimp eggs, and I was still raising a lot of fishes. I was, undoubtedly, also becoming a much better aquarist as I had also discovered that some live foods will more quickly and more effectively condition breeders than any frozen or prepared foods, and I was not nearly so dependent on any one product in my fishroom.

The other happy ending is that not only are

brine shrimp eggs available again, but the quality is better by far and the cost is very reasonable.

I know from many years of experience that nobody is safe in making an absolute statement on any subject, let alone one with so many facets as tropical fish. I will, however, take a position on one particular live food: white worms. I do believe this one easily cultured live food is more useful in conditioning more different kinds of fishes than any other food readily available to aquarists.

I feel as if I have the best of both worlds. I have the advantages of my live food cultures along with the convenience and utility of high quality brine shrimp eggs. I can also avail myself of commercially prepared fish foods that are both nutritious and readily accepted by my fishes. Things have never been better for me in particular or the tropical fish hobby in general.

White worms (*Enchytraeus albidus*)

In nature, white worms are widespread throughout the temperate zone. They prosper in heavily forested areas that provide cool, moderately damp areas with an abundance of soil rich in humus. By duplicating these conditions, we can readily culture these worms in our homes.

In the early years of the tropical fish hobby, most residences had unheated basements. A cool and dark corner to raise white worms was readily available and the culturing of them was quite popular. Nowadays, with central heating in almost every residence, those cool dark corners, even in those homes with a basement, are virtually nonexistent. The raising of white worms in a modern home requires a better understanding of them and a little ingenuity.

White worms have very few requirements to enable them to prosper, but these few are moderately rigid. They do best at a temperature between 12 and 16 °C (55 and 60 °F); they need high humidity and darkness, and, of course, food.

The most flexible of these three requirements is temperature. White worms will survive and even reproduce at a lower temperature but their metabolism slows to such an extent that a culture maintained below 10 °C (50 °F) is virtually useless. Additionally, anything over 18 °C (65 °F) will stress the worms and temperatures above 24 °C (75 °F) are lethal.

Almost without exception, every aquarist who has more than a year or two of fish keeping experience has become adept at both innovation and creativity. When I posed my problem of keeping white worms at a proper temperature to a few experienced fish keepers, not only was I given logical and proven suggestions, but one friend took me to his fishroom to demonstrate his solution: a refrigerator.

He had moved an old refrigerator into his fishroom and had adjusted the temperature selection to a warmer setting, and had thus created the ideal micro-climate for white worms. It was cool and dark in the refrigerator and the tendency for a refrigerator to dehydrate was offset by his feeding methods (see later).

He also showed me how easily the temperature knob can be prised off to reveal a set screw that will accommodate a wider range of temperatures.

As we had an old refrigerator in the garage that was being used for soda pop, beer, and watermelons, I was set up for white worm production in a matter of minutes. My experience has been that out-of-style but very serviceable refrigerators are readily available for free or at a very modest cost.

I eventually came to the conclusion that a neutral pH peat moss is the best medium for

Right: masses of white worms can be seen between the glass plate and the sides of the box; below: white worm cultures setup in an old refrigerator.
Centre: six cultures of grindal worms do not need much bench space; bottom: grindal worms attached to the plastic cover. All photos by Charley Grimes.

dampened with a mild yeast solution (2 ml of active dry baker's yeast in 1 litre of water) gives the most satisfactory results. The human food I use on an available basis is leftover pasta, rice, mashed potatoes, and cooked breakfast cereal. I avoid anything that has meat products, butter, or margarine. A word of warning: fish foods, such as commercial flaked foods, are very detrimental to white worm culture. I have tried almost everything that anyone suggested and some things I thought of but always came back to the neutral pH peat moss for the best results. I purchase a commercial worm bedding by the bale and find it perfect for various cultures. The cost is quite reasonable and I can get it delivered to my doorstep.

I always maintain six to eight cultures and, again, experience has proven that soft plastic storage boxes give the best service. The size is, of course, dictated by the refrigerator. My boxes measure 30 (length) x 40 (width) x 15 cm (depth) (12" x 16" x 6") . I fill the box about 10 cm (4") deep with damp (not wet) peat moss and add some white worms.

Experience has proven that white bread

worm cultures.

I place the bread in the centre of the culture and position a 20 x 30 cm (8" x 12") piece of glass or Plexiglass over the bread. This seems to maintain the humidity around the bread and in the culture.

The big advantage of using bread for feeding white worms is that it is placed on the surface of the medium and, in turn, the worms congregate to feed at the surface. As a result, the worms are easily harvested and are free of culture substrate.

As a general practice I don't use the container lids. The dehydrating effect of the refrigerator tends to dry the edges of the culture that the piece of glass doesn't cover, which, in turn, concentrates the worms near the food.

A good culture will totally consume one or two slices of bread per day. With eight cultures, I use two or three loaves of bread per week as white worm food. It doesn't take long to discover bakery surplus outlets and utilize two day old bread which is very inexpensive.

I feed my white worm cultures every day but harvest on a four day rotation which seems to maintain a high level of worm production. I harvest about a cup (1/4 litre) of clean worms every day, seven days a week, 52 weeks a year. As can be expected, with the pressure I put on a culture, there is a rapid build-up of waste in the white worm cultures. Every three or four weeks cultures seem to get heavy in the centre. I then thoroughly mix the entire culture to restore a looser and more aerated condition. This can be done to good effect four to six times before the culture is saturated with white worm waste.

One solution is to toss out the old culture and start a new one from scratch. The drawback of this method is that it takes a couple of weeks for the new culture to get into production. I think the delay results from a new culture being started with harvested adult worms. I prefer to split my cultures in half and either discard half or start two cultures. This method has the reconditioned culture back into production in three or four days and harvesting can be resumed. Never throw your old cultures in the trash. The worm enhanced peat moss is especially beneficial for your garden. Properly promoted, you might even be able to convince your spouse that there are positive aspects to your tropical fish hobby.

I have never experienced any negative effects from feeding white worms to my fish. I feel white worms are especially good for conditioning small and medium-sized breeders. I feed white worms every day to my pairs of *Julidochromis, Telmatochromis*, small *Lamprologus*, Killifish, and Rainbowfish to name a few. None of these fishes exhibit any negative effects; on the contrary, they are in robust good health. As an experiment, I fed four baby discus from a body size of a nickel (two centimetres) to one in excess of 8 cm (3") a diet of only white worms. The fishes exhibited normal growth, colour, and robust good health.

While I do not feel this experiment was sound from a nutritional viewpoint, —feeding a monotonous diet, especially of a kind which cannot be a natural food, is not a good idea, however much the fishes enjoy it— it did serve to confirm that white worms can provide a complete diet for tropical fish. For a modest investment in cost and time, white worms are an almost perfect and a very convenient food for small to medium size fishes. A diet containing large amounts of white worms is, however, not recommended since it may lead to fatty degeneration. It should be fed in addition to other (live) foods.

Grindal worms (*Enchytraeus bucholtzi*)

Grindal worms are one live food where I occasionally doubt that the results are worth the effort expended. My attitude and evaluation always changes to the positive side when

I observe a pair or group of small fishes turn themselves inside-out when they are fed grindal worms. I sometimes wonder if it is the taste, the size, the activity of the grindal, or that the fishes sense that grindal worms are more labour-intensive than any other live food I am willing to bother with, that makes the grindal so attractive to small fishes.

As for size grindal worms are a lot bigger than micro worms and a lot smaller than white worms. A grindal is about the same diameter as a human hair and up to one centimetre (0.4") in length.

Allow me to quickly temper the previous observation by stating that there are many positive facets to culturing grindal worms. I successfully culture mine in small containers on a shelf right next to my micro worms. Grindals prosper at fish room temperature and cost next to nothing to maintain.

I again utilise the clear, rigid plastic containers with the snap-on lids. For grindals I use shorter, wider containers which measure about 15 x 10 cm (6" x 4"). For the culture medium, I use the same kind of neutral peat that I use for white worms. I make a mound of damp peat, about 5 cm (2") deep in the container.

The starter grindal worms are placed on top of the mound where they tend to stay if they are fed daily. I have had excellent results by feeding baby cereal in the dry form. I put a heaped teaspoon of the dry cereal on the top of the mound, then wet the cereal using an eye-dropper and cover it with a small plastic lid, 8 cm (3") in diameter. After a few days of feeding the area covered with the lid, the underside of the lid will swarm with grindal worms and it can be dipped into tanks to feed your fishes. I maintain six cultures and feed from two each day on a rotating basis. This method maintains good production with cultures needing to be renewed about every 90 days.

What is the negative side of grindal worms? Cost is low, space required to maintain six cultures is minimal, fish room temperature is perfect, and fish love them. What could I find wrong with grindal worms? My main objection is the rather low productivity of the cultures for the daily effort invested. I will, however, keep using grindal worms because the fishes love them and the grindals produce good results from the fish.

Micro worms (*Tubatrix silusiae*)

Even though white worms are my favourite live food and the one I feed the most, I consider micro worms to be the most indispensable. The high quality of commercial foods, especially flaked foods, makes day to day maintenance of sub-adult and adult fish a matter of preference and convenience. In contrast, the feeding of fry is not as simple as opening a canister of flake food. The fry of some species seem to need to learn to eat. It is only common sense to assume that fry aren't born with the instinctive knowledge that commercially prepared foods will provide for their nutritional needs.

Live food, with natural and constant movement will, at least get the attention of the smallest fry. The constant movement of micro worms combined with their extremely small size makes them an ideal first food for almost any cichlid fry. By and large any fish, from the smallest of fry to the geriatric old lunkers, seem to relish a bite-sized morsel that is alive and has enough movement to attract the fish's attention.

The benefits of feeding live foods are never questioned by experts on fish nutrition. Interestingly, it is neither the protein nor the minerals that are the chief benefit offered by live foods. Quality dry foods provide both items in sufficient quantities and at a reasonable price. The nutritional superiority of live foods is that they are alive. While your cultured live food is not providing an exact duplicate of what the fish eats in nature, you are providing what the fish needs.

Since any uneaten live food stays alive and moving for hours in the aquarium your fishes get more and better nutrition for a prolonged period. This means faster growing and more robust fry as well as better conditioned adults that are much more inclined to spawn and raise healthy fry.

From the newly hatched fry's viewpoint, undoubtedly the most attractive feature of micro worms is their small size. Micro worms, while big enough to observe easily, are considerably smaller than newly hatched brine shrimp nauplii. Another positive feature is that micro worms, being very small, will settle slowly to the bottom of the aquarium and that is where most of the cichlid fry spend the first few days of their lives. Structure hugging fry like *Julidochromis* are drawn to micro worms within a few minutes of the first feeding and quickly learn to scout the aquarium bottom for uneaten worms.

They are prolific! Each micro worm is capable of producing over 300 offspring per day. Just one micro worm has the potential to produce 27 million micro worms in four days! Because of this phenomenal reproductive rate, it is almost impossible to overharvest a micro worm culture. Please believe me when I tell you that you will get more return from culturing micro worms than from any other live food. The method I am going to describe works better than any of the more than a dozen I have tried and it has worked for over twenty years for me.

Five minutes a week, tops, is all that is required to culture micro worms. The initial set-up cost is about US$5.00, including a year's supply of culture medium. In subsequent years, the cost is under $1.00 per year.

Micro worms do well at room temperature and require less than two feet of shelf space. Every serious aquarist can easily make room for a couple or three cultures. Almost any glass or plastic container from one litre up to about four litres will do nicely. I use the snap-top or screw-top food storage containers that hold about one litre and are about 12 cm (5") high. The semi-rigid plastic is durable, adequately transparent, easily cleanable, and provides a good surface for the harvesting of the worms. An air-tight container will kill off any live food culture in short order but is especially deadly for micro worms. To eliminate this situation, I cut a 2.5 cm (1") hole in the lid. I close off the hole with a porous sponge or a gob of filter floss. The hole allows for some ventilation and the plug both keeps the culture from drying out and excludes flies and other bugs.

The culture medium is yellow cornmeal. I have, over the years, tried a number of other media but always come back to cornmeal for the best results. Place ½ cup of cornmeal in the container and add enough warm water to turn the cornmeal into a porridge-like or ice cream milkshake-like consistency. It usually takes about an half hour for the cornmeal to become completely soaked. It is vital not to get the food on the sides of the culture else you end up feeding culture medium to the

Left: micro worms crawl up the sides of the container from where they can be harvested easily.
Right: earthworms are a very nutritious fish food.
Photos by Charley Grimes.

fishes, or else it cakes on and stops you harvesting the worms. When you are satisfied with the consistency and the medium has cooled off, you should add the starter culture of micro worms. A teaspoon is adequate to seed the new culture.

Without going into detail, the cornmeal provides nutrition for the yeast and the micro worms feed on the yeast. I purposely didn't mention yeast as something you need to provide because the micro worm starter culture will bring the yeast with it. Micro worms have yeast on them, in them, and around them; the starter culture will inoculate the new medium. Convenient!

Within three days the number of worms will have increased to the point where thousands will be swarming up the sides of the container. You can wipe your finger around the sides of the container to harvest them and then dip your finger into the fry tank. The micro worms will swarm up the sides of the hard plastic more readily than glass and are therefore more easily harvested. Wiping off the sides of the container yields worms and none of the medium. There is, of course, a tiny amount of yeast on the worms but I have never experienced any problems from that as long as I don't feed more worms than the fry can consume in an hour or so.

As a safeguard against a culture "crashing" and to maintain maximum production, I set up a new culture each week. The oldest culture is discarded and the container is thoroughly scrubbed. After the new medium is set up to my satisfaction, I incculate it with a teaspoon ful of culture medium from my two week old culture. I spoon it up out of the middle of the container. This way I get micro worms, yeast, and active cornmeal. The new culture is off and running right away. I haven't had a culture crash in years but it is better to be safe than sorry. Additionally, I confess that a culture will survive six weeks or more, so vacations and occasional lapses of attention won't spell disaster. Production from older cultures does, however, drop to almost nothing.

The only downside to this method of culturing micro worms is that the containers are small, handy, and easily carried away from your fish room. When you loan a container to a fish friend in desperate need, and, believe me, you will, it is almost impossible to recover the container. It seems like someone is always wanting or needing micro worms. Using the three culture system of weekly rotation that someone won't be you.

Earthworms

My first exposure to earthworms was, like most boys raised in a rural setting, as fishing bait and to utilise to tease girls. Earthworms were and still are tops for both purposes and probably have been for thousands of years. As a kid, I dug earthworms in the garden, raised them in buckets of rotting apples in the basement, and had a large worm bed under some shade trees which I maintained for years with leaves and garden trash. My worm bed got coffee grounds, egg shells, and table scraps. The result was lots of worms and worm dirt. Worms have an

amazing digestive system that converts almost any organic material into more worms and dirt.

I never thought about using earthworms to feed my tropical fishes until I had graduated from the ten gallon (40 l) community tank housing guppy-size fishes to larger tanks and Neotropical cichlids. As I became fascinated with more interesting fishes and their behaviour and, of course, misbehaviour, I began to haunt the libraries and reading all the aquarium books they had. I found that earthworms were a popular food for big and small cichlids. I read about how earthworms were fed whole, in pieces, chopped up, and minced. There were even details on purging the worms prior to feeding them to the fish. (I tried the purging and got a bunch of drowned worms.) Some authors suggested dipping the worms in boiling water prior to feeding as more humane and to make chopping easier. Another proposed partially freezing to make the worms more manageable.

The only good information I got from all of this research was that earthworms were a good fish food and if chopped up to the proper size, even small fishes can benefit. From experience, I can state that purging, boiling, or semi-freezing is a bunch of hooey.

Another personal experience that enables me to steer you away from a comical disaster: don't attempt to mince earthworms in a blender. Instead of minced worms the result is a brownish soup base that is ignored by the fish and is not appreciated by even the most understanding of spouses. The odds are also very high that the use of a kitchen tool, such as a blender or food processor (not much better than a blender on worms) on earthworms will cause more problems than you can ever talk yourself out of.

From my experiences, I can help you avoid choosing the wrong worm for reliable indoor, and especially fish room, culture. My experiences have proven the African Red worm or the Dwarf African Red worm (same thing), to be as good as any I have tried and much better than most.

Worms you can buy by the pound or by the thousands are a great fish food. Nutrition-wise there is overwhelming support for earthworms being the best single food you can feed your fishes, although it is not advisable to feed your fish one type of live or frozen food only.

Culturing earthworms is accomplished in the fish room utilizing only a small section of floor space under the fish tank racks. Container size is optional; I have had good results in everything from plastic shoe boxes to large plastic tubs that have about 200 litre (50 gallon) capacity. I get my best results in covered containers which allow me to control the humidity. For the medium I use my old stand-by, damp peat moss that has a neutral pH. I have fed the worms everything from commercially available worm food to shredded newspaper and cardboard. I do dampen the newspaper or cardboard and avoid any with coloured ink. Corn meal, oatmeal, mashed potatoes, dry instant potatoes, stale bread and leftover pasta also are eagerly accepted by the earthworms.

You can either feed on the medium surface or bury the food in the middle of the culture, which is my preference. Some people advocate feeding at the surface and then covering the food with damp newspaper or damp cardboard. The worms eat the covering in short order, which is beneficial. Basically, the worms are very accommodating and will adapt to your preferences.

I am currently using sweater boxes to culture earthworms. The size is 30 cm wide by 45 cm long and 12 cm deep (12" x 18" x 5"). I like these because they stack, have nice lids that are secure but allow the culture to breathe, but most of all because they were free. I have been successful in boxes one quarter this size. I have a friend who uses a spare 55 gallon tank with excellent results.

You will soon learn what a damp but not too wet medium is and to feed the earthworms only when they have eaten the previous meal. I feed mine every three or four days. After a few months the medium will be noticeably less loose and fluffy. This is a result of the worms efficient digestive system and an accumulation of worm casts. This is the time to start a new culture with your biggest earthworms; use the rest as fish food and repot all the house plants or vitalise your garden with the old medium. The worm casts will score big points with your spouse, especially if you also do the repotting: big points, yes, but not big enough to offset the negative ones if you are caught using any kitchen appliances to process your worms.

One piece of advice, especially if you start with a small starter culture of just a few worms. Getting usable production seems to take about three very long months. From then on the culture is a very steady producer if you avoid the temptation of over harvesting your breeder adults. Without reservation, I recommend earthworms to quickly bring your fish into breeding condition. Earthworms will often bring a sulking or listless fish out of the doldrums.

With earthworms and almost no patience you can train most medium or large Neotropical cichlids to hand feed. As a parlour trick, if you have a couple of Oscars —Mother Nature's natural gluttons— and a handful of earthworms, you can send the fish into a feeding frenzy that will amaze everyone present.

In closing on earthworms, I want to relate one special tug-of-war I witnessed between young adult cichlids over the same earthworm. This tussle involved two evenly matched Texas Cichlids and one tough worm. For what seemed to take five minutes, these two fishes dragged each over, around, and through the aquarium. It reminded me of a slapstick movie. Neither fish would release the worm. The worm finally snapped and each gladiator got a piece of the earthworm and retained its untarnished ego.

I feel this story speaks volumes on how strongly fishes are attracted to earthworms. Never mind that earthworms are not a natural food for most fishes, they just love them.

Daphnia

Daphnia are a luxury for any aquarist, useful for many cichlid breeders, and handy for Rift Lake cichlid breeders. There are many species of *Daphnia* but we shall consider only one, *Daphnia* magna. The merits of *D. magna* are many and account for its popularity with aquarists and universal acceptance in the scientific community as a test animal. *D. magna* has a large size, is steadily prolific, easily fed, fairly hardy, and readily available.

Daphnia have a reproductive trait that is the basis for their popularity. With regular feeding and weekly water changes, the culture is in a constant reproductive cycle. When conditions are not hostile to the *Daphnia*, the adult females give birth to live baby females. This process is called parthenogenesis, a miracle of nature that is to the aquarist's advantage. Basically, it eliminates the sexual and egg laying part of reproduction. This speeds things up and allows a newborn female *Daphnia* to become a reproductive adult in about two and a half weeks. The best *Daphnia* culturist I know does 50% **daily** water changes on his *Daphnia* culture and, of course, feeds them heavily, at least once a day. His culture tanks literally swarm with *Daphnia* and he takes a large harvest every day. This practice is not only reaping just rewards for his efforts, but it also eliminates the risk of a culture crashing from overpopulation.

When conditions in the culture are right, the population of *Daphnia* increases in an impressive manner. Within a few days there can be so many *Daphnia* that you can barely see half way through the tank. This apparent success is, however, balanced on the brink of disaster. I had a number cultures totally wiped out from nothing more than too many *Daphnia*. I had to learn that aggressive harvesting is one of the most beneficial things I could do for the cultures. As for size, *Daphnia magna* are the largest available; mature adults are about the size of a paper match head (three millimetres).

I culture my *Daphnia* in three 80-litre (20-gallon) aquariums and maintain the cultures in the fish room where maintenance and harvesting are convenient. I intend to do a 50% water change twice a week but actually get it done about once a week.

My culture water is siphoned through a very small mesh stainless hose strainer. A brine shrimp net, piece of old handkerchief, or drip-dry polyester dress shirt will also serve to keep even the smallest *Daphnia* in the tank while siphoning old culture water. If excessive mulm builds up, I siphon the bottom with an open ended hose, sacrificing a few *Daphnia*.

With attention to detail, you can raise *Daphnia* on yeast water. Simply dissolve a ¼ teaspoon of active (baking, not brewers) yeast in warm water and add enough to the culture to slightly cloud the tank. You next feed when the *Daphnia*, which are filter feeders, clarify the water. Be warned, however, that too much yeast can deplete the tank of oxygen and the entire culture will perish. A lot safer but not so effective is the "artificial plankton-rotifer". This powder-like stuff stays suspended in water where it is available to the *Daphnia* and is of a size they can consume easily.

Daphnia production is reliable but slow. My newest and currently best system is a combination of both of the above methods with an additional aquarium animal in the combination: the snail. My preference is the Columbia Rams Horn snail but the common Rams Horn works well too.

I feed a tablespoon of dried pea soup mix to each tank on a daily or every other day basis. The snails eat the pea soup mix and the incompletely digested material in the snail droppings feeds the *Daphnia*. At least once a week I add some yeast water left over from my white worm feeding method. The yeast provides something the *Daphnia* need as there is a "bloom" of newborn *Daphnia* the day after the yeast is added. I also add a ¼ teaspoon of "artificial plankton-rotifer" suspension once or twice a week, because it seems that the adult *Daphnia* size and its nutritional value is enhanced by the "artificial plankton-rotifer".

I have developed two reliable uses for *Daphnia* in my fish breeding procedures. When I establish a pair of dwarf cichlids, which I judge to be "ready to go", in a breeding setup, I want to feed them prior to, during, and after the actual spawning process. I feel a well-fed fish is a calmer fish that is more inclined to spawn successfully and less inclined to scrap or eat eggs and fry. *Daphnia* are a non-polluting food that will survive in the tank until eaten: perfect.

The use of *Daphnia* as a biological filter in newly hatched fry containers and tanks has been exceptional effective for me. I sometimes rob fishes of their fry to ensure that the fry survive. I have found the fry of both mouthbrooders and substrate brooders fare better the first few days in a small tank or container. To avoid the problems that a box or sponge filter may cause in an immature fry tank, and to prevent the potential disasters of an unfiltered environment, I employ one of nature's most perfect biological filters: *Daphnia*.

I use a weighted airline set to a slow bubble and add a few *Daphnia* to the container. I even feed the fry when they are ready to accept food. The water stays clean and both the fry and *Daphnia* prosper. As a general rule *Daphnia* are more sensitive to pollution than the fry. If the *Daphnia* aren't stressed, the fry aren't either. When the fry get larger, I dump the entire contents into a larger growing out tank with a sponge filter. Soon the fry start to pick off the smaller *Daphnia* and not much later the adult *Daphnia* are gobbled down. How could you ask more out of a bug?

Three final hints on culturing *Daphnia*: 1) Give them light for 24 hours a day; even a low wattage is beneficial. 2) Do regular water changes on your culture. 3) Harvest regularly to prevent overpopulation.

Brine shrimp (*Artemia sp.*)

It ever there was a product that deserves to be advertised as "better for less money" or "new and improved", brine shrimp eggs are that product. Improved harvesting and innovative processing has improved brine shrimp egg quality to such an extent that the best producers can confidently guarantee a 90% hatch rate. They actually get about 95% hatch in their quality control tests and the selling price is less than it was ten years ago....

(I know that the correct terminology is brine shrimp *cysts* and not brine shrimp *eggs*. In common usage, however, eggs is interchangeable with cysts as is baby brine shrimp with brine shrimp nauplii.)

All the hard work connected with brine shrimp eggs has already been done by the time you purchase the can of eggs. I want to share some hints to help you maximize your harvest. There are many factors affecting hatch rate. The first to consider is the hatching solution. The recommended density, which ranges from 1.010 to 1.020, is obtained by dissolving salt at a rate of a tablespoon of common salt (NaCl) per litre of tap water (which must have a pH above 7), a rule of thumb method which has proved acceptable. I haven't seen any measurable difference in hatch rate whether I use expensive sea salt mix or plain salt. I use inexpensive water softener salt. However, if your tap water is very soft you are advised to use sea salt because it will stabilise the pH at a necessary alkaline level.

I find that a tablespoon of brine shrimp eggs per 2 litres (½ gallon) of hatching solution is the proper ratio for maximum hatch rate. The culture must be aerated just enough to keep the eggs in motion. A too strong an aeration may kill newly hatched nauplii. The time for hatching is dictated by the temperature. At 25 °C (78 °F) the newly hatched brine shrimp can be harvested in 36 to 48 hours. The hatch rate is improved by maintaining a 24 hour light over the hatching container. The intensity can be as low 15 Watts.

Your hatch rate and ease of harvest can be improved dramatically by using an inverted cone or pyramid-shaped hatching container constructed of glass or, preferably, Plexiglas. This shape keeps the eggs in constant motion

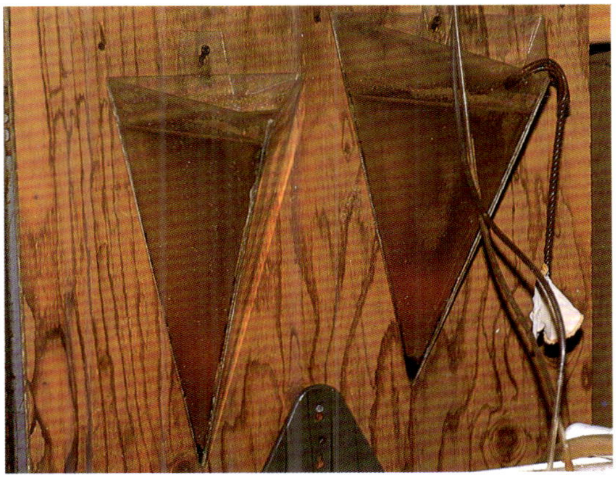

The inverted pyramid brine shrimp hatcher concentrates the hatched nauplii at a small area near the bottom (the bright orange colour represents millions of brine shrimp). Photo by Charley Grimes.

as there are no dead spots. With the inverted cone, harvest is simplified as the newly hatched brine shrimps settle to the bottom of the container and the egg shells float at the surface soon after the airline is removed. I use a large syringe to remove the newly hatched brine shrimps and drain off the salt water with a brine shrimp net. A siphon constructed of regular airline and a piece of rigid airline tubing also works well. I wash the drained baby brine shrimps into a small container with tap water and feed the shrimps to individual tanks with a small bulb syringe. This gives better control over the amount fed to each tank.

After every hatching, I thoroughly scrub the hatching container and rigid air line with a kitchen bottle brush. I feel it is well worth the effort and using new salt for each set-up is inexpensive.

Raising brine shrimps to adult size is not much more difficult than the hatching, just more time consuming. My experiences in raising brine shrimps to adult size was sort of "hit or miss" until I took my problems to Ocean Star International, a major supplier of brine shrimp eggs. Dr. Mark Lamon explained that the density of the water in the Great Salt Lake, Utah is over twice that of sea water or about 1.048. While brine shrimps hatch well at a density of about one third that of the Great Salt Lake, to raise them you must begin to increase the density to about 1.048 within 24 hours. He also recommended the use of Artificial Plankton Rotifer to feed the brine shrimp. When I followed his advice and used a sea salt mixture to provide the salinity rather than plain salt, my success in raising brine shrimps to adult size became predictable rather than random.

Is it worth your efforts to hatch brine shrimp eggs to feed your baby and juvenile fish? Definitely yes! Is it worth the effort of making or the expense of purchasing a cone or inverted pyramid shaped brine shrimp hatcher? Definitely yes! Is it worth your efforts to raise brine shrimps to adult size? Probably not, but it is fun to do and quite easy. I could raise fish without utilising brine shrimp eggs but I am sure glad I don't have to.

A final word on live food

One of the most popular live foods available at almost any pet shop is *Tubifex*. This is a thin, red worm which lives in the muddy substrate of rivers and is collected in areas where collection is profitable. Unfortunately these areas are found in heavily polluted rivers. The pollution in these waters is not restricted to waste water from housing areas but includes industrial wastes as well. Feeding such polluted worms to your fishes means that your are exposing them to various diseases. Therefore take this advice:

NEVER FEED *TUBIFEX*.

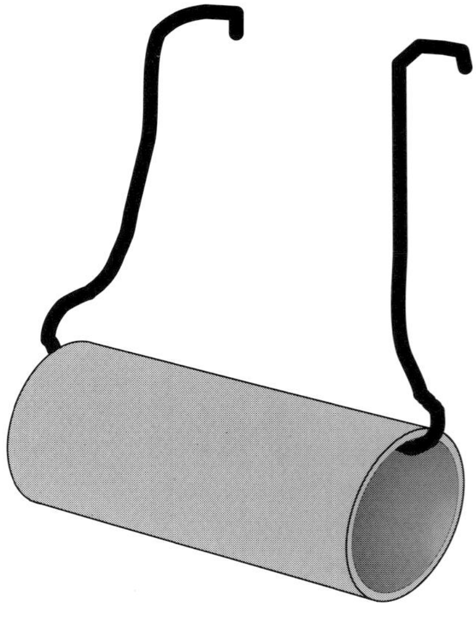

Breeding

by Ad Konings

Keeping cichlids is, of course, a very enjoyable pastime but most aquarists are not satisfied by just keeping their fishes healthy; they want to breed them. Most cichlids will, if their artificial environment allows, spawn in a community aquarium, but only a few species are able to raise a major part of their offspring to a size of 3-4 cm in the presence of other fishes. Almost all fry are eaten by other tank inhabitants, in particular during the first few days after hatching or release from the female's mouth. In order to breed cichlids in numbers a breeding or nursery tank is needed for most species. Typically a breeding tank houses only one species and the decor has been adapted to that particular species. It should provide at least one spawning site and plenty of shelter for the weaker individuals. Often harassed females seek shelter in the upper corner of the tank. A piece of plastic or clay pipe hanging from the rim of the tank (see figure at left) will provide them with a refuge. It is advisable to introduce the female into the breeding aquarium a few days before the male. Nursery tanks normally lack decoration. In the second part of this book you find many different groups of cichlids with their particular breeding requirements. This chapter contains some general information concerning the breeding of cichlids.

It goes without saying that the fishes we want to breed from should be in excellent condition. The female(s) in particular should be well-proportioned. Skinny females hardly ever produce eggs nor do overfed females. Several species have an internal clock and do not breed until their clock tells them to do so. Most such species breed only once or twice a year, and aquarists trying to breed them need to be patient. Although we can force-feed fishes, we cannot force-breed them!

In many instances it is wiser to start with a small group of juveniles and select a breeding pair or group while they grow up in the community aquarium. Juveniles, as a rule, are cheaper to purchase than adults. When adult individuals are wanted it is recommended that you try to obtain wild caught specimens, even if this is limited to one individual of the pair. Many cichlids are collected from their natural habitats and although a very few species are endangered this is not because of collection for the ornamental fish trade, but the result of environmental pollution (be it chemical or by exotic species).

Wild caught cichlids are frequently needed to introduce new blood to captive bred populations. This prevents deterioration of the captive species caused by inbreeding. Whenever more than 5% aberrant individuals appear among the offspring of a particular pair a change of one partner is strongly advised. The new partner must, of course, not be related to the previous male or female. Many species can be inbred to the fourth generation before aberrant individuals appear among the fry. The larger the group you start with the longer it takes before malformed offspring show up.

Sexing cichlids

In a large number of species pairs or breeding groups can be selected from a community by judging their behaviour and by the coloration of the sexes. Quiescent males of many mouthbrooding cichlids, however, have a coloration similar to that of females and are therefore frequently mistaken for them. On the other hand substrate brooding species may sometimes have very little sexual dimorphism (differences in shape between male and female), insufficient to determine the sex of an individual by just looking at it.

In many cases where the sex of a particular individual cannot be established by its colour, body shape, or behaviour, the shape of its vent may give a valuable indication. The vent contains of an anal pore and a genital papilla (a conical structure). The anal pore is the one closest to the pelvic fins and is similar in male and female. The genital papilla —which is closest to the anal fin— of females is wider than that of males, but one needs a lot of experience to determine the sex of a particular individual without examining and comparing other individuals of the same species. In some species, e.g. *Altolamprologus, Julidochromis*, *Ptychochromis,* and *Geophagus*, the genital papilla is pigmented (see photo of *Geophagus*) and therefore easier to examine. The slender, long-tapering papilla belongs to the male while the papilla of the female is shorter and much wider at the base.

Sexing cichlids should be learned on hardy cichlids, such as Mbuna. The individuals to be sexed are netted from the aquarium and placed in a bucket. **Fishes should be handled only with wet hands**. One by one the fishes are taken from the bucket and sexed. Large specimens are best kept in the net while examining the vent; small cichlids are held in the (wet!) hand. You need a bright light and for small species a magnifying glass. The females and males are put in separate buckets because it is likely that you are going to look at them again. The fish can be out of the water for about one minute and is then put back into the bucket. After a few minutes it can be taken out for a second time. Restrict such examinations to a maximum of three times per individual.

Bear in mind that the photographs in the right column are just an indication; to sex cichlids you need experience.

The care of eggs and fry

Most, if not all, young cichlids learn from the guarding efforts of the female how to behave when they are themselves mature and have to care for offspring. This is called

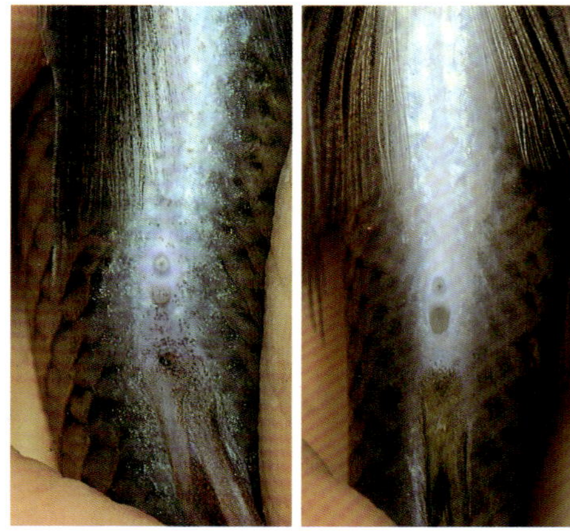

The two large photos above show the vent regions of a male (left) and a female (right) of a *Haplochromis* species from Lake Victoria. The anal pore (upper in photos) is the same size in males and females. The genital papilla (lower in photos), however, is wider in females and normally wider than the anal pore.

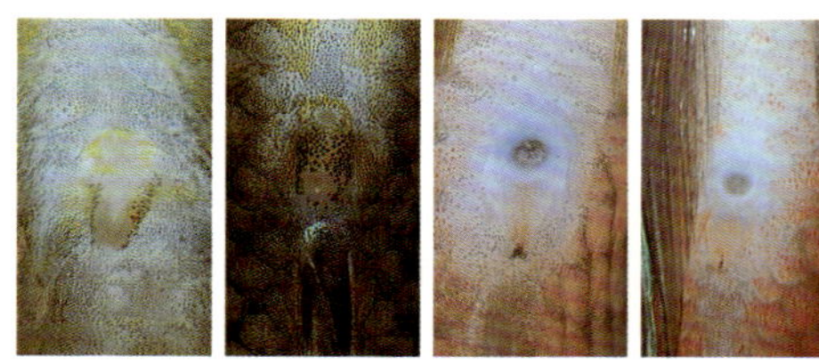

♂ *Geophagus* ♀ ♂ *Thorichthys* ♀

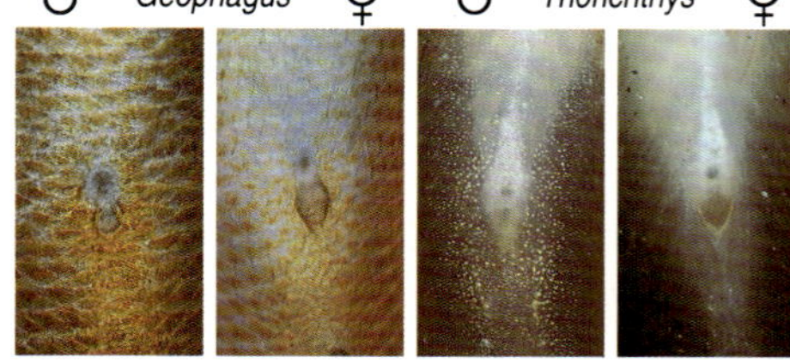

♂ *Neolamprologus* ♀ ♂ *Xenotilapia* ♀

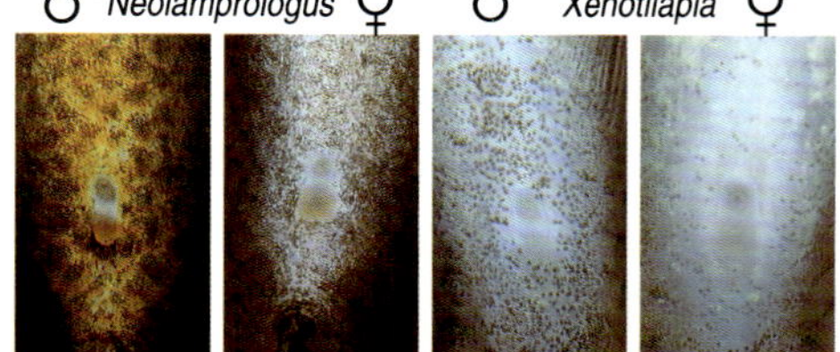

♂ *Pseudotropheus* ♀ ♂ *Stigmatochromis* ♀

imprinting. By taking the eggs away from the parent(s) —and therefore preventing the fry from being imprinted with the female's guarding and brooding behaviour— the fishes born from these artificially hatched eggs may not be good parents when adult. Their bad parenthood becomes evident when the eggs are eaten or when the female does not guard the fry or, in the case of a mouthbrooder, when the female does not hold the eggs until maturity. Such situations are clearly undesirable, even though after several failed spawnings such females may eventually raise some offspring. For this reason it is strongly advised to leave the eggs and fry under the protection of the female.

Unfortunately many professional cichlid breeders prefer to artificially hatch the eggs. Tank raised cichlids offered for sale in pet shops therefore have the potential of being bad breeders. In particular mouthbrooding females are stripped of their eggs before they are mature. In some species, especially those in which the female does not care for the fry after they have been released, artificial hatching does not seem to affect the fry's ability to raise offspring themselves. Fry of many other species, however, are affected by artificial methods.

Substrate brooders are normally bred in a special tank and the fry can be left with the female (and male) without any problem. If the parents continually eat the eggs before they hatch it is advisable to change the female and not to try and hatch the eggs artificially.

Many mouthbrooding species are bred in a community aquarium. When a female is holding eggs she should be removed to a nursery tank where she is allowed to brood and eventually release her fry. Sometimes the female spits out the eggs when she is handled with a net. In such cases the female should still be placed in the nursery tank together with the expelled eggs. In many instances she may pick up these eggs and continue brooding. However, if she does not pick up the eggs within two hours they are prone to rapid deterioration. In order to save such abandoned eggs from death they can be hatched artificially using an egg incubator.

Egg incubators have been developed by professional breeders who want maximum production from their breeding colonies. Although many different types and systems have been tried only a few have proven to yield maximum results. The incubator (adapted from Wang Kuo-Jung) sketched in the figure on the next page gives an almost 100% hatch rate and has the advantage that once installed no further maintenance is needed.

The incubator is filled with water from the aquarium. The eggs are siphoned out and

Deformed individuals should always be removed from a brood to preserve the vitality of the species kept in aquaria. Crippled and deformed cichlids frequently give birth to similarly crippled offspring, a practice which should be avoided at all costs. This monstrosity, a Siamese twin *Labeotropheus* species, was kept alive because of its rarety. Photo by Mark Smith.

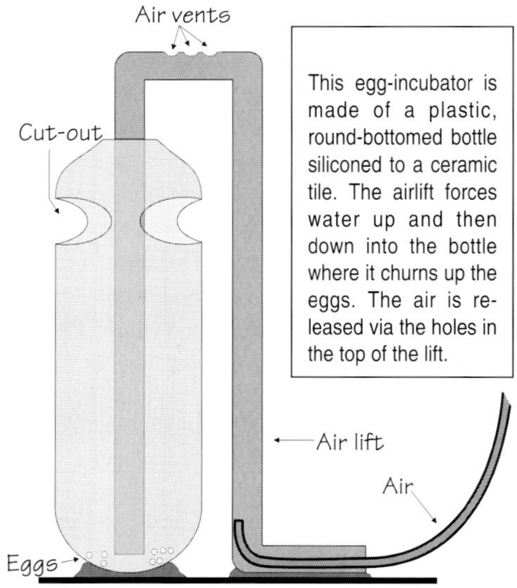

This egg-incubator is made of a plastic, round-bottomed bottle siliconed to a ceramic tile. The airlift forces water up and then down into the bottle where it churns up the eggs. The air is released via the holes in the top of the lift.

dropped into the incubator, which is then completely submerged in an empty tank with a capacity of about 50 litres. The aeration is adjusted to the lowest possible setting which still keeps the eggs churning slightly on the bottom of the incubator. Non-fertilised and deteriorated white eggs are lighter than live ones and are slowly "washed" out of the incubator. When the larvae are mature they are able to swim out of the incubator. When the first, completely mature (no yolksac visible) larvae are to be found outside the incubator the remaining fry can be removed as well. Never put eggs or larvae from different species in the same incubator nor eggs or larvae at a different stage of development.

Culling fry

Some substrate brooding species are very prolific and produce hundreds of fry. Fry of such fecund species are usually difficult to sell or give away. It is also difficult, costly, and space-consuming to raise all 2000 fry of a large Guapote knowing that they will not find homes once they are too big to be kept in your own breeding facility. It is much better for the perpetuation of the species in the hobby to select —specifically or randomly— a small number of healthy fry from large broods and expend your efforts on these. The simplest way to proceed is to take away part of the brood (about 100 babies) as soon as they start to swim free. The remaining fry will mostly be eaten by other tank inhabitants, but at the same time their parents can complete their breeding routine, thus avoiding stress between the couple. If the substrate brooder has spawned in a breeding tank you can reverse the sampling: take out most of the fry and feed them to other fishes. Leave about 100 which will be more than enough for the parents to take care of.

The fry are fed with live food small enough to be swallowed. Two types can be grown at home in small containers: brine shrimps (*Artemia* sp.) and micro worms (*Tubatrix silusiae*) (see pages 43 and 49 for further details). After a few weeks the fry are big enough to feed on *Cyclops*, small *Daphnia*, shrimp-mix, and on crushed flake food.

At any given stage in the growth of fry there are some individuals who can be seen to be deformed (in fins or body) or much smaller than their brothers and sisters. These runts should be removed from the brood. Individuals which seem to develop an apparently aberrant coloration (e.g. split bars or black blotches) should be removed as well. It is a waste of time to try and raise cichlids which are not 100% like their wild cousins. As aquarists we have the responsibility of maintaining nature's diversity and for this reason we should refrain from hybridizing or raising crippled individuals.

Two common diseases

by Mary Bailey

Although the brief of this book does not include discussion of all the diseases which may affect cichlids, there are two conditions which are rather common, and regarding which there is relatively little information available elsewhere in aquaristic literature.

It must be stressed that both conditions can largely be avoided by proper maintenance as set out in this book; with the best will in the world, however, things can sometimes go wrong, and coverage of these two problems has therefore been included.

Hexamitiasis

Hexamitiasis, or "Hole-in-Head Disease", is a problem which has beset cichlid keepers for as long as cichlids have been kept. It is often regarded as a disease primarily of Discus, but can affect any other cichlids as well. Some types, however, appear more prone than others, and the disease is relatively uncommon in African mouthbrooders. It should be mentioned, however, that the so-called "Tropheus Disease" (see page 58), which affects wild-caught *Tropheus*, is possibly a form of Hexamitiasis.

The best known sign of the disease is enlargement of the sensory pore openings on the head, which become filled with a whitish pus-like substance which may or may not ooze out in streamers —in my experience this is very rare. Often the lesions bear a resemblance to small mouth ulcers in humans, or slightly enlarged pores may exude small tufts of white. The "holes" sometimes appear in a symmetrical pattern corresponding to symmetry in the distribution of the sensory pores; they may sometimes become so large that they merge together to form a large cavity between and above the eyes, and can affect the orbit(s). Small holes in the head (with no whitish content), often the cause of much concern to novice cichlid-keepers who have heard of the disease, are no cause for alarm. These are simply the normal openings to the sensory pores. It is not unknown for the nostrils to be mistaken for Hole-in-Head!

It is not generally known that there are other signs of the disease —emaciation and poor appetite, whitish stringy faeces— or that the pores of the lateral line, especially anteriorly, may be affected as well as, or instead of, those of the head. The sensory system is not always affected at all, and the other signs are more reliable indications, especially if there is reason to believe the fish may be, or have recently been, subject to major stress of some type. Some, possibly many, unexplained deaths may be due to undiagnosed Hexamitiasis.

Scientists remain undecided about the exact cause of the disease. Cichlids showing the classic Hole-in-Head syndrome have been found to contain heavy infestations of a tiny flagellated organism belonging to the genus *Hexamita*, which also affects salmonids and some non-cichlid tropicals. It is not known whether the species found in salmonids (*H. salmonis*) affects these other fishes, or whether other types are involved. It has been suggested that each affected species may have its own specific form of the organism. One separate species (*H. symphodoni*), found in Discus, has been described but whether or not this is valid, or whether it is this which affects other cichlids is not known. Some authorities consider that Hole-in-Head in *Pterophyllum* (freshwater Angelfishes) is caused by *Spironucleus elegans*, a very similar organism which also affects carp; yet others consider all cichlid Hole-in-Head to be caused by *Spironucleus*. *Octomitus*, now normally regarded as an obsolete name, is still mentioned in aquarium literature. For the purposes of this article the name *Hexamita* is applied to flagellates referred to any of these three genera.

To confuse the issue even further it is unclear whether the disease is actually caused by the *Hexamita* organism, or by bacteria found in conjunction with it, or perhaps even by both. However, one may surmise that as treatment with antibiotics (which do not affect *Hexamita*) is ineffective, while anti-flagellate drugs usually effect a cure, the organism is at least partially responsible.

Hexamita is a normal inhabitant of the intestines of cichlids which have not been treated against it. It is a weak parasite, harmless under normal conditions, and perfectly healthy cichlids can, and do, carry the organism without any ill effects. Under conditions of abnormal stress, however, the fishes' resistance may be lowered; and it seems that *Hexamita* then multiplies, invades the bloodstream, and migrates to other areas of the body. If it reaches the sensory pores of the head then the classic symptom is seen. If the infestation proves lethal then this may be the result of damage to one or more of the vital organs (brain, liver, etc.). Progress of the disease is often slow, and death may not occur until months after the first signs are noted.

Stress may be physical (poor water quality; sudden change in water quality, chemistry, temperature; incorrect water chemistry; incorrect diet; excessive handling; attack by tankmates; other disease or parasitic infestation) or purely psychological (no suitable shelter; excessive illumination (strength and/or duration); intimidation by tankmates; transportation or change of tank; excessive disturbance of any kind). Of these the most important are probably

the psychological factors and those concerning water quality and chemistry. In addition Hole-in-Head may appear as a concomitant of old age, particularly in species from soft acid waters (including *Apistogramma, Astronotus*, and *Cichla* from South America, and *Pelvicachromis* from West Africa).

Prevention is the keyword, and this is obviously a case of avoiding stress, particularly in sensitive species. There is no evidence that high temperatures are effective as either a curative or preventative, as is often claimed. If a serious (i.e. evident) infestation is diagnosed this cannot be remedied simply by removing the stress. A cure can sometimes be effected by the use of Metronidazole or di-Metronidazole, prescription drugs obtainable from a veterinarian, who should be consulted regarding dosage using the particular form supplied. In the case of "Flagyl" (a brand name for Metronidazole) tablets, however, suggested dosage is 10 mg per litre, with 3 consecutive treatments given at 48 hour intervals. The tablets should be ground up and mixed with a little aquarium water, which is then dispersed through the aquarium. If the fishes are still feeding then a small amount of the drug can be mixed with the food. Biological filtration is not affected.

Unfortunately it appears that there are strains of *Hexamita* resistant to Metronidazole (possibly through excessive and/or ill-considered use), and in such cases di-Metronidazole may be tried instead. **No other effective treatments are known**.

Effectively treated fishes (and their offspring) will remain free of the disease unless re-infected by contact with untreated fishes (or water/equipment which has recently contacted them). The organism appears incapable of living for more than a few hours without a living host, so sterilisation of equipment and aquaria is not indicated.

Malawi Bloat and Tropheus Disease

This condition affects not only Lake Malawi mouthbrooders but also some of those from

Lake Tanganyika, especially *Tropheus*. The first and most important symptom is loss of appetite. Left untreated this is followed by gross distension of the body, particularly the ventral region; increased respiratory rate; the fish normally rests on the bottom, though may also hang at the surface. If these other symptoms are diagnosed it is usually too late to treat the fish, and death normally results within 24-72 hours of their onset.

It is unusual for more than a single fish to be affected at any one time in any tank, though deaths may occur at intervals of a few weeks or longer for months or even years if the cause is not identified and eradicated.

Three main causes, all "environmental", have been identified by evaluation of large numbers of cases over a period of 10 years or more; so that, where deaths are occurring on a regular basis, identification and elimination of the causative factor almost invariably ends the succession of cases immediately. This has been taken as empirical evidence that the putative causative factors are valid.

These causative factors are as follows: 1) The addition of large quantities (more than 6 grams/litre) of common salt (Sodium Chloride, NaCl) in the mistaken belief that this will help simulate natural water conditions. This practice is most common in areas with naturally soft tap water. The effects are the same in hard water. 2) Long term exposure to poor water quality (nitrate concentrations). 3) Incorrect diet: in particular a diet containing large amounts of beef heart; over-feeding with dried foods; or overfeeding with any food(s).

Cause 3) has been validated by scientific experiments (in Canada) involving heavy feeding of *Tropheus duboisi* with a single unsuitable food. Specimens which developed bloat were dissected and found to have severe inflammatory conditions of the intestines, with bacteria and protozoa present. The surviving fishes were treated with antibiotics, but as the diet was changed simultaneously the researchers' assumption that the drugs effected a cure has to be regarded as unproven; in practice correction of diet will normally prevent further cases.

More recently it has been suggested that Bloat may, like Hexamitiasis, be caused by a flagellate which becomes invasive when the fish is stressed. Where treatment has been initiated at an early stage a cure has been effected using Emtryl (Metrinodazole) or Flagyl (as for Hexamitiasis). The treatment should be preceded by a 30% water change and accompanied by increased aeration. It must be stressed that treatment must begin as soon as the first signs of illness are detected —once the abdomen has swollen irreparable internal damage is likely.

Tropheus Disease, which is also diagosed by the loss of appetite, mainly affects wild-caught *Tropheus*. It responds to a combination treatment with Metronidazole and Nifurpirinol (a powerful antibiotic; e.g. Aqua-Furan, Aquarium Münster, Germany), which should be administered only under veterinary supervision —immunity to antibiotics— and which is harmful to biological filters.

Except for very rare cases, probably with quite different "one-off" causes, Bloat can easily be avoided by eliminating the causative factors. My studies of the subject have been somewhat hampered by never myself having a case in my tanks, and a total reluctance to try and prove my theories by maltreating my fishes! Bloat did not arrive in the hobby together with its victims; it appeared when their availability increased without a parallel increase in availability of accurate information on their true requirements, or indeed, in awareness that they **have** any special requirements.

Treating cichlids

by Gary Kratochvil

Unpacking fish

After you have purchased the cichlids of your choice they need proper care, starting from the moment you unpack them. Fishes that have travelled for more than one hour in a bag, bucket, or box may have fouled the water with their excrement. In many cases the pH of the water in the transport container will have dropped to a level below neutral. Although the fishes seem to do fine, swimming in the often clouded water, they can easily be killed by pouring water from the aquarium into the dirty water of the bag. We have seen in the chapter about water (page 20) that ammonia (a toxic gas) is formed from waste products and that the speed of this process increases drastically with the raising of the pH above 7. When the pH of the dirty water in a bag with fishes is raised to above 7 there is a great risk of killing all the fishes in it.

In order to prevent sudden ammonia intoxication you have to measure the pH of the transport water when this is not crystal clear or when the fishes have been in it for more than two or three hours. If the pH of the aquarium water (in which the new fishes are to be placed) is above 7 then you should take the following precautions: prepare fresh water with approximately the same pH (but not below pH 6) as that of the transport water. The pH can conveniently be lowered by adding distilled vinegar (acetic acid, which is available from drugstores; do not use common vinegar!) to the water. Then the closed bag with the fishes is placed in this water to equalise the temperature. After about 10 minutes the fishes are taken out of the bag and placed in the fresh water with adjusted pH (and with airstone). None of the water in the bag should be poured into the bucket because often it contains drugs to sedate the fishes during transport. You have to go through this procedure to prevent the fishes from suffering pH-shock.

Only when the fishes are in clean water with a low pH can you mix this water with that from the aquarium until the fishes are adjusted to the higher pH. This should not take longer than about one hour.

If the aquarium water has a pH below or about 7 then the water in the bag can be mixed immediately with fresh water from the tank. After about 20 minutes the fishes can be placed in the tank. Never pour the transport water into the aquarium!

Quarantine

It is not a good idea to add any wild-caught fishes without a quarantine period to an existing community. Fishes that have been together in an aquarium for more than several months live in a kind of balance where each of them accepts or tolerates the other inhabitants. Such a balance is disturbed by adding new individuals to the community. It is almost certain that some fishes in the tank (not necessarily the new ones) will become stressed by the new situation and thus be more vulnerable to disease. Before fishes are added they should be cleaned of parasites and possible diseases in order to avoid stressed fishes in the community attracting these and dying. New fishes, in particular wild-caught individuals, should be placed in a small quarantine aquarium for about one month. Ideally such a tank should have a capacity of about 100 litres, but it all depends on the size of the fishes to be quarantined. The water in the quarantine tank should be changed (about 30%; do not forget the water conditioner) every week. The filtration of the water is best achieved with a sponge filter. Never add antibiotics or Metronidazole to the water as a prophylactic because this may stimulate the growth of resistant strains of bacteria or parasites which, once in the system, are difficult to get rid of. Prophylactic treatment may further stress your new fishes. The only preparations that can be added to the water are those that stimulate the formation of the fishes' mucus coating. Some of these preparations also condition the water and are thus ideal in such situations. If after the first few days your new fishes start showing signs of body or fin fungus, "ich", other parasitic or bacterial problems you should treat with the drug recommended by an experienced aquarist or veterinarian at this time (see below). Keep in mind that Malawi and Tanganyika cichlids are sensitive to medicines based on copper.

If, after one month of quarantine, the fishes show no sign of disease they can be added to the community. How fishes are introduced to an existing community is discussed on page 17.

Sick fishes

Almost all fish illnesses in captivity are of environmental origin. Keeping fish alive and healthy is largely a case of optimising their environment and minimising stress. Unfortunately sick fishes do occur and it is only natural to wish to cure them.

It is recommended that a sick fish be diagnosed by an experienced aquarist. Medicine can be obtained from a pet shop or veterinarian. A sick fish is placed in the quarantine tank —only a single fish per tank is treated. The most common way to administer medicine is to dissolve it in the aquarium water. If the medicine is to treat an internal disease a more direct approach is to let the fish eat it. Make a concentrated solution of the medicine (ask a veterinarian or an experienced aquarist about the appropriate concentration for the medicine in question). Take a few millilitres of this solution and let it be absorbed by pelleted food (some brands of pellets contain products of warm blooded animals: don't use them!). The treated pellets are fed to the diseased fish. When feeding the highly recommended shrimp-mix (see page 35) you could dissolve the medicine in the mix just before it hardens. Shrimp-mix has a natural attractant and is eaten by most cichlids the first time it is offered.

In many cases the diseased fish will not or is not able to eat. But in such cases you do not always have to resort to dissolving the medicine into the aquarium water. Treating the aquarium water is definitely the least effective method of treating internal problems and may disrupt the normal biological balance of the tank. Oral administration is a superior method of delivery. Fishes bigger than 10 cm can be force-fed with the aid of a syringe and a feeding tube. The dosage will vary depending on the drug used and the weight of the patient. To determine the weight of the patient, put it in a plastic bag and quickly weigh it on a gram scale. Substract the weight of the bag to get the net weight of the patient. Adult *Tropheus*, for instance, usually weigh approximately 50 grams, *Cyphotilapia frontosa* (20-25 cm) weigh 200-250 grams. Take the flake or pellets and crush them into a fine powder. Add the correct amount of medicine dilluted in distilled water and make this powder into a creamy paste. If you make the paste too thick it will be difficult to inject it through the feeding tube. If you do not have a scale to calculate the dosage, use commercially available medicated flake or pelleted food. The mixture is then put inside the syringe avoiding large air bubbles. The feeding tube should have a relatively wide diameter (about 1 mm (#16 gauge) or a plastic tube with a diameter of about 3 mm) to allow the passage of the mixture. The diseased fish is netted from the tank and held firmly in one (wet!) hand. The mouth is held open with a finger and the feeding tube is passed just beyond the pharyngeal bones, 5 mm into the gullet (see photo). The mixture is slowly expelled into the stomach. A large *C. frontosa* needs about 1-2 cc of mixture once a day. A fish with a length of about 10 cm cannot be fed more than 0.5 cc of the food-medicine mixture per day.

Some old cichlids may eventually recover from a disease but are then too weak to eat. Such individuals have also been successfully cured by force-feeding them for a few weeks. By the time they regained a normally rounded abdomen they were feeding by themselves.

A word of warning is necessary: only after an experienced aquarist or veterinarian has diagnosed a disease in your fish is it worthwile to try to force-feed it. One of the main criteria is that it has not eaten and excreted for at least THREE weeks. Unnecessary handling of fishes is stressful and may weaken them (even more).

Wounds

Wounded fishes should be treated to prevent an outbreak of disease. Small wounds such as a ripped off scale or a bite off a fin

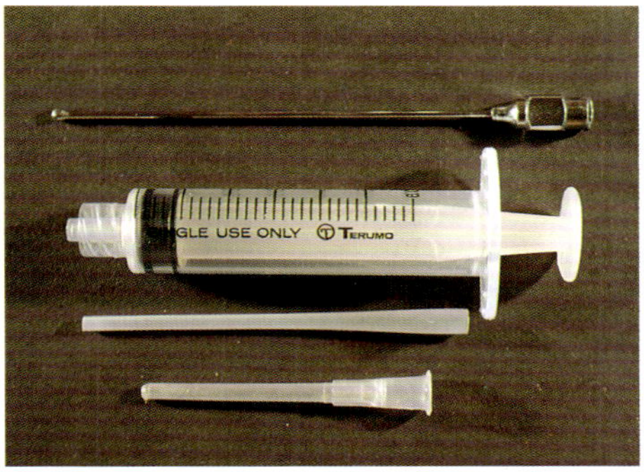

Force-feeding is advisable only when the sick fish has refused to eat for at least three weeks and no signs of excrement have been seen.
Left: the feeding tube, through which the food is forced into the fishes' gullet, should have a rounded tip and a wide diameter (one metal and two plastic tubes shown).
Below: Force-feeding *Cyphotilapia frontosa.* The fish is held firmly in one (wet!) hand while the other carefully brings the feeding tube into the gullet. The medicine-food mixture is gently expelled into the stomach. Photos by Gary Kratochvil.

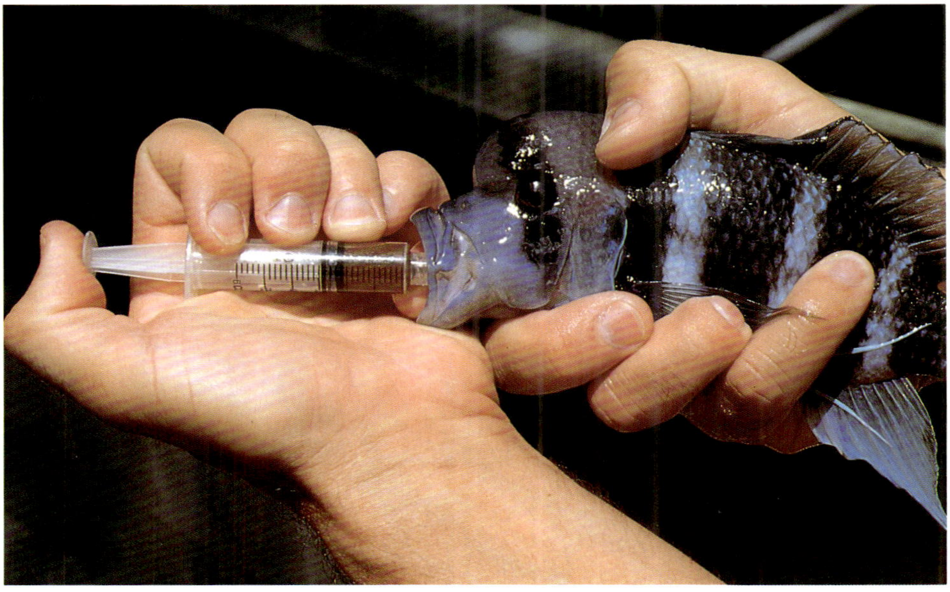

usually do not need special attention when the water of the aquarium is clean and regularly changed. Only in very dirty tanks is fungus likely to develop on such small wounds.

Large wounds caused by fights should be treated. The wounded fish should be separated from the others, preferably in a quarantine tank. Once a day it is netted from the tank and the wound is treated with an antibiotic ointment. Such ointment is available from a veterinarian. It usually contains a cocktail of antibiotics. For wounds to the eye an antibacterial ophthalmic ointment should be used (ask your vet). The wound and the skin around it is blotted dry with a tissue. The antibiotic ointment is smeared thinly on the wound and the patient is held by hand out of the water for one minute and then gently released back into the tank. Most of the ointment will be washed off upon contact with the water but enough remains to heal the wound. Repeat this treatment daily until the wound shows signs of healing.

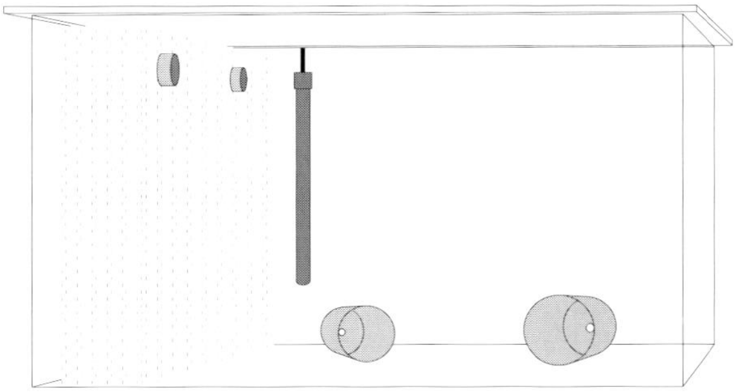

A quarantine tank. The filtration consists of a piece of coarse sponge which fits tightly at one end of the tank. Two airlifts supply enough circulation for it to work properly. A quarantine tank should be placed in a quiet spot and preferably not have a bright light above.

Transporting cichlids

Shipping cichlids is no problem when the following points are taken into consideration. When fishes have to remain in a bag for more than two hours it is advisable to pack them under oxygen. When no oxygen is available one should pack the fishes at low density (single pack or very large bags) or supply the water with oxygen using a battery operated air pump (only necessary when the fishes are confined to the bag for more than 12 hours). Fishes that have to be packed for a long journey need to be "cleaned" before shipment. The fishes to be shipped are put in buckets or bare tanks and not fed for two days. Twice (or more times) a day the wastes are siphoned off until the water stays crystal clean. When the fishes have emptied their guts completely they can be bagged for shipment. Do not add antibiotics to the transport water. Fishes larger than 7 cm (3") can be sedated by adding a fish calmer, such as "Hypno", to the water, but this is necessary only when more than one fish is packed in a bag AND when the journey is longer than 12 hours. The plastic bags used for transport should be sturdy and must have rounded corners. Always double bag fishes. A second bag is put over the first and tied with a second rubber band. Plastic bags with pointed corners can still be used for shipment if the corners are sealed off or closed by tying a rubber band around them. When packing bags in a box do not place them on top of each other. During transport the upper bags may push the oxygen and, eventually, the water out of the lower ones. Clearly mark the box that the contents are live tropical fishes and that it should not be placed in excessively hot or cold areas.

Some examples

For those of you who would like an idea how many and what kind of cichlids can be kept in a community aquarium we give here some examples for five different groups, together with references (which can also be used for identifying your fishes) in which you should find colour photographs of most of the species mentioned.

It is assumed that the aquarium has a regular shape and that its decor includes the necessary shelter.

Tanganyika cichlids

KONINGS, A. & DIECKHOFF, H.W. (1992) *Tanganyika Secrets.* Cichlid Press, St. Leon-Rot, Germany. 208pp; 351 colour photos. ISBN 3-928457-09-8.

Aquarium 100 litres: pair *Neolamprologus brichardi*; pair *N. brevis*; pair *Julidochromis ornatus.*

Aquarium 200 litres: pair *Neolamprologus leleupi*; pair *Neolamprologus buescheri*; pair *Lamprologus ocellatus*; 5 *Paracyprichromis nigripinnis.*

Aquarium 400 litres: group of 12 (4 males, 8 females) *Tropheus duboisi,* pair *Eretmodus cyanostictus*; pair *J. transcriptus*, group of 10 *Neolamprologus multifasciatus.*

Malawi cichlids

KONINGS, A. (1990) *Cichlids and all the other fishes of Lake Malawi.* TFH Publications, Neptune, New Jersey, USA. 495pp. ISBN 0-86622-527-7.

Aquarium 100 litres: group (one male, three females) *Aulonocara ethelwynnae.*

Aquarium 200 litres: pair *Melanochromis johanni*; 1:2 (1 male, 2 females) *Labidochromis caeruleus* (yellow); 1:3 *Pseudotropheus saulosi.*

Aquarium 400 litres: group (1:3) of *Copadichromis borleyi*; pair *Aulonocara jacobfreibergi,* pair *Sciaenochromis fryeri* (Electric Blue), 3 pairs *Labid. caeruleus* (yellow).

West African cichlids

LINKE, H. & STAECK, W. (1981) *Afrikanische Cichliden I. Buntbarsche aus Westafrika.* Tetra Verlag, Melle, Germany. 142pp; 118 colour photos. (English text available).

Aquarium 100 litres: pair *Pelvicachromis taeniatus*; pair *Anomalochromis thomasi.*

Aquarium 200 litres: pair *Steatocranus casuarius*; pair *S. tinanti*; pair *Teleogramma brichardi.*

Central American cichlids

KONINGS, A. (1989) *Cichlids from Central America.* TFH Publications, Neptune, New Jersey, USA. 223pp; 550+ colour photos. ISBN 0-86622-700-8.

Aquarium 100 litres: pair *Herotilapia multispinosa*; pair *Thorichthys aureus.*

Aquarium 200 litres: pair *Thorichthys meeki*; pair *Theraps coeruleus.*

Aquarium 400 litres: pair *Herichthys carpintis*; pair *Amphilophus longimanus*; pair *Neetroplus panamensis.*

South American cichlids

LINKE, H. & STAECK, W. (1984) *Amerikanische Cichliden I.* and *II.* Tetra Verlag, Melle, Germany. 194pp; 120 colour photos (English text available).

Aquarium 100 litres: pair *Microgeophagus ramirezi*; pair *Dicrossus filamentosus.*

Aquarium 200 litres: pair *Biotodoma* sp. "Santarem"; pair *Krobia guianensis*; 1:3 *Apistogramma steindachneri.*

Tanganyika cichlids

by Ad Konings

The popularity of Tanganyika cichlids has been steadily growing since the first fishes were imported in the late fifties. In the beginning Tanganyikans were considered difficult. Until more information about the chemistry of the water in Lake Tanganyika became known, aquarists kept these species in water which was too acidic. The most important factor in keeping Tanganyika cichlids properly is the pH of the water; it should always be higher than 7.5, preferably between pH 7.8 and 9.5.

The temperature of the water should be between 23 and 27 °C. Water with a temperature higher than 29 °C can be lethal to Tanganyika cichlids!

The water in the lake is very clear and in the upper 40 metres oxygen-rich. The oxygen content of the aquarium water is very important and should be as close to saturation as possible. This means that frequent water changes (30% each week) should dilute the waste products which may otherwise produce a too high concentration of noxious gases (carbondioxide and ammonia) and compete out the oxygen. Aeration of the water is a must and for larger aquaria a trickle filter is recommended. The requirement for oxygen increases dramatically when the temperature of the aquarium water rises above 29 °C. Above 30 °C the oxygen content must be near saturation otherwise the cichlids will die of suffocation. If outside temperatures on a hot summer day may raise the aquarium water temperature above 30 °C remedial action must be taken. The aquarium (or room) must then be insulated to prevent overheating or the water must be kept cool by daily changes and kept saturated with oxygen. Tanganyika cichlids are more likely to die of overheating than from too low a temperature.

Coarse sand is recommended as a substratum for the bottom of the aquarium, unless an undergravel filter is used. Sand-dwelling cichlids need sand and can therefore not be housed properly in an aquarium with an undergravel filter. Several other species dig crater nests and they too are better housed in an aquarium with sand on the bottom.

Real plants, especially *Vallisneria, Anubias,* and *Ceratophyllum* can be kept with most Tanganyika cichlids. These have tough leaves and are normally left unharmed. In the lake water plants are only found in shallow bays.

Aquarists who wish to breed Tanganyika cichlids or who want to introduce wild caught fishes to an established aquarium need at least two small extra aquaria. These are used as quarantine or nursery tanks. When only one fish at a time is kept in such tanks decoration or bottom substratum is not necessary. A heater, an inside filter-box and a cover are the only items needed to render these tanks, which should have a contents of about 50 litres, suitable for their purpose.

Photos facing page; top: *Julidochromis marlieri* in its natural biotope (Magara, Burundi). The elongated cichlid lives in narrow recesses of the rocky habitat.
bottom: A female *Chalinochromis brichardi*; another rock-dwelling elongated cichlid preferring the dark caves in the rocky habitat.

***Julidochromis*-group**	max. size in cm	shallow bays	deep mud	sand	empty shells	rocks and sand	surge	steep rocks
Chalinochromis brichardi	14							
C. sp. "Bifrenatus"	14							
Julidochromis dickfeldi	11							
J. marlieri	15							
J. ornatus	9							
J. regani	15							
J. transcriptus	7							
Telmatochromis bifrenatus	7							
T. brichardi	8							
T. dhonti	15							
T. temporalis	10							
T. vittatus	11							

Julidochromis-group

This group consists of small, elongated cichlids which are best kept as pairs.

Behaviour in the wild

Julidochromis and *Chalinochromis* are normally found in pairs when adult or solitary when younger. They remain close to the rocks which they need for protection. *Telmatochromis* is usually found in small groups except *T. dhonti* which lives in pairs when adult. *T. temporalis* is frequently seen on its own.

Behaviour in the aquarium

Julidochromis and *Chalinochromis* are best kept as pairs. The sexes can be determined by examining the vents (page 52), even in sub-adult individuals. Avoid keeping pairs of two or more species of *Julidochromis* (or *Chalinochromis*) in the same aquarium. Otherwise there is a strong possibility of continuous fighting or hybridisation. It is possible to keep one pair of a *Julidochromis* sp. and one pair of a *Chalinochromis* sp. in the same tank.

Telmatochromis dhonti can be kept only in pairs and need to be housed with robust tank mates. *T. temporalis* and *T. vittatus* are best kept in pairs, but *T. bifrenatus* and *T. brichardi* also do well in small groups of about 5 individuals.

Apart from *T. dhonti* and, in some cases *T. temporalis*, all of these species are relatively peaceful towards other cichlids in the aquarium and can be added to almost any type of Tanganyika community tank.

Aquarium

For one pair of *J. transcriptus* or *J. ornatus* a 40-litre tank is usually sufficient, but pairs of the other species prefer a tank with a capacity of at least 75 litres. *T. bifrenatus* and *T. brichardi* will use empty shells —do not use sea shells— as shelter, as long as the fishes fit into them.

Feeding

In the wild these fishes feed on various kinds of food. They are, however, predominantly predatory species feeding on items ranging from tiny snails (e.g. *J. marlieri*), eggs from other, much larger cichlids (e.g.

T. brichardi), to algae (*T. temporalis*).

The recommended food is frozen or live *Cyclops* or *Daphnia*. Larger individuals can be fed with shrimp mix (see page 35), *Mysis* or other crustaceans. Dry food is readily taken but must be of a good quality (see page 34) to result in colourful and healthy fishes.

Breeding

Although spawning will take place in a community aquarium these species should be bred in a special breeding tank if one wants to obtain reasonable numbers of offspring. *Julidochromis* has two different breeding strategies. A pair may produce large clutches (50 to 100 eggs) every five to seven weeks or small ones (5 to 20 eggs) every week. *Julidochromis* likes to spawn in narrow caves. To provide a pair with a suitable spawning site a slate (at least 25 cm long for the larger *Julidochromis*) is placed against a dark side of the tank. It is even better to lay such a slate on the bottom with one end raised slightly by means of a small stone underneath. The narrow horizontal cave thus created should not be higher than a few centimetres. The eggs are deposited on the ceiling of such a cave. The tank should also contain a small clay flowerpot or a few small rocks which can be used as a refuge by a harassed partner. Once the pair has settled peacefully in the breeding tank, it is strongly advised not to change the arrangement of the rocks because these mark the boundaries of the territories of both male and female.

When several breeding pairs have to be accommodated it is suggested that breeding tanks such as those described by John Szwechlowicz (1991) should be set up. The rockwork in such a tank is glued onto an elevated shelf. The idea is that every two to three months the fry are removed from the breeding tank to give the parents more space and incentive to produce more offspring. The catching of the fry is facilitated by lowering the water to below the shelf. The big advantage is that the position of the rocks does not change, which would otherwise provoke territorial problems between male and female.

Chalinochromis, *T. dhonti*, and *T. temporalis* prefer a spawning site between some rocks or inside a flowerpot (or ceramic cave). The breeding tank must be of at least 75 litres capacity and have separate refuges for both partners.

The preferred spawning site of *T. brichardi*, *T. vittatus*, and *T. bifrenatus* consists of a tiny cave into which the pair can only with difficulty enter at the same time. When the pair is still small such a cave can be provided by an empty snail shell. Large pairs can be accommodated with flowerpots, ceramic caves or heaps of rock. The best time to remove the fry is when they are about six weeks old, and at the latest when the parents start chasing them.

Neolamprologus brichardi group

The species of this group are normally kept in pairs in a community aquarium where they require a relatively large territory.

Behaviour in the wild

N. buescheri, *N. falcicula*, and *N. savoryi* are most frequently seen in pairs. They defend a small cave between the rocks as a territory and remain rather close to these rocks. Pairs of *N. brichardi*, *N. crassus*, *N. gracilis*, *N. pulcher*, and *N. splendens* also defend territories but these are so close together that it appears that they live in schools. Groups of territorial *brichardi*-types may

***N. brichardi* group**	max. size in cm	shallow bays	deep mud	sand	empty shells	rocks and sand	surge	steep rocks
Neolamprologus brichardi	10							
N. buescheri	9							
N. crassus	7							
N. falcicula	8							
N. gracilis	10							
N. pulcher	10							
N. savoryi	8							
N. splendens	8							

number several hundred individuals.

Behaviour in the aquarium

In aquaria larger than 150 litres it is possible to house a small group of one of these species. In a community tank one pair of these cichlids may take a large part of the rocky decoration as territory thereby limiting the space for other territorial species.

It is possible to keep *N. brichardi* together with *N. buescheri* and also with *N. crassus, N. gracilis*, or *N. falcicula*. However, it is better to avoid keeping *brichardi*-types that resemble each other in the same aquarium. When *N. brichardi* is put together with *N. pulcher* hybridisation may occur, and this can also be the case with the other species of this group. It is therefore wiser to have one species per aquarium. *N. buescheri* can be housed with any of them. In general each pair of these species needs a territory with a diameter between 40 and 70 cm. Groups (three pairs or more) of one species need relatively less space; but not much less.

Photo facing page: The princess of Burundi (*Neolamprologus brichardi*) in its natural habitat (Magara, Burundi).
Photo top: *Neolamprologus buescheri* has become a very popular Tanganyika cichlid since its discovery in 1982.

Aquarium

There should be as many caves in the tank as there are territorial fishes. Caves can be created by piling small rocks or using ceramic caves. The minimum size of tank for a pair of a *brichardi*-type cichlids is approximately 40 litres. A pair of *N. buescheri* need about double that volume.

Feeding

In the wild these cichlids feed predominantly on zooplankton and on tiny invertebrates in the biocover.

The recommended food is frozen *Cyclops, Artemia*, and other planktonic crustaceans. White worms are eagerly taken but have a high fat content and should be given in limited quantities. Dry food is accepted but will not be sufficient for *N. buescheri* to maintain breeding condition.

Breeding

The *brichardi*-type cichlids are easily bred in a small breeding tank. A breeding tank of less than 50 litres capacity will accommodate only a single pair. The sexes can easily be distinguished by examining the vents (see page 52). Let an experienced aquarist sex your fish if you are not certain you can handle the fish without harming it.

There are two methods of breeding *N. buescheri* successfully. One is to give the pair a large breeding tank, at least 100 litres, and many hiding places. When the pair is adult, it is better to place the female in the breeding tank a few days before the male is introduced. After the male has been placed with the female check the tank frequently, for the male may harass the female during the first few days. When the pair have accepted each other they may stay together peacefully for several years. In that case it is important never to change the lay-out of the decoration. A flowerpot or ceramic cave will be fine as a spawning site. The male does not necessarily need a separate refuge.

A safer option is to introduce a few small individuals into a community aquarium and let one pair form. Then remove the other bueschéri and provide the pair with a spawning site. When other cichlids are around a *bueschéri*-pair is too busy defending their territory to quarrel among themselves.

The brood-size of *N. brichardi* and similar species ranges between 30 and 100 fry, that of *N. buescheri* between 5 and 50. The latter may spawn small clutches every two weeks or so or larger ones every six to eight weeks.

Neolamprologus leleupi group

The species of this group are solitary predators, with males as well as females chasing conspecifics from the feeding site. This behaviour makes them difficult aquarium residents.

Behaviour in the wild

The cichlids of this group are usually seen searching for prey among the rocks of their environment. Both males and females are solitary. Although in some places some of these species can be common, most of them are rare or live a hidden life. The fact that these species have to search for food over a large area indicates that their prey is not abundantly available. This is the reason why they don't like to see competitors feeding in their domain. At breeding time, however, a male and female must tolerate each other in order to propagate the species. When a male and female of any of these species are observed together they will be guarding eggs or fry. Aggression during the breeding period is mostly directed against fry-eating intruders and, of course, conspecifics; other species are ignored as long as they don't resemble conspecifics.

Behaviour in the aquarium

These species can readily be kept in a community aquarium. Care must be taken not to house *Lepidiolamprologus* species with small fishes which they may consider as food.

Only one pair of any species can be housed in the same aquarium, and avoid keeping the

***N. leleupi* group**	max. size in cm	shallow bays	deep mud	sand	empty shells	rocks and sand	surge	steep rocks
Lepidiolamprologus elongatus	20							
L. kendalli	18							
Neolamprologus cylindricus	11							
N. fasciatus	14							
N. furcifer	16							
N. leleupi	11							
N. modestus	12							
N. mondabu	11							
N. mustax	9							
N. niger	7							
N. nigriventris	10							
N. obscurus	9							
N. pectoralis	12							
N. petricola	12							

following species together (because of their similar morphology and behaviour): *L. elongatus* and *L. kendalli*; *N. furcifer* and *N. pectoralis*; *N. modestus* and *N. petricola*; *N. mustax, N. leleupi* and *N. cylindricus*; and *N. niger* and *N. obscurus*. The latter two are better not housed together with *N. leleupi* as well.

As mentioned before these species are harmless towards other species but can be extremely pugnacious towards their own. It is very important to be sure of having a male and a female. See therefore the photos of the vents on page 52. If juveniles are introduced into the aquarium a small group can be housed together, but as soon as the sexes can be differentiated a pair should be selected and the remaining individuals removed. It is difficult to introduce an adult pair into a tank. The best way is to first let the female adjust to the new environment before placing the male with her some days later.

Aquarium

L. elongatus, L. kendalli, N. fasciatus, N. furcifer, N. pectoralis and *N. petricola* need an aquarium which is at least 125 cm long and which has a minimum capacity of 300 litres. In the case of *L. kendalli* it is very important to have a tightly fitting cover because individuals may jump out of the tank when chased.

The other species need a tank which is at least 75 cm long. The decoration of the aquarium should contain many caves to protect the female from harassment. Additional shelter can be provided by a small plastic pipe suspended from the top of the tank (page 51) or by water plants (*Ceratophyllum*).

Feeding

In the lake these cichlids feed on invertebrates which are found on the substratum. *L. elongatus* and *L. kendalli* also feed on small fishes.

Although flake food and pellets are accepted by most of these species, live or frozen crustaceans (shrimp mix), mosquito larvae (white and black, but not red!) or plankton are recommended. *N. leleupi* needs to have *Cyclops*, *Mysis* or other carotene-containing food (not *Daphnia*) if it is to show a bright orange-yellow colour.

Breeding

If care has been taken when selecting a pair and decorating the tank, breeding follows if a suitable spawning site is present. In a community aquarium a pair usually chooses a dark site among the rocks. In a breeding tank a flowerpot or ceramic cave normally gives the best results. It is important to leave the fry as long as possible with the pair because the male may become aggressive after the eggs or fry have been removed. As long as the pair is in breeding condition they can live in harmony in the same tank. However, if the female has not yet recovered from a previous spawning she should not be exposed to a sexually active male. When breeding any of these species in a special breeding aquarium the following procedure gives the most satisfying results:

The breeding tank should be well decorated with plenty of rocks and at least two flowerpots placed at opposite corners. The female alone is introduced into such a set up and conditioned with suitable food. Only after the female has become fuller around the abdomen should the male be placed with her. The best time to do this is shortly before the lights go off. The next day the tank must be checked because the male must be taken out if the female is not in her favourite hide-out or does not have free access to it. When things have gone wrong, the female hangs in one corner with the male patrolling the tank. After about a week the male can be put with the female again, and the same procedure must be repeated until the pair accept each other. When the female is ready to spawn she can withstand the male's aggression and will lead him into her cave. After the eggs have been attached inside the cave the male may be removed to ensure a successful outcome to the spawning. A compatible pair, however, should be left with the fry. If the breeding set-up has additional females in the conditioning phase the male can be placed with another female three days after spawning. Except in *N. niger*, the clutch size of which rarely numbers more than 25 eggs, these species have relatively large spawns numbering between 50 and 250 eggs.

The larger species are best bred in a community aquarium and some of the fry taken out when they become free-swimming. The presence of the remaining fry guarantees continued harmony between male and female.

Photo facing page; top: *Neolamprologus cylindricus*. This species should not be kept with *N. leleupi* in the same aquarium.
Bottom: *N. mustax* in its natural habitat (Moliro, Zaïre)
This page; top: *L. attenuatus* with fry.
Bottom: A *N. tretocephalus* pair in front of their excavated nest.

Neolamprologus tretocephalus group

This group contains cichlids which are normally found in pairs and which need a rather large territory when breeding.

Behaviour in the wild

N. tetracanthus breeds in shallow water in the sandy habitat. When not breeding it moves about on its own over the sand searching for prey. The other species are found in the intermediate habitat where they, almost permanently, occupy a territory. The territory is defended vigorously against all intruders. They are rather common and all of them can be found together at a single locality.

***N. tretocephalus* group**	max. size in cm	shallow bays	deep mud	sand	empty shells	rocks and sand	surge	steep rocks
Lepidiolamprologus attenuatus	12							
Neolamprologus moorii	10							
N. tetracanthus	16							
N. toae	10							
N. tretocephalus	16							

Behaviour in the aquarium

Any one of these species needs a large territory when breeding in an aquarium. Intruders are also chased when no breeding is imminent but the area from which they are chased is much smaller.

Never put two males of the same species in the same aquarium. *N. tretocephalus* needs a very large community aquarium (larger than 600 litres) when kept as a pair. The sexes can be distinguished by examining the vents (see page 52).

Aquarium

The aquarium should contain sand as well as rocks. The rocks should be placed in small heaps about 60-100 cm from each other. Such a heap will be adopted as a territorial site by a pair of these cichlids. A shelter in the form of a flowerpot or a ceramic cave is immediately accepted as a territory. *L. attenuatus* is even satisfied with a large snail shell. A pair needs about 60-100 cm of the length of the aquarium from which all other species are chased when the owners are breeding. As these species are bottom oriented, herring cichlids (*Cyprichromis*) would be a good combination in a community tank.

Feeding

These species are predators feeding mainly on invertebrates. *L. attenuatus* may occasionally feed on small fishes but small snails and crustaceans are the main items on the menu. *N. tetracanthus* seems to feed more frequently on fishes but also on small snails and crustaceans. *N. toae* feeds at night on crustaceans. *N. tretocephalus* feeds on crustaceans and also small snails.

In the aquarium these species need more than pelleted food although they will survive in fairly good condition on such a diet. If we want to breed these species we have to feed them more natural foods such as planktonic crustaceans (e.g. *Cyclops, Mysis, Artemia*) or mosquito larvae (white and black, but not red!). *N. tetracanthus* can be brought into breeding condition by feeding it feeder guppies or other small fishes.

Breeding

For breeding *L. attenuatus* uses a small cave dug by the pair, usually between a few small rocks. A large snail shell would be a suitable alternative, on the *outside* of which most of the eggs are deposited —they are clearly visible. The fry find shelter inside the shell. In a breeding tank, which should have a capacity of at least 125 litres, the pair can be accommodated in a flowerpot placed upside-down on the sand.

N. tetracanthus needs a small heap of rocks or a large flowerpot with a relatively narrow entrance. When the pair has been placed in the breeding tank —at least 150 litres— a few days feeding with feeder guppies may stimulate spawning activity. Before the eggs are deposited the pair dig a cave under the rocks or clear the entrance of the flowerpot.

N. moorii, N. toae, and *N. tretocephalus* need a relatively large breeding tank (at least 200 litres) or can be bred in a community

***A. compressiceps* group**	max. size in cm	shallow bays	deep mud	sand	empty shells	rocks and sand	surge	steep rocks
Altolamprologus calvus	14							
A. compressiceps	14							
Neolamprologus prochilus	12							

aquarium. It is advised that *N. tretocephalus* be bred in a large community aquarium. A large flowerpot, ceramic cave, or simply a heap of rocks is usually accepted as a territory. A lot of shelter is needed for the weaker partner as not every male and female put together forms a harmonious pair. A good method is to place the female in the breeding tank a few weeks before the male. When bred in a community aquarium the other fishes usually divert the attention of the chasing male.

Of these species, only *L. attenuatus* spawns every six to eight weeks; in the case of the rest spawning frequency is more like twice a year, but as a result they produce larger clutches —upwards of 400 eggs.

Altolamprologus compressiceps group

These species are best kept and bred as pairs in a community aquarium.

Behaviour in the wild

These three species are predators specialised in snatching prey —young fishes and invertebrates— from narrow cracks in the rocky substratum. Their laterally extremely compressed bodies facilitate entering such crevices. These predators always operate on their own and the only time more than one individual is seen is when they are spawning or guarding their offspring. The thick scales of *Altolamprologus* give an efficient protection against attacks by fry-guarding cichlids while the predator feeds on their offspring.

Behaviour in the aquarium

As indicated in the previous paragraph these predators may feed on juvenile cichlids, especially very young ones, and on eggs from some mouthbrooders while they are spawning. *O. ventralis* males are usually strong enough to keep *Altolamprologus* at bay but the smaller mouthbrooders like those of the genus *Xenotilapia* may suffer egg-stealing attacks. Substratum brooders are rarely successful in raising a large number of fry in a community aquarium even when predators like the ones discussed are not present.

Apart from feeding on fry and eggs when the opportunity is given, *Altolamprologus* and *N. prochilus* are a welcome addition to a community aquarium. They are not territorial and not aggressive towards other cichlids of similar size. When *Altolamprologus* is introduced to a new tank it may hide for weeks before it is acclimatised. Although in the wild these species can be found together at a single locality it is not recommended that more than one of these three species be kept per tank.

Aquarium

The aquarium should be at least 100 cm long, but larger is better. It is important that other cichlids are present and that only one male and one female is kept in the aquarium. The sexes are easily identified by examining the vents (see page 52). Females are much smaller than males, so selecting a pair from one spawn can be done simply by taking a small and a large individual. However, "venting" the fish gives a more reliable result.

A very important object in the aquarium is a receptacle in which the female can deposit

Left: a male *Altolamprologus compressiceps.*
Opposite page:
Top: Male and female of *Neolamprologus brevis* hide in the same shell.
Small photo: a male *Lamprologus signatus* from Zambia.

her eggs. This site must have an entrance too small for the male to enter! Empty snail shells from Lake Malawi (*Lanistes nyassanus*) are very satisfactory, but small ceramic caves with a narrow entrance may also work.

Feeding

The three laterally compressed cichlids are predators feeding on cichlid fry and invertebrates. In the aquarium they can be given any type of frozen or live food, especially crustaceans. Dry food is rarely accepted and not sufficient to bring the female into breeding condition.

Breeding

As already mentioned earlier a receptacle for eggs is a very important item in the aquarium. It is possible to breed these cichlids using flowerpots but if regular breeding is desired empty shells give the best results. A wild caught pair of *A. calvus* that was kept for more than two years in a large community aquarium with a flowerpot as cave spawned only once in that period, but after an empty *Lanistes* shell was placed in the tank the pair spawned every five to six weeks. Similar results have been obtained with *A. compressiceps* and *N. prochilus* as well. Never place a large sea shell in the aquarium because the male may chase the female all the way down into the shell where she may get stuck and die of suffocation. Although the female is normally seen in and around the shell (or ceramic cave) she comes up to feed. When the female stays in the shell during feeding time —usually the male is then also to be found near the shell— one can be almost certain that she is guarding eggs. It takes more than a week before the eggs hatch and the larvae mature enough to move out of the shell. If the fry are to be raised the shell with female is simply taken out of the tank and placed in a nursery tank. A week after spawning the fry can be washed out of the shell even when the female is still stuck inside it. The fry —spawns may number as many as 200— are quite large but take a very long time to grow to maturity. When the fry are left in the community aquarium they become vulnerable to predatory attacks, even by the male!

Lamprologus ocellatus group

The cichlids of this group belong to the smallest existing today. Most of them are conchicole —i.e. they live in empty snail shells.

Behaviour in the wild

The group can be split into two. On the one hand *L. kungweensis, L. signatus,* and to a lesser extent *L. ornatipinnis,* live over and in the muddy substratum, sometimes in shells. The other species are always found in the neighbourhood of or inside empty snail shells. Males of *L. ocellatus, L. ornatipinnis*, and *N. calliurus* usually have more than one female in their territories; the other species are normally found in pairs. *N. brevis* is the only species known where male and female share the same shell as shelter and brooding site. In all other species male and female have their own shell and spawning takes place inside that of the female. Adult males of *N. calliurus* and *L. ornatipinnis* are too large to fit inside the shells that their females have chosen to breed in. *N. calliurus* males do not hide inside shells but are found among the rocks near the shell-beds. *L. ornatipinnis* males hide in large shells when these are available.

Behaviour in the aquarium

In captivity these small cichlids all accept an empty snail shell as refuge and spawning site. Those species living over muddy substrata, in which the female digs a tiny hole, readily accept an empty shell as hiding-place in the aquarium. All these species can be kept in pairs. The females are smaller than

***L. ocellatus* group**	max. size in cm	shallow bays	deep mud	sand	empty shells	rocks and sand	surge	steep rocks
Lamprologus kungweensis	5							
L. ocellatus	5							
L. ornatipinnis	6							
L. signatus	5							
Neolamprologus brevis	5							
N. calliurus	10							
Telmatochromis burgeoni	7							

the males, including when they are still in the juvenile phase. The shelter —the shell— is defended against other possible inhabitants, and when fry are being guarded these little cichlids show an astonishing vigour in their chasing of intruders. All these species are territorial, which means that each individual needs a free area around its shell. They are ideal aquarium inhabitants and, because they are so small, the only problem is that larger, piscivorous, cichlids may consider them live food. Several of these species do not simply accept the empty shell as it is but adjust the position of it to their liking and cover it or dig it into the sand so that it lies inconspicuously in the substratum.

Aquarium

When only one pair is maintained a tank with a capacity of just 25 litres is sufficient. However, these shell-dwelling species are very good additions to a community aquarium where they will defend a shell placed on the sand. It is better to keep only one male of a particular species because territories can be relatively large (50-70 cm is not exceptional). For each individual at least one empty snail shell must be available. Of course the original snail species, *Neothauma*, from Lake Tanganyika, gives the best size shells but in delicatessens one can obtain empty escargot snail shells which are perfectly suitable for these shell-dwellers. It is quite possible to house several species in one tank.

Feeding

In the lake the food consists of small invertebrates which are taken in mid-water (zooplankton) or from the substratum.

In captivity these small species are best fed with frozen or live *Cyclops*, *Artemia*, *Daphnia*, and similar small crustaceans.

Breeding

A few empty snail shells —do not use larger sea shells— and a sandy substrate are the only prerequisites needed to breed these cichlids. Fine gravel (1-3 mm) is accepted as well, but —in particular for those species that bury their shells— coarse sand is a better choice. Breeding normally takes place in the community aquarium, and fry can be removed by taking the shells out of the water. Approximately 20 to 50 fry are produced per spawn. Not only the fry but also the adults hide in the shells and are sometimes difficult to remove. A possible method of removing the fry is to hang the shells in a wide meshed net in the top of a nursery tank. After a while the fish come out of their shelter and the smaller ones may swim through the net to the bottom of the tank. If we place some shelter on the bottom most of the smaller shell-dwellers will leave the shells in the net and take refuge in those on the bottom. The shells with the adult cichlids are placed back in the breeding or community tank.

Neolamprologus multifasciatus group

The smallest cichlids of Lake Tanganyika live in groups or colonies in the remains of snail shells or among the rubble of the intermediate biotope.

Behaviour in the wild

N. multifasciatus and *T.* sp. "Vittatus Shell" inhabit the heaps of empty shells which accumulate at certain places on the lake floor.

***N. multifasciatus* group**	max. size in cm	shallow bays	deep mud	sand	empty shells	rocks and sand	surge	steep rocks
Neolamprologus multifasciatus	5							
N. similis	5							
Telmatochromis "Vittatus Shell"	5							

Individuals live so closely together that it appears they are not territorial, but in fact each fish has its own shell which is defended as a territory. The same is true of *N. similis,* but this species is found mainly among the small rocks and pebbles of the intermediate habitat at a depth of 20 metres and deeper. At some localities, however, it inhabits heaps of empty shells in the same way as *N. multifasciatus.*

The colonies of *T.* sp. "Vittatus Shell" are smaller than those of *N. multifasciatus* and *N. similis,* and they are also found in shallower water.

Behaviour in the aquarium

These shell-dwellers can be kept in a community aquarium together with many other different cichlids. Given a good quantity of empty snail shells —do not use large sea shells— they can live in harmony with much larger species. These three species do not cover the shell with sand to conceal it from the outside world. However, *N. multifasciatus* is an avid digger which is halted only by the glass bottom. The digging takes place directly beside the shells. As a result the shells sink into the depression which is completely cleared of sand. In order to prevent *N. multifasciatus* from digging up the entire aquarium some rocks can be placed around the group of shells. When some of the shells lie against the glass of the aquarium it is easier to observe the daily life of these interesting shell-dwellers. *N. multifasciatus* and *N. similis* are better not kept in the same aquarium.

Aquarium

An aquarium of 40 litres is sufficient to house a small colony of one of these species. The accommodation for the fishes must consist of as many shells as possible, but at least two per individual. *Neothauma* shells, which form the natural environment of these shell-dwellers, may be obtained from a specialised pet shop. A good alternative can be obtained in a delicatessen where they sell empty shells of escargot snails. If another source of shells is chosen, care should be taken to boil the shells before use. Only shells of snails which are not bigger than two inches in diameter should be considered.

Feeding

In the wild zooplankton forms the major part of the diet of these small cichlids.

In captivity dry food is usually accepted but the fishes are best fed with shrimp mix (page 35), *Cyclops, Artemia* and other small crustaceans. Live micro worms are also eagerly taken. When these fishes are housed in a community aquarium the place where the food is administered needs to be chosen carefully. These shell-dwellers fear larger cichlids and may not venture far from their protective shells, even at feeding time.

Breeding

Given the right environment these cichlids cannot be prevented from reproducing. In the course of time fry appear among the shells

and are tolerated by all inhabitants. Although male and female seem to each have their own shell, fry can enter shells belonging to other individuals as well. The number of eggs per spawn varies between 8 and 15.

It is difficult to collect the juveniles from the aquarium because they hide inside the shells —sometimes more than five fishes can be found in one shell. A good but time consuming method of separating juveniles from adults is to put all shells in a large-meshed net and to hang this in the upper part of a nursery tank. As described for the previous group the small fishes are able to escape the net while the adults remain with the shells.

Neolamprologus caudopunctatus group

These small cichlids are best kept in pairs and need a small receptacle for spawning, which, in the case of some species, can be provided by an empty shell.

Behaviour in the wild

The species of this group are cave brooders, some of which need an empty snail shell as a permanent home (*A.* sp. "Sumbu" and the females of *L. callipterus, N. boulengeri,* and *N. meeli*). The other species dig a small hole under or between the rocks and use that as their brooding site.

A. sp. "Sumbu" is a predator feeding on small, shell-dwelling cichlids and operates on its own. Only during breeding may we find a pair. *L. callipterus* has an unusual life history: it is only the females and juvenile males that live in empty shells. Males, which grow to about three times the females' length (to about 12 cm), gather in large schools at a size of approximately 6 cm and roam through the habitat feeding on anything that can be

Left: a pair *Neolamprologus caudopunctatus* over their nest which is an upside-down flower pot.
Right: *Telmatochromis* sp. "Vittatus Shell" lives in empty snail shells.
Centre: The male *Lamprologus callipterus* is about three times bigger than the female and is not able to hide inside the empty shells of his territory.

swallowed. Adult males defend a harem consisting of three to ten females which reside inside shells. Males are not content merely to possess those females which choose to live in their territories, but may also steal shells containing females from other males. *N. boulengeri, N. hecqui,* and *N. meeli* normally live in pairs. The female (sometimes together with the male) digs a pit in which lies one or a few shells. Such a pit can be as large as 30 cm in diameter or hardly

***N. caudopunctatus* group**	max. size in cm	shallow bays	deep mud	sand	empty shells	rocks and sand	surge	steep rocks
Altolamprologus sp. "Sumbu"	6				▓			
Lamprologus callipterus	12	░			▓	░		
Neolamprologus boulengeri	8			░	▓			
N. caudopunctatus	8	░				▓		
N. hecqui	7			░	▓			
N. leloupi	8	░				▓		
N. meeli	7			░	▓			

visible. The female takes refuge inside a shell but the adult male, although staying close to the female, flees away over the sand when danger threatens. *N. caudopunctatus* and *N. leloupi* are rarely found near shells; they live in pairs —the pairs can be so close together as to give the illusion of a school— and excavate their nests between and under small rocks.

Behaviour in the aquarium

In captivity a pair of these cichlids usually defends a territory. The territory of *A.* sp. "Sumbu", *L. callipterus, N. boulengeri, N. hecqui*, and *N. meeli* is situated around an empty snail shell. *N. caudopunctatus* and *N. leloupi* normally defend a cave which they have dug between some stones. When provided with a cave (flowerpot or a ceramic one) the pair cover this entirely with sand but leave the entrance open. Apart from defending their possession against all other inhabitants, these cichlids do not hunt or deliberately chase other species. *A.* sp. "Sumbu", however, may feed on tiny fry from other fishes when these venture close to their shells.

Aquarium

It is recommended never to put more than one pair of any of these species in the same aquarium. The sexes can be identified by examining the vents (see page 52). The territories of *A.* sp. "Sumbu", *L. callipterus, N. boulengeri, N. hecqui*, and *N. meeli* can be determined by placing the shells where we would prefer them to be! Although aesthetically not always a success, a flowerpot can be positioned, upside-down, on the sand at the spot where we want *N. leloupi* or *N. caudopunctatus* to establish their territory. Ceramic caves are accepted as well and should be placed with the entrance facing upwards. The size of the tank can be relatively small when only one pair of these species is kept —as small as 50 litres. They are, however, easily kept in a community aquarium where they can inhabit the sandy part.

Feeding

In the lake the cichlids of this group feed on invertebrates and small fishes (*L. callipterus* males and *A.* sp. "Sumbu"). *N. caudopunctatus* and *N. leloupi* are frequently found feeding from the zooplankton.

The recommended food for these predators is *Artemia, Cyclops, Mysis*, and other planktonic crustaceans (frozen or live). *N. leloupi* and *N. caudopunctatus* can be fed with a good quality dry food (flakes and pellets, without mammalian fat).

Breeding

A special breeding tank is not necessary to breed these species. For the shell-dwellers a few empty snail shells are mandatory —do not use large sea shells. Breeding *N. leloupi* and *N. caudopunctatus* is achieved simply by placing a flowerpot upside-down on the sand. The small hole in the bottom of the flowerpot should be enlarged to allow entrance by both partners.

The number of eggs laid per spawn varies between 20 and 50, except in *N. leloupi* and *N. caudopunctatus* whose clutch size may be about 100 eggs.

***L. cunningtoni* group**	max. size in cm	shallow bays	deep mud	sand	empty shells	rocks and sand	surge	steep rocks
Bathybates	40							
Boulengerochromis microlepis	70							
Lamprologus lemairii	25							
Lepidiolamprologus cunningtoni	25							
L. profundicola	30							
Neolamprologus sexfasciatus	18							

Lepidiolamprologus cunningtoni group

This is a group of large piscivorous cichlids which should be kept with cichlids of similar size and temperament.

Behaviour in the wild

Bathybates, *Boulengerochromis microlepis, Lepidiolamprologus cunningtoni*, and *L. profundicola* are pursuit predators which means that they chase down their prey. They operate on their own and only rarely form small groups. *Lamprologus lemairii* is an ambush hunter which is normally found resting on the substratum. *Neolamprologus sexfasciatus* is an opportunistic piscivore feeding on fish when it is readily available. It feeds on other prey as well.

Behaviour in the aquarium

Bathybates has rarely been kept in the aquarium but the few individuals that have been exported seemed to need a lot of swimming space. They don't bother other cichlids much unless they are small enough to be eaten. When sub-adult or adult *B. microlepis* can be kept only on its own in small groups. It regards any fish smaller than 20 cm as food. *L. lemairii* and *N. sexfasciatus* can be kept only in pairs. They are relatively peaceful towards tank mates unless these are small enough to be eaten. A 15 cm-long *N. sexfasciatus* can eat a 10 cm-long *Enantiopus melanogenys*; the first bite engulfs half the victim's body! So avoid keeping sand-dwelling cichlids with these predators.

Aquarium

L. profundicola, L. cunningtoni, N. sexfasciatus, and *L. lemairii* should be housed with other cichlids otherwise too much aggression is directed towards the weaker partner. For this reason the aquarium should be at least 200 cm long. *B. microlepis* needs an aquarium larger than 1000 litres but can be kept in small groups. *Bathybates* also needs a very large aquarium.

Feeding

In the lake these predators feed on fish. *Bathybates* feeds on herring-like fishes of the open water (*Stolothrissa* and *Limnothrissa* species) whereas the other species feed mainly on sand-dwelling cichlids.

In captivity *Bathybates* and *B. microlepis* can be kept in condition by offering them live fish. The other species can be fed with larger crustaceans such as frozen shrimps or mussels.

Breeding

Bathybates has not yet been bred in captivity. *B. microlepis* has been spawned in a very

large concrete vat at a breeder's in Taiwan (Wang Kuo-Jung, pers. comm.) but there is no record of it having been bred in an aquarium. *L. cunningtoni* and *L. profundicola* are open substratum brooders but records of their breeding in captivity are not known.

L. lemairii and *N. sexfasciatus* are cave brooders. The female *L. lemairii* is much smaller than the male and selects a spawning cave into which only she can enter. A flowerpot with an entrance too narrow for the male or a large sea shell may be accepted as a spawning site. Such sites can easily be removed from the community tank while the female is inside caring for her eggs or larvae and can then be placed in a small nursery tank.

There are three known variants of *N. sexfasciatus*: the blue, the golden, and the yellow Zaïre variants. While the yellow and golden variants have been bred in captivity, the blue variant from Zambia has not been recorded as doing so, although I kept a harmonised pair in good condition for more than 7 years. The blue *sexfasciatus* is one of the few Tanganyika cichlids which have apparently not been bred in captivity. A breeding tank for the golden *sexfasciatus* should have a capacity of at least 500 litres. First the female should be placed in the aquarium —the sexes can be distinguished by examining the vent (see page 52). The tank should have a large cave, a flowerpot or a slate, where the female can attach the eggs to the ceiling of the cave. After the female has familiarised herself with the tank, the male can be introduced. When both fishes are in the breeding tank the female should stay in, or at least be allowed free access to, the spawning cave. If this is not the case the male should be removed from the tank and re-introduced a few weeks later. In the meantime the female should be conditioned with protein-rich food. Only when the pair accept each other's presence in the tank may a spawning result. A spawn may contain more than 700 eggs. A similar number is found in spawns of *L. lemairii, L. profundicola,* and *L. cunningtoni*. The spawns of *B. microlepis* range between 5000 and 12,000 eggs.

C. frontosa group	max. size in cm	shallow bays	deep mud	sand	empty shells	rocks and sand	surge	steep rocks
Cyphotilapia frontosa	35							
Grammatotria lemairii	18							
Tylochromis polylepis	30							
Oreochromis tanganicae	35							

Cyphotilapia frontosa group

These four cichlids have a mild temperament and relatively large size in common.

Behaviour in the wild

C. frontosa is sometimes found in large groups —it is better not to speak of schools because each individual in the group behaves independently from the others. Although it is a predator it is never found chasing prey or behaving energetically. *O. tanganicae* is often found in very large schools feeding on algae and detritus in the shallow water. Breeding males have not been observed in the wild. *T. polylepis* is mostly found solitary, and forages in the muddy substratum. *G. lemairii* is a sand-dwelling cichlid which is often found in small groups foraging in the sand.

Behaviour in the aquarium

Just as in the wild these cichlids are rather peaceful —towards other tank inhabitants— in the aquarium and aquarium size does not need to be based on their maximum length. Any of these species can be kept together in the same aquarium. *C. frontosa* is best kept in small groups of one male and two or more females. The sexes can be determined with certainty by examining the vents (see page 52). Do not rely on other characteristics like a large hump or long fins. There are several geographical variants known and several of them are regularly exported. It is advised, in order to avoid interbreeding, that only one variant be kept in the same aquarium.

Male *O. tanganicae* in captivity show aggression towards conspecific males but are perfectly harmless with other cichlids. The

Photo facing page: juvenile *Lepidiolamprologus cunningtoni*. Right: *Cyphotilapia frontosa* from Kigoma, Tanzania. There are several different geographical races of this species which should not be kept together in the same aquarium.

sexes are somewhat difficult to determine since most *O. tanganicae* are offered for sale when still very small. Breeding male *O. tanganicae* construct crater nests in the aquarium.

Male *G. lemairii* do not form territories but stay in the school with the females. This is a very peaceful cichlid which is best kept in groups of about five individuals. *T. polylepis* can also be kept in small groups, but little is known about this mouthbrooder.

Aquarium

Although the temperament of these species is rather mild they need enough space to move around. The aquarium should be at least 150 cm long and, when keeping *G. lemairii* or *O. tanganicae,* contain fine sand on the bottom. Real plants are not recommended when maintaining *O. tanganicae* or *T. polylepis*; they are regarded as food. In tanks larger than 750 litres *C. frontosa* can be kept in groups of 10 individuals or more. Such a group may even contain several males.

Feeding

C. frontosa is a piscivore which appears to feed at night or dusk. In captivity it is a slow eater, preferring shrimps (or shrimp mix (page 35)), mussels, and earthworms. Some wild caught specimens may feed on tank inhabitants too! It can also be fed on frozen fish. Feeding can take place at any time of the day. Pelleted food is sometimes taken but this hardly conditions the fish. *T. polylepis*, an omnivore feeding on plants and invertebrates in the lake, can be fed the same fare as *C. frontosa. G. lemairii* and *O. tanganicae* need somewhat smaller foods. Pellets are readily accepted and may keep *O. tanganicae* in good condition. In order to breed *G. lemairii* other items such as frozen *Mysis* and plankton, or live earthworms, should be fed.

Breeding

In general these four species need an open space on the bottom of the aquarium where spawning can take place.

O. tanganicae has been bred at least once in captivity. The female produced 65 fry after four weeks of incubation. Since males build nests in the sand this should be available in the tank. *T. polylepis* has been bred in captivity but the actual spawning was not observed. *G. lemairii* needs a large open space on the sand where the male can display in front of the females. Spawning takes place at any suitable site. Mouthbrooding females should be removed from the aquarium and placed in a nursery tank in order to produce a reasonable number of fry. The clutch size of the few spawns known varied between 24 and 75 eggs.

Large *C. frontosa* spawn frequently when a free space of at least 30 cm in diameter is available on the bottom of the tank. A male ready to spawn has a blue colour which is more intense than normal. The females of the group do not need shelter but the male, usually the largest but shyest fish of the group, will appreciate a large cave. Mouthbrooding females are best left with the group and the babies (between 25 and 100 per spawn) stripped from their mouths after an incubation period of four weeks.

P. nigripinnis **group**	max. size in cm	shallow bays	deep mud	sand	empty shells	rocks and sand	surge	steep rocks
Cyprichromis leptosoma	9							
C. sp. "Leptosoma Jumbo"	12							
C. microlepidotus	12							
Paracyprichromis brieni	9							
P. nigripinnis	11							

Paracyprichromis nigripinnis group

The species of this group —sometimes called "herring cichlids"— live in large schools and feed in mid-water. In the aquarium they are usually found in the open space above the rockwork.

Behaviour in the wild

Cyprichromis males defend a three-dimensional territory in mid-water near large rocks. Their breeding colonies consist mainly of males, while the females form separate schools. *P. nigripinnis* is a cave-dweller in which males defend a territory near the ceiling of a cave. Females form schools in the open water of the cave. *P. brieni* groups in schools, with territorial males found alongside large rocks.

Behaviour in the aquarium

Males are pugnacious among themselves and for this reason one should keep more than three males in an aquarium (this will spread their aggression). The sexes are distinguished as shown on page 52. Juvenile herring cichlids are not easily sexed. Therefore a group of at least 8 juveniles should be introduced to the aquarium. A stable group can be formed by putting five males and five or more females together. Most of the time the herring cichlids move about in the open space of the tank and are thus a good addition to a community tank in which mainly bottom-oriented cichlids are housed. It is recommended that only one species be kept per tank although in the lake several species can be found together. *Paracyprichromis* has a milder temperament than *Cyprichromis*; the former will not display its full range of behaviour when housed together with the more robust *Cyprichromis*. *P. nigripinnis* prefers a dark aquarium or at least a dark bottom and side walls. When kept in a well-lit tank the splendid colours of the males fade to a light beige and the species loses much of its attraction.

Aquarium

The herring cichlids need a much larger aquarium than their small sizes seem to suggest. Each breeding male needs a territory with a diameter of about 40-50 cm. Aquaria should be longer than 150 cm for a group of herring cichlids. It is possible to fill the open space in a smaller tank with water plants, such as *Ceratophyllum*, to obstruct the males' view of each other. Nevertheless even a densely planted tank should not be smaller than 100 cm if it is to house a group of herring cichlids. The aquarium should also contain some large rocks, which males need as reference points for their territories. Some species —*P. nigripinnis* and *P. brieni*— need larger rocks for a territory and for spawning.

Feeding

In the wild the herring cichlids feed on zooplankton which is found in the open water.

In the aquarium these species can be fed with a good quality dry food. One has to try several brands —Spirulina-type flakes (without mammalian fat) are recommended— to find out which one maintains the beautiful colours on the males and conditions the females. A much better choice is live or frozen *Cyclops* and *Artemia*. Once the fishes are used to eating frozen or live plankton it is difficult to get them to eat dry food.

Breeding

Because of the space a (breeding) group of herring cichlids requires, they are normally bred in a community tank. If fry are to be produced in reasonable numbers the mouthbrooding females should be taken out of the community and placed in a nursery tank. Several mouthbrooding females can be placed together in such a tank. Another possibility is to keep the herring cichlids by themselves and give the mouthbrooding females protection in the form of floating waterplants or something similar. These females release their offspring

"Featherfins"	max. size in cm	shallow bays	deep mud	sand	empty shells	rocks and sand	surge	steep rocks
Cunningtonia longiventralis	20							
Cyathopharynx furcifer	20							
Ophthalmotilapia boops	16							
O. heterodonta	14							
O. nasuta	18							
O. ventralis	15							

in the aquarium where they find shelter among the plants. *Paracyprichromis* can be successfully bred in such a tank even when no shelter for the fry is available. The fry school together in a corner and are left in peace by the males.

As soon as the fry are released by the female —clutch size varies from 6 to 25 larvae— they are able to feed on *Cyclops* (and, of course, *Artemia* nauplii).

"Featherfins"

These mouthbrooding cichlids are called "featherfins". Males have a very attractive colour and a boisterous temperament.

Behaviour in the wild

At several localities these species form breeding colonies where territorial males are found grouping. It may appear that there are many territorial males close together, but most territories are more than 2 metres apart. Females form small to large schools and are usually found close to the males' breeding arenas.

Behaviour in the aquarium

Males are very vigorous in their territorial defence and therefore need ample space. Best

Photos facing page; top: *Paracyprichromis nigripinnis* became popular under the trade name of "Blue Neon". When kept under subdued light this cave-dweller shows its best coloration.
Centre: A male *Cyprichromis microlepidotus*.

Right: Tank raised male *Cyathopharynx furcifer* show their breeding colours at an early age.

results are obtained by keeping one dominant male, a much smaller male, and five or more females in the same aquarium. In *C. furcifer* two or three small juvenile males can be kept together in the same tank; when grown up together sometimes two breeding males may tolerate each other. These species are difficult to house with other cichlids. Tank mates should be larger than 8 cm or should be pairs of substrate brooders, for instance from the *Neolamprologus brichardi* group. When housed with much larger or more robust cichlids the male loses his colour and stops breeding. The females of the group are often huddled into one corner of the aquarium.

Aquarium

The aquarium must at least be 150 cm long, preferably 200 cm or longer. It must contain some large rocks and 30 to 50% of the bottom must be sand.

Feeding

In the wild these species feed on small particles floating in the water column or from the sediment on the substratum. These cichlids are easy to feed and readily take any type of food.

For keeping the male in good shape and colour a good dry food is sufficient (no mammalian products), but in order to breed this species the females need frozen or live food. Shrimp mix (page 35), *Artemia, Cyclops, Mysis* and other small crustaceans are recommended.

Breeding

A special breeding tank is not required for these species. When a male is dominant in a community tank, breeding will take place in such an aquarium. At night mouthbrooding females can be taken from the aquarium —during the day the catching of a female causes too much stress to the whole group— and put on their own in small nursery tanks. When left with the male she will spit out the eggs or eat them. Once a male has been defeated by a newly matured younger male, he usually retreats to the corner farthest from the young male's territory. When placed in another aquarium he may refuse any type of food and slowly die from starvation. One apathetic male *O. ventralis* didn't eat for months before it finally died of starvation. An autopsy revealed that all its internal organs had dramatically shrunk. This may be the natural course of things in species where younger males replace the "burnt-out" males.

The clutch size of the featherfins ranges between 15 and 40 eggs.

Sand-cichlids

These sand-dwelling cichlids are delicate and need a bottom of fine sand in the aquarium. When breeding males of most species display a conspicuous coloration.

Behaviour in the wild

All these sand-dwellers live in schools and most of them show a seasonal peak in their breeding activity. When not breeding both male and female have a beige-yellow coloration with a silvery sheen. The males of these species, except *X. ornatipinnis, X. sima*, and *M. tenuidentatus*, construct a nest in the sand and do this in breeding colonies. When danger threatens these cichlids flee over the open sand towards deeper water.

Sand-cichlids	max. size in cm	shallow bays	deep mud	sand	empty shells	rocks and sand	surge	steep rocks
Enantiopus melanogenys	15							
Callochromis macrops	12							
C. melanostigma	12							
C. pleurospilus	10							
Cardiopharynx schoutedeni	12							
Ectodus descampsii	10							
Lestradea perspicax	12							
Microdontochromis tenuidentatus	7							
Xenotilapia bathyphilus	10							
X. ochrogenys	10							
X. ornatipinnis	12							
X. sima	17							

Behaviour in the aquarium

In the aquarium the non-breeding individuals stay close together in a group when other more robust cichlids are present. When kept with similar species males will soon start to build their nests in the sand and court females. Although males are quite determined to defend their properties, they are rarely found in pursuit of unresponsive females. Nevertheless it is better to keep more than one female per species. When several males are present in the tank they develop a deeper breeding (territorial) coloration. *M. tenuidentatus* males do not construct a nest and do not change much in colour when breeding.

These sand-dwelling cichlids belong to the most difficult to keep cichlids from Lake Tanganyika. Therefore the community tank should be decorated to suit the sand-dwellers living in it.

Aquarium

An aquarium for sand-dwelling cichlids does not need to be large. The only essential is fine sand on the bottom and enough space to build nests. Most of these nests are no bigger than 20 cm in diameter. The nest of *E. melanogenys*, however, can be 50 cm across. In an aquarium with a length of 120 cm a group of 5-7 individuals of any of these species (except *X. sima*, which needs at least 150 cm) can be kept without difficulty. A small group of *M. tenuidentatus* can be housed in a 75 litre aquarium.

Feeding

In the lake all these species, except *M. tenuidentatus*, sift the sand through their gills, retaining anything edible. *M. tenuidentatus* feeds on zooplankton in the free water near the bottom.

In captivity some of these species may eat dry food but it is not recommended that they be fed on dry food alone. They are predators and need plankton, *Artemia, Cyclops, Daphnia* and the like. Also white worms are eagerly taken and nutritious. Females in breeding condition are distinctly fuller-bellied than young or non-ripe individuals.

Breeding

The sexes are difficult to differentiate,

especially when dealing with small species like *M. tenuidentatus*. With the aid of a magnifying glass the sexes can be determined by examining the vents of (sub-)adult specimens. Breeding these sand-dwelling cichlids is best done in a special breeding tank in which is placed a group of a single species. *Callochromis* species may breed precociously, at a size of only about 6 cm.

Mouthbrooding females should be removed from the breeding tank after two weeks of incubation. Avoid catching females during the daytime because they are easily frightened, causing them to shoot frantically through the tank and spit out any eggs or larvae they may be holding. At night the mouthbrooding females can be gently lifted out of the water and carefully placed in a nursery tank. This must have a closely fitting cover and should be positioned so that the females cannot be disturbed.

Always keep some offspring from the first clutches —clutch size ranges from 15 to 70 eggs except in *M. tenuidentatus* which does not have more than 8 eggs per spawn— and grow them on to adulthood. These sand-dwelling cichlids usually breed during just one year and then stop; thereafter the females produce hardly any eggs and the fertility of the males seems to diminish as well. Replace the breeding stock every year and one can enjoy these beautiful but delicate species for a long time.

"Sunflower" group

These four species are delicate biparental mouthbrooders which need special care when housed in a community aquarium.

Behaviour in the wild

Adults of *A. leptura, X. papilio*, and *X. spilopterus* are normally found in pairs; sub-adults sometimes in small groups or on their own. They feed from the sediment on the sand or rocks. They are very vulnerable to predation and therefore prefer the deeper areas of the habitat. They do not have a territory when they are not guarding offspring, but nevertheless move around in pairs. *X. flavipinnis* occurs in large schools outside the breeding period but in pairs during such a period.

"Sunflower" group	max. size in cm	shallow bays	deep mud	sand	empty shells	rocks and sand	surge	steep rocks
Asprotilapia leptura	12							
Xenotilapia flavipinnis	9							
X. papilio	9							
X. spilopterus	11							

Behaviour in the aquarium

Although these cichlids seem to be very fragile when handled, squabbling between the partners is rather common. The best way to house these species is to keep two to three pairs in a tank (including the schooling *X. flavipinnis*). A single pair is also possible but may lead to a long period of squabbling between male and female —and it is not always the male who is intolerant. When two pairs are present enough aggression is diverted to the other couple. Having more than four pairs in a tank does not always seem to work well. Pairs that want to spawn may have difficulty finding a quiet spot where they are not disturbed by conspecifics.

The sexes have to be determined by examining the vents (see page 52) or by selecting pairs from a larger group (they usually separate from the group). When you are not certain tha: you can handle these fragile cichlids without harming them, ask an experienced aquarist to sex them for you. A secondary sexual characteristic may be used with adult individuals: the anal fin of males is slightly larger and its edge more pointed than in females. Venting, however, remains the better procedure.

Photo facing page:
The "Kilesa" is closely related to *Enantiopus melanogenys* and needs a bottom substrate of fine sand.
Right: This small sand-dwelling cichlid became known under the trade name of "Sunflower". It is a biparental mouthbrooder which should be kept in pairs.

None of these species shows aggression towards other fishes in the aquarium.

Aquarium

Although these cichlids are rather small the aquarium should not be smaller than 100 cm, in which two pairs can be kept without difficulties. In the case of a single pair a smaller tank may suffice, but adequate shelter and/or other fishes (as a distraction) should be present as well. A thin layer of fine sand on the bottom is necessary for the pair to spawn —a nest is not constructed, however.

Feeding

In the wild *A. leptura* scrapes the algae from the biocover on the rocks, especially large rocks. The *Xenotilapia* species feed on invertebrates which they find in the sand or in the sediment covering the rocks.

In captivity all these species are best fed with frozen or live *Cyclops, Mysis*, or other planktonic crustaceans. *A. leptura* should not be given frozen *Artemia*, mosquito larvae, or other soft structured food, because this may upset their digestive systems. These cichlids can be taught to eat Spirulina flakes but it does not seem to bring them into breeding condition.

Breeding

When housed with calm, gentle cichlids these biparental mouthbrooders are likely to spawn in a community aquarium. In this case do not remove the female! After about 10-12 days, all being well, the male takes over the larvae and carries them to maturity, which takes another 8-10 days. It is possible to catch the male during this period and place him in a nursery tank. Leave the female in the community tank. There may be some "marital" problems re-introducing the male into the community aquarium after he has released the fry, but such marital strife is normally settled in a few days. It is, however, recommended that all tanks in which these cichlids are housed should have tight fitting lids. In particular *A. leptura* and *X. papilio* have been known to leap through a tiny hole in the cover.

The clutch size of these biparental mouthbrooders varies from 10 to 30 eggs.

Limnochromis auritus group

These rather large, predatory species have a mild temperament when kept as pairs in a large aquarium.

Behaviour in the wild

G. permaxillaris, G. christyi, L. auritus, and *R. calliurus* live in small groups or are solitary. They are bottom oriented cichlids foraging in or over the muddy substratum. *H. microlepis* lives in the free water column alongside large rocks and feeds on small fishes and zooplankton. Observations in the lake indicate that these species rarely display territorial aggression. Although *G. christyi, R. calliurus*, and *H. microlepis* are piscivorous their prey consists of very small fishes which are stalked either where they school in the upper layer of water (*H. microlepis*) or from the bottom. *G. permaxillaris*' daily activity consists mainly of "vacuum-cleaning" the loose sediment off the bottom. *L. auritus* lives in tunnels dug in the muddy substratum.

Behaviour in the aquarium

G. christyi and *H. microlepis* are best kept in pairs in large aquaria. The other species can be kept in groups of 4 to 7 individuals although it is recommended that these too be kept in pairs. When the other inhabitants of the aquarium are larger than 5 cm there is no objection to housing a pair of these predators with them. Avoid keeping territorially aggressive species together with these "peaceful" predators. Their rather peaceful behaviour is disrupted only when two conspecific males find themselves in the same aquarium. The difference between the sexes can be detected only at the vent (see page 52), secondary sexual characters are not present. When the sexes cannot be distinguished after examining

***L. auritus* group**	max. size in cm	shallow bays	deep mud	sand	empty shells	rocks and sand	surge	steep rocks
Gnathochromis permaxillaris	20							
Greenwoodochromis christyi	22							
Haplotaxodon microlepis	25							
Limnochromis auritus	15							
Reganochromis calliurus	15							

the vents, it is better to let about 5 individuals pair off by themselves. When a pair has formed the remaining individuals should be removed to another aquarium.

Aquarium

Because of their mild temperament a pair of these large cichlids can be kept in an aquarium which contains 500 litres or more. The tank should be at least 125 cm long. *G. permaxillaris, L. auritus*, *R. calliurus* and *G. christyi* prefer to hide in a dark cave which can be provided by placing wide plastic or clay pipes behind the rockwork. The pipes should be closed at one end. The best indication that the male and female are living in harmony is when both hide in the same pipe. Initially two male *G. permaxillaris* may hide inside the same cave, but after they have acclimatised to their artificial environment, the dominant male will chase the weaker fish. *H. microlepis* does well with *Cyphotilapia frontosa* or other placid fish but is intimidated by species like *Tropheus moorii* or *Neolamprologus tretocephalus*. They don't need caves although disturbed individuals like to hide.

Feeding

The natural food of *G. permaxillaris* consists of tiny invertebrates, that of *L. auritus* of larger invertebrates. The other species are mainly piscivorous but feed on invertebrates (zooplankton) as well.

L. auritus, R. calliurus, and *G. permaxillaris* readily accept *Cyclops, Artemia, Mysis* and other planktonic crustaceans. Mosquito larvae (white and black, but not red!) are also worth feeding. It may take a while for *G. permaxillaris* to accept the regular aquarium fare but eventually they eagerly feed on flake food as well. However, it is recommended to feed these predators live or frozen crustaceans. *G. christyi* and *H. microlepis* do not accept flakes or pellets and can be finicky about other foods as well. Frozen *Artemia* may stimulate them to accept other foods.

Breeding

The species of this group are biparental mouthbrooders and difficult to breed. The reasons are not very clear but may be connected with the age at which and the frequency with which these cichlids spawn in the wild. *L. auritus* has been bred in captivity more often, but success with the other species has been limited to a few aquarists. At the time of writing *H. microlepis* has not been bred in captivity, but not many adult individuals are being kept in aquaria. Since *H. microlepis* is a piscivore breeding may be stimulated by feeding it feeder guppies or other small fishes.

The other species of this group need a dark cave for breeding. A good way to stimulate the pair to spawning activity is to offer them a wide —10 cm in diameter— plastic (or clay) pipe filled with fine sand. While they are digging, the cave is formed according to their specifications. If the pair stays together after they have completed their cave then everything has been done that can be done to stimulate these cichlids to spawn.

Even though these species are mouthbrooders, spawns with more than 200 fry are normal.

Aulonocranus dewindti group

These mouthbrooding species are common in shallow, often turbid waters and need to be kept in groups.

Behaviour in the wild

A. dewindti has the mildest temperament of these three species. It is very common in many shallow intermediate habitats. Males construct, using coarse gravel, half crater-nests against rocks. Females and non-breeding males forage in groups on the sand. Their sensitive acoustic system enables them to locate invertebrates in the sand without seeing them. *"G." pfefferi* males sometimes defend a spawning area but do not construct a nest. Females are courted whenever they are close to the male. Spawning occurs at any site in the habitat. *"G." pfefferi* is a piscivore mainly feeding on small cichlids. Like most piscivores it operates on its own.

Ct. horei is the most aggressive of the three. Males vigorously defend their territories between the rocks against all intruders. Females and non-breeding males forage in small, loose groups on the sand and between the rocks of the habitat.

Behaviour in the aquarium

Because of the natural behaviour of these cichlids it is better to keep only one male with several females in the same aquarium. The sex of small individuals can be determined by examining the vents (page 52). Adult male *"G." pfefferi* can be recognised by the small red spots on the anal fin. Adult Ct. horei males have a yellow colour on the lower part of the head. Male *A. dewindti* have a bluish sheen on the flanks and elongated ventral fins. The latter species is a good aquarium resident

Left: *Limnochromis auritus,* although among the first cichlids exported from Lake Tanganyika, never became a species which is easy to breed in captivity.
Right: *Aulonocranus dewindti* is a common cichlid in the wild, but in captivity it is kept only by a few specialists.

A. dewindti group	max. size in cm	shallow bays	deep mud	sand	empty shells	rocks and sand	surge	steep rocks
Aulonocranus dewindti	12							
Ctenochromis horei	15							
"Gnathochromis" pfefferi	14							

and can be kept with many different cichlids. *Ct. horei* has a rather boisterous temperament towards both its own and other species. It should therefore be housed with cichlids with similar behaviour. *"G." pfefferi* is reasonably peaceful towards other species but males approach females in a rather rough way. Small cichlids should not be housed with this piscivore.

Aquarium

Since a small group should be kept in the aquarium this should be at least 150 cm long and have a capacity of at least 350 litres. An *A. dewindti* male needs rocks against which to build a nest. Coarse gravel is appreciated by the male and is carried from all corners of the aquarium to construct the nest. Females of all three species need plenty of shelter which can be provided by heaps of rock or by piling other decorative materials.

Feeding

The food of *A. dewindti* and *Ct. horei* consists mainly of invertebrates. The latter species also feeds on vegetable matter, but there is not much nutritional value to be extracted from plants. *"G." pfefferi* hunts cichlid fry which it finds among the cracks between and in excavations under the rocks.

These three species are easily satisfied with the regular aquarium fare. Dry food is as well accepted as frozen or live food. *A. dewindti* and *"G." pfefferi* can be brought quickly into breeding condition by feeding them frozen or live food.

Breeding

The key to breeding these species is to have at least three females with one adult male. Spawning regularly takes place in the community aquarium without the need for any special treatment. Mouthbrooding females should be removed and placed in a nursery tank. In a large aquarium female *A. dewindti* may be left with the male and stripped three weeks after spawning. Female *Ct. horei* and *"G." pfefferi* guard their offspring after they have been released. The clutch size ranges from 25 to 60 eggs.

Benthochromis tricoti group

The three genera of this group are delicate and other tank inhabitants should be carefully selected.

Behaviour in the wild

B. tricoti lives in the deep to very deep regions of the rocky habitat. When not breeding they form foraging schools in the free water column. Before breeding adult individuals migrate to shallower water (25 to 50 metres) where males defend a territory on top of a rock.

Trematocara species are rarely exported for the ornamental trade. They appear to live in the very deep, muddy habitats but migrate to much shallower areas at night where they forage in the bottom.

T. otostigma are collected mainly in shallow, muddy bays where they appear to feed entirely on the muddy substratum.

Behaviour in the aquarium

B. tricoti is a beautiful aquarium resident but it needs peaceful company to keep it in optimum condition. The long filaments on the fins are chewed off by most Lamprologines, *Tropheus,* and other robust species. The best company for *B. tricoti* consists of the many different sand-dwelling cichlids of the genera *Xenotilapia, Ectodus, Enantiopus*, etc. Of the herring cichlids only *Paracyprichromis* species are recommended as tank mates. Only one dominant male should be kept, maybe together with a smaller one. Males court females and lead them to their nest, but in general they are very mild towards females. All other species are ignored. It is possible to keep just a single pair in an aquarium but three females and one male are better. The sexes can best

***B. tricoti* group**	max. size in cm	shallow bays	deep mud	sand	empty shells	rocks and sand	surge	steep rocks
Benthochromis tricoti	20							
Trematocara	12							
Triglachromis otostigma	12							

be told apart by examining the vents (see page 52).

Trematocara species —only *T. nigrifrons* has been kept in captivity so far— need a calm environment where several males and females are kept together.

T. otostigma's main occupation appears to be digging. A single individual is able to completely turn over the sand in the aquarium in a single day. *T. otostigma* is a biparental mouthbrooder but several pairs can be housed in the same tank. They seem to like to live in colonies. The avid digging is in part due to their feeding behaviour. Another reason is that they like to live in tunnels or caves. The sexes can be distinguished only by checking the vents.

Aquarium

B. tricoti needs an aquarium which is at least 150 cm long. More important is the height of the tank, which should be at least 60 cm. A large stone with a flat top is readily accepted by the male as spawning site. The lighting above the tank should not be too strong; one small fluorescent tube is more than adequate.

The aquarium for *T. otostigma* and *Trematocara* does not need to be large; a capacity of about 250 litres is sufficient for a small group of four to five individuals. *T. otostigma* appreciates the provision of a wide pipe filled with sand. Such a pipe can be hidden between some rocks. The sand is carried away and piled in front of the cave. Such a dark shelter also promotes breeding activity.

These three species cannot be kept successfully with other cichlids unless these are very peaceful and placid themselves.

Feeding

B. tricoti feeds predominantly on zooplankton and is therefore best fed with *Cyclops, Daphnia*, and *Artemia*. Dry food is accepted, but will not bring the females into breeding condition. *Trematocara* feeds on invertebrates in the lake and needs live food in the aquarium. Frozen food, such as *Cyclops* and *Mysis*, is taken only while it falls to the bottom. When it is on the bottom it does not seem to be noticed by *Trematocara*. *T. otostigma*, a mud eater, is easily satisfied with any type of aquarium food available, but live or frozen *Cyclops, Mysis, Artemia*, and other planktonic crustaceans are recommended to bring them into breeding condition.

Breeding

When kept on its own *B. tricoti* spawns after the females have recovered from their journey from Africa. It seems, however, that their breeding season in the wild (probably July to October) is adhered to in the artificial environment as well. Offspring may breed throughout the year but no information is available at the time of writing. It is important to feed *Cyclops*-like invertebrates in large quantities to keep a well-rounded appearance on the females. For its relatively large size the number of eggs produced per spawn is rather small: 10 to 25.

Nothing is known of how to induce breeding

Left: a male *Benthochromis tricoti.*
Facing page; centre: *Tropheus moorii*, the so-called Murago variant;
bottom: *Tropheus duboisi.*

in *Trematocara. T. otostigma*, a biparental mouthbrooder, needs a dark cave and a quiet environment before breeding takes place. This species too has rarely been bred in captivity. The clutch size appears to be quite large and numbers more than 100 eggs.

Tropheus moorii group

Males of these mouthbrooders are rather aggressive in their attempts to coax females to spawn. None of them should be kept as a single pair in a community or breeding aquarium.

Behaviour in the wild

These herbivorous species are rather common in their preferred habitat. They spend most of the time feeding from the biocover (algae) on the rocks. When disturbed they immediately hide among the crevices of their biotope. Some species, such as *P. trewavasae*, are very shy and can be observed only from a distance.

Males are territorial but chase only conspecifics from their (feeding) territory. *Petrochromis* species, which are the most dominant cichlids in the upper rocky habitat, chase not only conspecifics but also other *Petrochromis* species. *Petrochromis* and *Simochromis* species vigorously defend their territory and never venture far from it. The territoriality of some *Tropheus* species is less obvious: males frequently chase conspecifics but they can also be found side by side grazing from the same rock.

Behaviour in the aquarium

In the aquarium males of all these species are clearly territorial and relentlessly chase conspecific males from their domain. Females are courted continuously and often aggressively chased when they are not ready to spawn.

The only correct way to keep these species in captivity is in a group of ten or more individuals. The sexes of *Tropheus* and *Simochromis* can be relatively easily determined by examining the vents (see page 52). *P.*

***Tropheus moorii* group**	max. size in cm	shallow bays	deep mud	sand	empty shells	rocks and sand	surge	steep rocks
Petrochromis trewavasae	18	●						○
Simochromis babaulti	12	●				○		
S. diagramma	18	○				●		
S. marginatus	12	●						
S. pleurospilus	12	●				○		
Tropheus annectens	12					○		●
T. sp. "Black"	12					○		●
T. brichardi	11	●				○		○
T. duboisi	11					●		○
T. moorii	12					○		●

trewavasae males have bright egg-spots in the anal fin at a size as small as 3 cm. Never put more than one species of *Petrochromis* or *Simochromis* in the same aquarium. *T. duboisi* can be kept with any of the other *Tropheus* species but is better kept by itself. Never put different geographical races of *Tropheus* or individuals from different localities together in the same tank. It frequently leads to unwanted hybridisation. *Simochromis, Petrochromis, T. polli* and *T. brichardi* are best kept with just one dominant male in the aquarium. A small male may be added as a replacement whenever the leading male "gives up". The other *Tropheus* species should be housed with as many males as females.

Aquarium

S. pleurospilus and *S. babaulti* may breed at a size as small as 6 cm, but need, like the other species of this group, an aquarium —at least 150 cm long— with a capacity of more than 500 litres. In order to provide enough shelter for persecuted individuals, a large quantity of rocks, pots or other decorative materials should be placed in the aquarium. When the decoration does not reach to the top of the tank or nearly so, additional shelter can be provided by water plants (*Ceratophyllum*) or by pieces of plastic pipe hanging from the top in the upper reaches of the tank (see page 51). This plastic pipe should be small, just large enough to hold one female.

Feeding

As mentioned earlier all these species feed on vegetable matter which they scrape, pick, and comb from the biocover on the rocks.

Feeding these species is the most difficult part of keeping and breeding them. The safest food one can give these vegetarians is shrimp mix (page 35) or Spirulina flake food. When a good quality flake is chosen —absolutely no products of warm blooded animals among the ingredients!— it is sufficient to get these cichlids into breeding condition. A few other foods are also recommended: *Cyclops, Mysis* and other planktonic crustaceans.

It is important that the (frozen) food must feel rough to the touch and not soft or slimy. Feeding red or white mosquito larvae, *Artemia*, beef heart and other soft, easily digestible food is lethal for these fishes (see also chapter about food, pages 34-37). We are well aware of the fact that many aquarists feed their herbivores the wrong food, and some of them even claim to be successful. It is not denied that some cichlids may survive such a treatment for a long period of time, but if the recommendations given in this book are not followed one is likely to bring about an early death in one's fishes. This advice is not based on scientific investigations but on the experience of professional breeders who have dealt with thousands of these herbivores over many years. If you wish to experiment with different kinds of food keep in mind that you cannot feed steak to a cow or grass to a lion.

Do not feed more than once a day. All the commercially available dry foods contain lots of protein and fat. In the aquarium the cichlids can eat more of these nutrients in two minutes than they could eat in an entire day in their natural environment. Of course it is possible to feed these fishes small amounts 3 to 5 times a day, but these portions should total no more than can be eaten in two minutes if fed as a single portion! Please, do your fish a big favour and don't give more than can be eaten in TWO minutes. Algal growth on the aquarium decor, promoted by strong lights in the canopy, provides an additional source of food.

Breeding

Breeding *P. trewavasae, Simochromis,* and *Tropheus* species is rather difficult for several reasons. The most important is that the male wants to spawn every minute of the day. Another reason is that females are not easily conditioned. They don't need a lot of food but just the right type. In a breeding tank a large pile of pipes (plastic or clay) provides ample shelter for the females. As long as the weaker fishes are out of the male's sight he will not chase them. Mouthbrooding females can be removed and placed by themselves in a nursery tank. But care must be taken not to take too many females from the breeding tank as the remaining females may then have to cope with increased "courting" by the male. In a large aquarium (>1000 litres) with plenty of shelter mouthbrooding females can be left with the group. They can be stripped about 25 days after spawning. There are indications that stripped fry, because of the lack of a proper imprinting period, become bad mouthbrooding females when mature. Such females may need up to six spawnings before they hold the eggs to maturity, while naturally released females usually hold the eggs from the first spawning on. It is therefore better to put mouthbrooding females in nursery tanks and let them take care of the fry until a week after their release. The most elegant and efficient solution to this problem is to build a "balcony" onto your tank. Gerard Tijsseling has described this feature in *The Cichlids Yearbook* (2nd volume). It provides the mouthbrooding females with a very shallow area in the tank where they can release the fry without fear of their being eaten immediately by the other inhabitants.

P. trewavasae females may hold up to 35 eggs per spawn, but the clutch size of the other species of this group varies from 8 (or less) to 20 eggs.

Another very important point when keeping and breeding these cichlids is **never** to add new individuals to an existing group. If a breeding group has to be expanded then all the individuals of the new, expanded group must be placed at the same time into a new aquarium or one where the decor has been rearranged so as to obliterate previously existing territories.

Goby cichlids

The species of this group are biparental mouthbrooders and often called goby cichlids. They prefer to live in the surge and therefore need oxygen-rich water.

Behaviour in the wild

Most adult goby cichlids move around in pairs in the upper rocky habitat. Juveniles are found in extremely shallow water. Their daily activity is dominated by picking and scraping the biocover from the pebbles and rocks. Although conspecifics are chased from the feeding site none of these species seems to have a permanent territory.

Behaviour in the aquarium

In captivity goby cichlids are best kept as pairs. It is possible to keep more than one pair in the same aquarium but it should be realised that they can be quite pugnacious among themselves. The sexes can only with certainty be told apart by checking the vents (see page 52). Adult females are smaller than males. During the first phase of mouthbrooding the female holds the eggs for 10 to 12 days. The male then broods the larvae for a similar period. All the time the pair stays close together. Finally it is the male who releases the fry and guards them for about a week thereafter.

In the aquarium goby cichlids are normally found in the middle and upper parts of the rockwork.

Aquarium

The aquarium must have an excellent aeration system because goby cichlids need oxygen-rich water. When they are frequently

Goby cichlids	max. size in cm	shallow bays	deep mud	sand	empty shells	rocks and sand	surge	steep rocks
Eretmodus cyanostictus	10							
Spathodus erythrodon	8							
S. marlieri	12							
Tanganicodus irsacae	7							

found around the filter outlet there is probably not enough oxygen in the water. Although excellent surface turbulence can be provided in many ways —frequently involving airstones and or power heads— a trickle filter gives very good results in oxygenating the aquarium water.

The size of the tank should be more than 100 litres for a single pair of goby cichlids. A harmonised pair can make do with a smaller tank but usually pairs are formed after the fishes have been introduced into the aquarium. The gobies are good company for cichlids like *Tropheus* and *Simochromis*.

Feeding

The upper rocky habitat offers a rich biocover from which all goby cichlids feed. *Spathodus* and *Eretmodus* have a more herbivorous diet than *T. irsacae*. The latter species also feeds on invertebrates.

Because goby cichlids are mainly vegetarians Spirulina flake food is a good choice. Planktonic crustaceans such as *Cyclops* and *Mysis* are recommended but *Artemia* and other soft food should not be given as this may upset the digestive system. Algae growing on the aquarium rocks provide supplementary food, and their growth can be encouraged by placing a strong light directly over the rocks which are near the surface. The goby cichlids will reward such effort by showing their best colours and by frequent spawnings.

Breeding

Although it is possible to breed these species in a special breeding tank, the simplest way is to leave them with other species in a community aquarium. When a male and female have been introduced into the tank they normally form a pair and stay together most of the time, including when they are not breeding. Mouthbrooding females are easily recognised by their swollen buccal pouch. About 10 to 30 eggs are laid per spawn. Never remove the mouthbrooding female from the tank because the larvae are transferred to the male 10 to 12 days after spawning. When the male holds the larvae we can catch him (at night) and place him in a nursery tank.

Another possibility is to build a balcony onto the aquarium (Tijsseling, 1992) and leave the mouthbrooding male with the female. The fry are released in the very shallow water of the balcony. When lights are placed directly over the small stones on the balcony a lush algal vegetation welcomes the newborn gobies.

Petrochromis group

The cichlids in this group are not ideal aquarium residents; they are best kept by themselves.

Behaviour in the wild

Petrochromis species are the most dominant cichlids in the upper five metres of the

Photo top: *Eretmodus cyanostictus*, like all other goby cichlids, needs oxygen-rich water.
Right: Large *Petrochromis* sp. "Kasumbe" are common in the lake. In captivity it can be kept only by experienced aquarists.

***Petrochromis* group**	max. size in cm	shallow bays	deep mud	sand	empty shells	rocks and sand	surge	steep rocks
Petrochromis famula	15					■		▒
P. fasciolatus	14	■				▒		
P. macrognathus	20						■	▒
P. orthognathus	15	▒				■		
P. polyodon	14					■		▒
P. sp. "Kasumbe"	18							■
P. sp. "Texas"	20							■
Lobochilotes labiatus	45	▒				■		

rocky habitat. At most locations we may find more than three species, at some as many as nine! Most of them behave towards other *Petrochromis* species as they would towards their own: with aggression. Apart from *P. fasciolatus,* males of these cichlids defend a very large territory with great vigour. In the wild most other species (excluding *Petrochromis*) are ignored unless they intrude into the male's hide-out. *P. fasciolatus* also shows aggression towards conspecifics but is sometimes seen in large schools feeding in areas from which they would be chased if they were on their own.

L. labiatus is a common cichlid feeding on invertebrates from rocky substrata. It is mostly seen on its own roaming through the habitat.

Behaviour in the aquarium

P. polyodon, the closely related *P. famula*, and *L. labiatus* are the only species of this group which can be kept with other robust cichlids in a community aquarium. The best company for *L. labiatus* is *Petrochromis*.

The other *Petrochromis* species need a special aquarium in which only one species is kept. Only one male can be kept per tank. The sex of *Petrochromis* can be determined relatively easily by examining the vent (page 52).

Aquarium

When kept with other cichlids *P. polyodon* and *P. famula* need an aquarium at least 200 cm long and filled with many rocks to provide the females (and other fishes) with plenty of shelter.

Only one male of any of these species can be kept in the same aquarium unless it is bigger than 10,000 litres. *L. labiatus* needs a very large tank as well, at least 1000 litres.

Feeding

Petrochromis combs the loose material, mostly algae, from the rocky substratum. The length of the intestinal tract is in some species more than 10 times the standard length. This indicates that the food has a low nutritional value and is slowly digested.

In captivity *Petrochromis* is best fed with shrimp mix (see page 35) or Spirulina flake food (no mammalian products in the ingredients!). *Cyclops* and *Mysis* are also recommended. Never feed them red mosquito larvae, *Artemia*, and other soft food. It will sooner or later cause damage to the long intestines, perhaps eventually leading to the death of the fish.

L. labiatus feeds on large invertebrates in the wild and readily accepts any type of food offered in captivity.

Breeding

Information about breeding *L. labiatus* in captivity is not available.

Petrochromis can be bred in captivity not only at random in the community but also in a special tank. Such a breeding tank should be at least 150 cm long and have plenty of hiding places. These can be provided by placing clay or plastic pipes on top of each other. At least 25 pipes are necessary to provide enough shelter for 5 to 10 females. The females should be well fed with Spirulina flake and/or *Cyclops* and *Mysis*. When several females seem to be in breeding condition or when a female starts to act territorially, the male should be introduced into the group and watched continuously! After an adjustment period of about 5 minutes the male starts courting the females. If only a few females are available the male's attention can be distracted by placing a mirror in the tank (being very careful that it is not going to cause toxicity). He will fight his reflection for a few hours and from time to time court some females. The male can be left in the tank for a few days or until he begins to molest the females. The mouthbrooding females are removed to a nursery tank where they are left with the fry until at least one week after release. About 20 to 50 eggs are laid per spawn. The length of the brooding period is about four weeks.

Scale-eaters group	max. size in cm	shallow bays	deep mud	sand	empty shells	rocks and sand	surge	steep rocks
Perissodus microlepis	13							
Plecodus straeleni	14							

Scale-eaters group

These two species are scale eaters and rarely kept in the aquarium. Because of their particular feeding behaviour only a few species can be kept with them.

Behaviour in the wild

The behaviour of these two scale eaters is obviously not to the liking of other species. *P. microlepis* mainly attacks herbivorous species which are busy scraping or combing algae from the biocover. *Tropheus* and *Petrochromis* form the main part of their victims, but *Ophthalmotilapia ventralis* females are also regularly attacked. *P. straeleni* usually feeds from somewhat larger, silvery coloured cichlids such as female *Cyathopharyn*x furcifer and larger sand-dwelling cichlids.

Behaviour in the aquarium

As can be expected with scale eaters, housing such species with other cichlids is almost impossible. Even though they accept regular aquarium fish food they still attack other species. Even their own kind are not spared sudden attacks. Only when a pair is living in harmony will they restrict their attacks to all the other fishes in the tank. Not all fishes are attacked with the same frequency and they also learn to evade the strikes of the scale-ripper. Newly introduced fishes are attacked with a much higher frequency than other individuals of the same species which have been living with the predator for some time. It is, however, recommended that just one pair be placed by themselves in a special aquarium.

Aquarium

A special aquarium for these fishes should be longer than 100 cm and contain plenty of shelter.

Feeding

Their natural food seems to consist 100% of scales of other cichlids —this is in adult fishes; juveniles feed on plankton or on material they find in the biocover.

In captivity they can be fed either by putting surplus fishes in the tank or on planktonic crustaceans such as *Cyclops*, *Daphnia*, *Mysis* etc. Care must be taken not to use "food-fishes" that are large enough to swallow the scale eater. Having scales ripped from one's flank can be annoying and lead to unexpected aggression in an otherwise placid, herbivorous victim.

Breeding

Both species are biparental mouthbrooders. *P. microlepis* has been bred in captivity (Hans-J. Herrmann, pers. comm.). Special treatment is not required but a diet of scales may be a prerequisite. A typical spawn may contain as many as 200 fry.

Malawi cichlids

by Ad Konings

The coloration of many Malawi cichlids has pleased aquarists all over the world and has made these fishes very popular.

The water in Lake Malawi has an alkaline pH (~8.3). Malawi cichlids are rather robust and can stand some fluctuation in the pH, but it is recommended that the pH of the aquarium water be maintained between 7.0 and 8.5 (see page 19 for pH adjustments).

The temperature of the water in Lake Malawi fluctuates with the seasons. In the dry season it can be as low as 20 °C and in sheltered bays in the rainy season as high as 30 °C. The flexibility of Malawi cichlids regarding temperature should not be tested in the aquarium. It is thus advisable to keep the temperature constant at a value between 23 and 28 °C. Overheating to about 32 °C can be sufficient to kill these cichlids. If the outside temperature might influence the temperature of the aquarium water, care must be taken to insulate the tank or to change the water frequently enough to keep the temperature within an acceptable range.

When the light in the aquarium is very bright a dark substratum on the bottom brings out the best colours in the fishes. Coarse sand or fine gravel is recommended and this can be mixed with fine gravel with a dark colour, such as lava (basalt) split. Avoid using white gravel or coral sand because it promotes pale colours, is unnatural, and seems to cause gill irritation.

Real plants, in particular *Vallisneria, Anubias* and *Ceratophyllum,* can be kept with many Malawi cichlids. *Anubias* can be grown on rocks and thus positioned at a higher level. In such sites they are away from digging cichlids which might cover the leaves with sand.

At least two nursery/quarantine aquaria are needed if one wishes to breed Malawi cichlids or to introduce wild caught fishes to an established aquarium. When only one fish is present in such tanks decoration or bottom substratum is not necessary. These tanks should have a capacity of about 50 litres and be fitted with a heater, a sponge filter, and a cover.

Most Mbuna are rock-dwelling cichlids. A typical rocky habitat is shown in the large photo. The Mbuna are divided into several groups (complexes). The photo at right shows a species of the *Pseudotropheus zebra* complex. The often markedly differences between the sexes, such as in *Ps. sp. "Tropheops Chilumba"* (insets previous page; upper: male; lower: female), made many Mbuna very popular among aquarists.

Mbuna group	max. size in cm	muddy bays	sandy shores	deep sand	rocks and sand	surge	rocks	open water
Cyathochromis obliquidens	13							
Cynotilapia	11							
C. axelrodi	8							
C. *sp. "Lion"*	8							
Gephyrochromis	15							
Labeotropheus trewavasae	16							
Melanochromis	15							
Pseudotropheus	15							
Ps. *sp. "Acei"*	14							
Ps. livingstonii	10							

Mbuna group

This group contains most of the Mbuna. Although many differences can be found between these cichlids, the "rules" for maintaining them in an aquarium are similar.

Behaviour in the wild

Except for *Melanochromis, Gephyrochromis* and *Ps.* sp. "Acei", males of all these Mbuna are permanently territorial. Some Mbuna females also defend a feeding territory, e.g. some species of the *Ps. elongatus* complex. Most individuals of *Ps. livingstonii* defend an empty shell as shelter. *Gephyrochromis* males and males of *Ps.* sp. "Acei" forage together with females over the sand.

Cyathochromis obliquidens inhabits the vegetated areas and feeds primarily on the algae growing on the leaves of *Vallisneria. Cynotilapia* males are normally found near their cave between the rocks but females gather in large schools in mid-water where they feed on plankton. *C. axelrodi* and *C.* sp. "Lion" males normally excavate their nest under a few small rocks on the sand. *Labeotropheus trewavasae* lives in the somewhat deeper reaches of the rocky habitat. Most males of this species are weakly territorial. *Melanochromis* species are relatively common in the rocky and intermediate habitats. Only a small percentage of the males are territorial and show their breeding coloration. *M. johanni* and *M. joanjohnsonae* are grouped with the less boisterous Mbuna on page 114.

Gephyrochromis moves over the sand and feeds from the layer of silt covering it. *Ps.* sp. "Acei" is found in the sandy habitat near tree trunks or branches.

Behaviour in the aquarium

The behaviour of these Mbuna in captivity shows a similar pattern. Males are territorial, including those of *Melanochromis*, *Gephyrochromis* and *Ps.* sp. "Acei". It is strongly recommended never to put more than one male of a species from this group in the same aquarium. The sex of Mbuna can easily be assessed by checking the vents (see page 52).

Another important factor to consider is choosing tank inhabitants which do not resemble each other in male breeding coloration, as males will respond more aggressively towards look-alikes. When only one or two different Mbuna species are kept together, males should be housed with three or more females. This avoids continuous chasing of the single female by the ever-active male.

Mbuna can be kept with larger haplochromines unless there is a danger that they will be regarded as live food. They do not mix well with Utaka, *Aulonocara*, and sand-dwelling species like *Lethrinops* and *Nyassachromis*.

Aquarium

A special Mbuna aquarium should at least be 125 cm long and contain numerous caves. Shelter can be provided by piling rocks against the back of the tank. The substratum on the bottom is not important unless aquatic plants are grown in the tank (see page 12). Coral sand, which is frequently used in Mbuna aquaria, is, however, not recommended in any cichlid aquarium. It is unnatural, promotes paler colours in males, and seems to cause gill irritation.

Feeding

The Mbuna of this group feed on vegetable matter, mostly on algae from the biocover but also on phytoplankton in mid-water. The biocover contains a large number of invertebrates, although these are eaten as well they don't appear to be the main source of food. *Ps.* sp. "Acei" seems to feed mainly from the algae on the bark of tree stumps and branches that have been washed into the lake.

The recommended food for Mbuna is shrimp mix (see page 35). In captivity Mbuna are probably the easiest cichlids to adapt to feeding on dry food —never use dry food made with animal products. They can process copious amounts of food several times a day. Such a regime must, of course, be avoided. Many of them grow much larger than their counterparts in the lake which indicates that they receive much more food (rich in nutrients) than their wild cousins. Adult Mbuna should be fed once every other day, yes, every other day! If it seems "cruel" to see the hungry fishes racing up and down the glass as soon as they see somebody moving in the room, we can compromise by feeding **tiny** bits twice a day. Remember, we don't do them a favour by overfeeding (see page 34 for further discussion). The recommended food for Mbuna is *Cyclops, Mysis, Daphnia*, and Spirulina flakes. Of course, *Tubifex*, red mosquito larvae, beef heart, and other products made from organs of warm blooded animals are forbidden for cichlids (or any other fish for that matter).

Breeding

Mbuna will spawn in any community aquarium which is suitable for Malawi cichlids. No special steps have to be taken. On the contrary, when sufficient shelter is available, young Mbuna released in the tank may evade predatory attacks and overpopulate the aquarium in a relatively short time. When numbers of fry are wanted mouthbrooding females should be removed to a nursery tank. About 30 eggs per spawn is normal but as many as 96 eggs were once recorded for a medium sized Mbuna (*Ps. tropheops*). *Melanochromis* seem to be larger-brooded than *Pseudotropheus*. Two to three weeks after a female has released the fry and regained her strength she can be returned to the community aquarium. Re-introduction should take place at night or shortly before the lights go off, and if possible several females should be re-introduced together to spread any aggressive reaction from the resident fishes.

Photo top: *Cynotilapia* sp. "Mbamba" not only closely resemble *Pseudotropheus zebra* in coloration but also in aquarium behaviour.
Centre: Probably the most popular Malawi cichlid, *Labidochromis caeruleus*, is very rare in the wild.
Bottom: The so-called orange-blotched (OB) morph of *Ps. zebra*.

Melanochromis johanni became very popular probably because of its easy maintenance and the contrasting colours of male (right) and female (above).
Photo bottom: *Iodotropheus sprengerae* is better known as the "Rusty Cichlid".

***Labidochromis* group**	max. size in cm	muddy bays	sandy shores	deep sand	rocks and sand	surge	rocks	open water
Iodotropheus	11							
Labidochromis	12							
Melanochromis joanjohnsonae	10							
M. johanni	11							

Labidochromis group

These cichlids are the smallest from Lake Malawi and can be kept together with any other Malawian cichlid provided they are not regarded as food by other tank mates.

Behaviour in the wild

Iodotropheus is normally found on its own or in very small groups. Males are not territorial but may chase conspecifics from the feeding site. The herbivorous *Labidochromis* (e.g. *L. freibergi, L. gigas*, and *L.* sp. "Hongi") are territorial, but the insectivorous species (e.g. *L. pallidus, L. chisumulae*, and *L. caeruleus*) roam through the habitat searching for prey. Both males and females of the latter group may chase conspecifics from the feeding site.

M. joanjohnsonae behaves like an insectivorous *Labidochromis* and is not territorial. *M. johanni* males are weakly territorial. Males, which show their "breeding" colours even when not defending a territory, frequently leave their domain to feed.

Behaviour in the aquarium

In captivity the species which are non-territorial in the lake become territorial. Males defend a small territory from which mainly conspecifics are chased. In a community tank several conspecific males can be kept together provided they are each given an opportunity to occupy their own cave. This means that enough shelter must be available and all the males should be introduced at the same time. In the case of most of the *Labidochromis* it is recommended that several males are kept in the same tank —which should be large enough to house these comfortably— because then the dominant male will be in full colour most of the time.

Sex is not always easily determined in small individuals, but should pose no problem in adults (see page 52). More than one female per male is, of course, advisable but a 1:1 ratio or even more males than females is possible. The same holds true for *Iodotropheus* and *M. joanjohnsonae*. It is not recommended that more than one male *M. johanni* is kept in the same aquarium unless many other Mbuna are present as well.

Aquarium

A breeding tank for, for example, *L. caeruleus* can be as small as 150 litres, but a community aquarium which holds several Mbuna should be at least 125 cm long and have a capacity of about 250 litres. These small Mbuna need plenty of hide-outs which can be provided by small rocks piled against the rear glass.

Feeding

As mentioned before *Iodotropheus* and some of the *Labidochromis* feed on vegetable matter while *M. joanjohnsonae* and the other *Labidochromis* feed on crustaceans, insects, and insect larvae. *M. johanni* is an omnivore which feeds on the algae on the rocks as well as on invertebrates.

In captivity these small Mbuna can easily be overfed. The herbivorous species are especially prone to obesity. Instead of dry food, *Cyclops, Daphnia*, *Mysis,* and shrimp mix (see page 35) are a good choice and provide a balanced diet for these lively cichlids. It is recommended that the food consist of small items which are quickly distributed over the aquarium. This allows the shy females to feed sufficiently without running the risk of overfeeding the males.

Breeding

Spawning takes place in the community aquarium when sheltered spawning sites are available. Mouthbrooding females can be left in the aquarium until three weeks after spawning. About 10 to 30 eggs are laid per spawn. After three weeks of incubation the fry are normally released from the female's mouth when she is netted. The advantage of this is that the female can be placed back immediately in the community whereas re-introduction after a few weeks absence may cause extra stress on the female. If, however, females have to be re-introduced it is best done at night when the lights are off or about to go off, and with several re-introduced simultaneously to spread any aggressive reaction.

Labeotropheus fuelleborni group

This group of medium sized cichlids consists of species which have a dominating behaviour. They need a larger aquarium than other Malawi cichlids of this size.

Behaviour in the wild

Astatotilapia calliptera is found predominantly in shallow water where it prefers the vegetated areas. Small groups of foraging females are not uncommon, while males are normally found defending a territory within the *Vallisneria* beds.

Labeotropheus fuelleborni is commonly observed in combat with other cichlids during territorial disputes. It is a herbivore and scrapes algae from the rocks.

Melanochromis melanopterus is a predator which normally feeds on small cichlids. It is a solitary species which chases conspecifics from its feeding territory.

Petrotilapia species are known for their boisterous behaviour. *P. genalutea* may sometimes form large groups and forage in areas which would be inaccessible if it approached them on its own. *Petrotilapia* are herbivores which comb the loose material from the biocover on the rocks. Territorial males defend their terrain energetically against all intruders.

Behaviour in the aquarium

These species have in common the fact

***L. fuelleborni* group**	max. size in cm	muddy bays	sandy shores	deep sand	rocks and sand	surge	rocks	open water
Astatotilapia calliptera	13							
Labeotropheus fuelleborni	18							
Melanochromis melanopterus	15							
Petrotilapia	22							

Photos facing page:
top: A so-called orange-blotched (OB) female *Labeotropheus fuelleborni*. Males (centre) have very large territories which are defended aggressively.
bottom: *Aulonocara maylandi* in its natural habitat which consists of sand and rocks.

Photos this page:
top: This strain of *Aulonocara jacobfreibergi* is better known as "Eureka Peacock". It was selected from offspring of the race found near Otter Point, Cape Maclear.
centre: In their natural environment Chitande Type *Aulonocara* —the photo shows a male from Masinje— are weakly territorial. In captivity they cannot be kept together with Mbuna or other boisterous cichlids.
bottom: *Aulonocara* sp. "Maleri". In captivity *Aulonocara* species grow much larger than their counterparts in the lake.

that males, whatever size of aquarium they are kept in, will always fight for a larger territory. For this reason it is impossible to keep more than one male (of a species) in the same aquarium without having one damaging the other(s). It is possible to keep *L. fuelleborni* together with *L. trewavasae* (which has a milder temperament) in the same aquarium —one male of each species— but they should come from the same area of the lake so that they recognise each other as belonging to different species. When one isn't sure about the origin of *Labeotropheus,* putting these two species together should be avoided, because it may lead to hybridisation. The same is true of the *Petrotilapia* species; never put together species in which the males resemble each other in their breeding coloration.

M. melanopterus and *A. calliptera* may behave aggressively towards other tank inhabitants which should therefore be robust and able to withstand these boisterous cichlids. Most of their aggression is, however, directed towards conspecifics. It is advised that these cichlids be housed in a community aquarium.

The sex of these cichlids can easily be determined by "venting" them (see page 52). Don't rely on the colour or size of the specimen. A small, colourless fish may grow into a territorial male in the aquarium.

Aquarium

Because of the male's temperament *A. calliptera* and *Labeotropheus* need an aquarium with a length of at least 150 cm. *Petrotilapia* and *M. melanopterus* should be housed in a tank at least 200 cm long. Plenty of shelter should be provided for the females —it is advisable to have more than one female even when other species are present to divert the male's attention. The caves created by the rockwork must be large in order to avoid a harassed female getting stuck between the rocks. When enough shelter is available there is no problem keeping these cichlids.

Feeding

In the wild *A. calliptera* feeds on insects, crustaceans, and also on plant material. *Labeotropheus* and *Petrotilapia* are herbivores. *M. melanopterus* is a predator.

The problem with keeping Mbuna is not only their territorial aggression but also their relentless appetite. Most of them are herbivores and usually graze from the biocover all day long. The food we offer our fishes in captivity contains far more nutriment than the material ingested in the lake. Adult Mbuna should therefore be fed only every other day. The food we give them must contain a lot of fibre or else material which can be digested only slowly and with difficulty. Flake food, in particular flakes containing Spirulina, pelleted food (not containing mammalian fat!), shrimp mix (see page 35), *Cyclops*, and *Mysis* are recommended for feeding these Mbuna. The amount of food given must be eaten within TWO minutes. Professional breeders make their own fish food in which a lot of fibre is included. Most of them feed only once a day.

Breeding

Depending on the situation in the community aquarium breeding takes place whenever the male is able to defend a territory and a female becomes ripe. When a male doesn't show colour or when he is repeatedly chased by other species spawning cannot be expected to occur. In such cases a special breeding tank should be used. The breeding tank for these species must, however, have the same minimum size as recommended for the community aquarium. Another possibility is to remove the most dominant male from the community tank for a while and let other species breed in his absence. A single male can conveniently be placed in a 50-litre aquarium with good filtration to keep the water quality under control. In many instances a slightly overcrowded community aquarium appears to be the best method of keeping and breeding Mbuna.

Mouthbrooding females must be removed from the main tank when fry are wanted. They are placed by themselves in a small nursery tank until they release the fry. The number of fry per spawn ranges between 25 and 40.

Aulonocara group

Aulonocara species are probably the group of Malawi cichlids with the mildest temperament. This group, which is very popular among aquarists, cannot be kept with large or boisterous cichlids.

Behaviour in the wild

Aulonocara feed from the sand and are therefore always found in the neighbourhood of sandy substrata. Because of their relatively small size they need the protection of rocks. Almost all rock sand habitats at depths between 5 and 40 metres in the lake are populated by at least one species of this genus. Characteristically males as well as females hover a few millimetres above the sand and remain in a motionless position. With the very sensitive enlarged sensory pores on the lower part of their head they are able to detect tiny movements of invertebrates under the sand. Whenever such prey is located, a quick bite in the sand secures it inside the predator's mouth. In Lake Malawi this behaviour is typical of *Aulonocara*. Silhouettes of fishes hovering motionless above the sand can thus easily be identified as belonging to *Aulonocara*. Males are weakly territorial and leave their territory to feed. Males of most of these rock-dwelling *Aulonocara* defend a cave as territory; some species (the so-called Chitande

***Aulonocara* group**	max. size in cm	muddy bays	sandy shores	deep sand	rocks and sand	surge	rocks	open water
Aulonocara auditor	14							
A. baenschi	12							
A. sp. "Chitande Type"	11							
A. ethelwynnae	10							
A. hansbaenschi	14							
A. hueseri	11							
A. jacobfreibergi	13							
A. kandeensis	12							
A. korneliae	14							
A. sp. "Maleri"	15							
A. maylandi	12							
A. sp. "Mbenji"	14							
A. saulosi	15							
A. stuartgranti	14							
A. sp. "Yellow Collar"	12							

Type *Aulonocara*) may instead defend a small depression in the sand near or between rocks. In the lake *Aulonocara* can be very abundant but aggression towards other cichlids has never been observed.

Behaviour in the aquarium

The typical feeding behaviour of *Aulonocara* is not exhibited in the aquarium. This could be due to the fact that the bottom in most aquaria still consists of coarse gravel and that nothing moves about in this substratum. Even though *Aulonocara* males are peaceful towards other cichlids it is recommended that only one male per species is kept in the same aquarium. Males are not very aggressive but *Aulonocara*s are easily damaged when chased. More than one female is not necessary, but, of course, possible. The sexes, even of small individuals, can be determined by examining the vent (see page 52).

Although many rock-frequenting species of *Aulonocara* are known only a few can be kept together in the same tank. The only reason is that several species may hybridise and we aquarists have the responsibility of keeping every race and population pure. It is possible, however, to keep different species together provided these are chosen from the different groups into which the genus can be subdivided (one species only from each group). These groups are: *A. jacobfreibergi* with all its geographical races; the Chitande Type *Aulonocara*s; the blue and/or yellow coloured *Aulonocara*s (*A. stuartgranti* types); and the sand-dwelling *Aulonocara*s. Apart from the sand-dwelling *Aulonocara*s, several species of which can be found together in the wild, only one geographical race per group should be kept in a single aquarium. In a community tank one could therefore house for instance *A. jacobfreibergi, A. ethelwynnae, A. stuartgranti*, and *A. guentheri* without fear of hybridisation between these species. When, however, the blue-coloured Chilumba *Aulonocara* is kept together with the yellow-coloured Usisya *Aulonocara* one can expect hybrids between these two variants. Always be sure of the purity of the strain or obtain wild caught individuals only.

Rock-dwelling *Aulonocara* can be kept together with other *Aulonocara, Lethrinops*, Utaka, and medium-sized "haps" (non-Mbuna). **They should not be housed with Mbuna**

such as *Labeotropheus, Petrotilapia, Ps. zebra*, and *Ps. tropheops.*

Aquarium

The tank should be at least 100 cm long and have a capacity of at least 200 litres. The substratum on the bottom is best composed of sand and fine gravel. Rocks should be piled at several places in the tank to provide caves for the males.

Aulonocara stuartgranti occurs in several different geographical races which should be kept separated in captivity in order to avoid loss of bio-diversity. The most recent discovery is that of the "Ngara Peacock" (photo facing page).
Right: *Aulonocara rostratum* grows to a maximum size of about 20 cm, but, because of its mild temperament, should not be kept together with boisterous Mbuna.

Feeding

Aulonocara in the wild feed on sand-dwelling invertebrates.

In captivity *Aulonocara* species usually grow to a much larger size than in the wild. This is because of the enormous quantities of food these and other cichlids are given in the aquarium. *Aulonocara*s are very placid cichlids and as such don't expend very much energy living in the artificial environment of an aquarium. When the contours of the fishes start getting rounder and fatty bulges become visible behind the head, they have clearly been overfed. *Aulonocara* accept any type of food and can be kept in breeding condition by feeding a good quality dry food only. It is important that a small quantity of food is administered only once a day or once every other day. **Never feed more than can be eaten in two minutes**.

Breeding

Breeding *Aulonocara* does not require luck or patience. In a balanced community aquarium spawning takes place at regular intervals. This is true for fishes in good condition. The argument that larger fishes breed more often or have larger spawns is correct only when large doesn't mean fat. Fat *Aulonocara* may have wonderful colours but are usually too busy eating to breed. The spawning frequency of large, fat females is clearly lower than that of healthy females. When fat females are dissected the ovaries are found to be embedded in thick layers of fat. It then becomes clear that such females have problems producing eggs. Such obese specimens can fast for at least two weeks before some of the fat is absorbed. After they have recovered their normal outlines they may still be able to spawn. The spawns of most Aulonocara number between 25 and 50 eggs; those of the Chitande Type *Aulonocara*, however, may have as many as 90 eggs.

***Lethrinops* group**	max. size in cm	muddy bays	sandy shores	deep sand	rocks and sand	surge	rocks	open water
Aulonocara guentheri	16							
A. rostratum	20							
A. sp."Jumbo Blue"	17							
Lethrinops	23							
Nyassachromis	18							
Tramitichromis	15							

Lethrinops group

The cichlids in this group are sand-dwellers with a mild temperament and need a bottom of fine sand in the aquarium.

Behaviour in the wild

Nyassachromis species live in mid-water above a sandy bottom. They feed on zooplankton and are normally found in groups or schools. Most of them have a breeding season during which territorial males gather in breeding colonies. In such colonies the nests, which consist of a sand cone with a small depression at the top, are one to three metres apart.

The other species in this group are much more bottom-oriented. *Aulonocara* species are predators feeding on insects and crustaceans which they locate in the sand using their elaborate sensory system. *Aulonocara* usually occur in groups or in small schools. Many males defend a territory all year round, but sometimes individuals with male-specific coloration are observed together with females foraging in the sand. *Lethrinops* and *Tramitichromis* species feed on insects and crustaceans as well but obtain their food by sifting the sand through their gills. Anything edible is retained and swallowed. Females of these characteristic sand-dwellers have a silvery coloration which forms a perfect camouflage when living over sand. Species of the genus *Lethrinops* and, to a somewhat lesser extent, of the genus *Tramitichromis* breed only during a specific season. Breeding males of *T. brevis*, however, are found throughout the year. *Lethrinops*-like cichlids are some of the most delicate fishes from Lake Malawi.

Behaviour in the aquarium

Like the rock-frequenting *Aulonocara* (page 119), these three sand-dwelling *Aulonocara* are ideal aquarium residents which can be kept with any other Malawi cichlids apart from large predators and the more boisterous Mbuna,. Even keeping two or more conspecific males in the same aquarium should not give rise to serious problems, although this practice is not recommended. Females are rather peaceful among themselves but it is not really necessary to have more than one in order to preserve the harmony of the tank.

Nyassachromis males can be quite determined when it comes to defending their territory, but against most other Malawi cichlids their efforts are fruitless. It is therefore better to house these cichlids with their own kind in a special aquarium or with *Aulonocara*, Utaka and/or *Lethrinops*-like cichlids. More than one *Nyassachromis* male can be kept in the same tank but normally only one male will show breeding coloration. When *Nyassachromis* species are kept in a community aquarium a single female would be sufficient if not ideal. In a breeding tank three or more females are necessary to keep a peaceful balance between chasing and courting.

Lethrinops-like cichlids are difficult to sex when not fully mature. Territorial males can be quite pugnacious towards conspecific males but totally ignore other species. It is not necessary to keep more than one female per male but a few females is always safer, especially when only a few fishes are kept in the aquarium. Some species (e.g. *L.* cf. *micrentodon* and *L. microstoma*), which have a specific breeding season in the wild, breed throughout the year after they have adjusted to the artificial environment.

Aquarium

One of the most important factors in keeping these cichlids is to provide them with fine sand on the bottom and with enough space to build a nest. *A. rostratum* should be kept in an aquarium with a length of at least 150 cm; the other species of this group can be housed in smaller tanks with a length between 100 and 125 cm. When several nest-building cichlids are kept together enough space should be available for them to build nests or at least to defend a territory. A typical aquarium for these cichlids will have a few solitary rocks, maybe some plants, and a bottom of fine sand. Because of their behaviour and habitat preference rock-dwelling Mbuna do not belong in such a tank.

Feeding

All of these species are predators feeding on insects, zooplankton, and crustaceans. Some *Lethrinops* feed on snails as well.

In captivity they all relish dry food which can make them grow beyond normal proportions and stop them from breeding. These cichlids need shrimp mix (page 35), white worms, live or frozen *Cyclops, Artemia, Mysis*, and other planktonic crustaceans.

Breeding

To breed these species we first have to be patient and wait until their internal clock tells them to do so. Apart from *Aulonocara*, males of which may exhibit breeding colour all year round, these cichlids are collected when they are breeding. This guarantees that the right females are collected with the males. After transport most males may have lost their breeding "mood" and need to be acclimatised to their new environment. In the aquarium several species of this group may not breed again before their natural season, a year later. In the meantime males do not show their best colours but this does not mean that they don't feel well. Malawi cichlids that breed during a restricted season do not do so year after year; two, maybe three seasons is the maximum in captivity. In the lake they may breed for a single season only.

In the aquarium an imminent spawning is indicated by the territoriality of the male and his enhanced coloration. When other fishes prevent the male from exhibiting his natural breeding behaviour they should be temporarily removed from the tank, unless offspring are not wanted. Mouthbrooding females

—when more than one female is present they all seem to spawn within a few days— can be left with the male for a few days and then removed to a nursery tank. Several brooding females can be put together but it is always better to keep them separated. Keep some of the fry and grow them to maturity to replace the breeding stock which may not breed again. The clutch size of these species varies between 30 and 150 eggs.

Utaka group

These cichlids are sometimes referred to by their African name, Utaka. The females in particular are rather delicate and for this reason these species need to be housed in an aquarium devoted to the group or with other mild-tempered cichlids.

Behaviour in the wild

Utaka are characterised by their schooling behaviour and by the fact that they feed on zooplankton in mid-water, usually close to a rocky habitat. Males of *C. azureus, C. likomae, C. mbenjii, C.* sp. "Mloto Likoma", *C. pleurostigma*, and *C. virginalis* use sand to construct their nest; *C. borleyi, C. quadrimaculatus*, and *C. verduyni* defend a nest on the rocks while *C. chrysonotus* males defend territories in mid-water.

Females and young males gather in large schools —frequently consisting of several different Utaka species— and feed from the zooplankton in the open water above or beside a rocky reef. The protrusible mouth, characteristic of this group, is an adaptation for picking prey from mid-water.

Most *Lethrinops* species have a specific breeding season. When born in captivity males of some species, such as *Lethrinops* cf. *micrentodon* (centre facing page: male; bottom left: female) may show their breeding coloration throughout the year.
Aulonocara sp. "Jumbo Blue" (facing page bottom right) would be a popular cichlid if it could be exported in larger numbers.
Right: *Copadichromis verduyni* is a very popular Utaka. It is better known as "Borleyi Eastern".

Utaka group	max. size in cm	muddy bays	sandy shores	deep sand	rocks and sand	surge	rocks	open water
Copadichromis azureus	17							
C. borleyi	18							
C. chrysonotus	16							
C. likomae	17							
C. mbenjii	15							
C. sp. "Mloto Likoma"	15							
C. pleurostigma	20							
C. quadrimaculatus	24							
C. verduyni	14							
C. virginalis	14							

Behaviour in the aquarium

Utaka are good aquarium residents, because they are mild tempered and males have a bright coloration almost year-round. Males of different species can be placed in the same tank with all the females forming a school. It is, however, recommended that only species in which the females can be easily distinguished are kept in the same tank. Some energetic males are able to attract heterospecific females to their nest and may even spawn with them. When the females of the other species in the aquarium are quite different in appearance such hybridisation occurs only in exceptional cases.

Utaka can be housed with *Aulonocara* and with mild tempered Mbuna, such as *Labidochromis* species. Large, more boisterous Mbuna and large haplochromine predators are a bad choice as tank mates for Utaka. Even if housed with Mbuna of meek temperament, Utaka can be intimidated if outnumbered by Mbuna. For this reason it is advised that no more than 50% of the tank occupants be Mbuna in such a mixed community.

Adult male Utaka do not always show breeding coloration. In order to determine the sex of these cichlids one has to inspect the vent (see page 52).

Aquarium

The aquarium should have a lot of swimming space because these cichlids do not naturally hide among rocks. For many of the Utaka fine sand is needed on the bottom and a few solitary rocks as well. In the case of smaller Utaka, with a maximum length of about 15 cm, an aquarium with a length of about 100 cm may be sufficient. The other species should be housed in a tank which is at least 150 cm long. If Utaka are housed together with Mbuna both habitats should be provided. This may necessitate a larger aquarium.

It is recommended that a few dither fishes, such as *Aulonocara* or *Lethrinops* species, are kept together with Utaka to prevent them from becoming shy and easily frightened. For the same reason it is not advisable to keep Utaka in an aquarium sited at a low level. Near the ground many cichlids appear to be uncomfortable (although this may be restricted to the times when we stand in front of the tank).

C. chrysonotus needs an aquarium with a height of at least 70 cm if we want to observe its typical mid-water spawning behaviour. In captivity most males defend a rock as territory but in the wild males have three-dimensional territories in mid-water, a few metres above the rocks.

Feeding

As mentioned before Utaka feed on zooplankton.

In captivity most species readily accept dry food, especially flakes. Although some species, such as *C. borleyi* and *C. verduyni*, can be fed entirely on dry food —no mammalian fat as part of the ingredients— it is recommended that they be fed planktonic crustaceans instead. Males of many Utaka will not regain or acquire their breeding colours when fed exclusively on dry food.

Breeding

Some Utaka have a specific breeding season outside which males don't show their breeding coloration or defend a nest. Wild caught individuals usually show such seasonal behaviour in the aquarium as well. *C. virginalis, C. quadrimaculatus, C. pleurostigma*, and *C. chrysonotus* have a restricted breeding season and may therefore need a much longer acclimatisation period before they start breeding in captivity. Offspring of wild caught Utaka, however, do not seem to be restricted to a certain period and may breed throughout the year.

A few other species are found breeding the year round in the lake but for some reason need a very long time to get used to the artificial environment of an aquarium or perhaps simply need to mature fully before they are able to produce offspring. There is little we can do to speed up their acclimatisation period, other than feeding them as varied a menu as possible and giving them the right environment to let them develop their natural behaviour.

Mouthbrooding females should be removed from the breeding or community aquarium and put in a nursery tank. Such females may be put together when they have spawned on the same day and when the nursery tank is large enough to give each female about 50 litres of water. It is better to divide a larger tank into several compartments and give each mouthbrooding female her own. The spawn size of most Utaka varies from 30 to 75 eggs and is dependent on the size of the female.

"Happies" group

This large group of cichlids consists of species which can be kept with almost any other Malawi cichlid.

Behaviour in the wild

Apart from *C. euchilus, P. milomo, Sc. fryeri* and some predatory *Mylochromis*, these cichlids are commonly found foraging in small groups or even in large schools. Breeding males are often found in colonies although several exceptions exist within this group. Territorial males, which defend their terrain energetically against all intruders, are common. Territories are, however, quite small.

Behaviour in the aquarium

It is recommended that several different species be kept in the aquarium. The temperament of these species does not allow the presence of more than one breeding male in the same tank unless it is bigger than 2000 litres. Young males may be housed together with the group but as soon as they start to colour they bear the brunt of the territorial aggression of the dominant male. When several species are kept together in a reasonably balanced (no regular casualties) community aquarium, one female is usually sufficient. When only one of these species is kept (together with Mbuna or *Aulonocara*) three or more females are necessary to spread evenly the effect of the male's belligerence.

The sex of sub-adult individuals can be determined by examining the vents (page 52). Individuals that lack the typical male coloration are not necessarily females. Males of many species have exactly the same coloration as females when they are dominated by another male.

Photos facing page:
top: *Cyrtocara moorii*, one of the old favourites and still very popular among aquarists.
centre: *Placidochromis milomo* became known as "Super VC 10".
bottom: The "Electric Blue" has recently been described as *Sciaenochromis fryeri.* It is one of the mainstays in the hobby although in the wild it is not at all common.

Photos this page:
top: "Steveni Taiwan" has also been found along the Tanzanian coast of the lake.
centre: *Otopharynx heterodon* has been exported as "Royal Blue". It is found throughout the lake but most aquarium specimens are caught at Chizumulu Island.
bottom: The "Mbenji Thick Lips" is found only around the Mbenji islands.

"Happies" group	max. size in cm	muddy bays	sandy shores	deep sand	rocks and sand	surge	rocks	open water
Chilotilapia euchilus	25	light			dark			
C. rhoadesii	25	dark	light					
Ctenopharynx	20				light		dark	
Cyrtocara moorii	20	light	dark					
Fossorochromis rostratus	35		dark		light			
Hemitilapia oxyrhynchus	20	dark						
Mylochromis	25	light	light	light	dark			
Otopharynx	25		light	light	dark		light	
Placidochromis	20	dark			light			
Pl. milomo	25						dark	
Protomelas	20				light	light	dark	
Protomelas similis group	20	dark	light					
Sciaenochromis	20			dark	light			
Sc. fryeri	18				light		dark	
Taeniolethrinops	30		dark	light	light			
Trematocranus	25	dark	light					

Aquarium

The minimum length of the aquarium should be at least 125 cm for species with a maximum size of about 20 cm; all the other species of the group need aquaria longer than 175 cm. A tank with a length of 200 cm, a capacity of 600 litres, and an excellent filtration system may house 10 to 15 individuals of this group. Smaller aquaria are not advisable when more than one species of this group is being kept. Although several of these cichlids are found in the rocky habitat, rocks in the tank have mainly a decorative function unless Mbuna are also kept in the same tank.

Feeding

This large and varied group contains piscivores (e.g. *Sc. fryeri*), insectivores (e.g. *P. milomo*), as well as herbivores (e.g. *H. oxyrhynchus*).

In captivity these species feed on anything offered. When only dry food is given it is recommended that this be restricted to flake food (of course without animal fat). Sticks and pellets are usually made of the same ingredients but the fishes can eat much more in a very short time. Correctly feeding these cichlids is not an easy task because they seem to be hungry all the time. As was recommended in an earlier chapter (pages 34-35), feeding adult cichlids should be restricted to once a day or once every other day. Flake food is a better choice because it can be distributed through the aquarium more evenly and give every fish a chance to feed. Several cichlids of this group can be bred only when fed with live or frozen food. *Mysis*, shrimp, mussels, white worms, earthworms, *Daphnia*, *Artemia*, and most other kinds of planktonic crustaceans can be given in appropriate quantities. When males lose their colour and acquire a deeper-than-normal body, too much food has been given.

Breeding

In a special breeding tank one male needs to be accompanied by at least four females. In a community aquarium, in which more than one species of this group is kept, a single female may be sufficient. Care must be taken that the male does not direct his entire repertoire of territorial aggression towards that single female. If this seems to be the case then additional females will usually relieve the pressure. Mouthbrooding females must be removed from the community or breeding aquarium, and placed in a nursery tank. After the fry have been released for the first time they are still guarded by the female. During this time the female can regain her strength before she is placed back in the aquarium with the male (two to three weeks after she has released the fry). Spawns usually contain 50 to 100 fry.

Piscivores group

This group of cichlids includes relatively large fishes which may become dominant in a community aquarium.

Behaviour in the wild

These predators usually roam around their particular habitat on their own. None of them has a territory that is permanently defended. Feeding territories are very large and therefore other species are tolerated within their boundaries. Conspecifics are normally chased from the feeding area but foraging individuals of *Ch. caeruleus, N. polystigma*, and *Stigmatochromis woodii* are sometimes found in small groups. Breeding males may defend a temporary territory, especially when other males are around. Such males are very shy towards divers but rather aggressive towards conspecific males.

Piscivores group	max. size in cm	muddy bays	sandy shores	deep sand	rocks and sand	surge	rocks	open water
Aristochromis christyi	25							
Buccochromis	35							
B. heterotaenia	40							
Champsochromis caeruleus	40							
C. spilorhynchus	30							
Dimidiochromis	25							
Exochochromis anagenys	30							
Hemitaeniochromis	25							
Naevochromis chrysogaster	20							
Nimbochromis	23							
N. polystigma	20							
Rhamphochromis	40							
Stigmatochromis	30							
S. modestus	20							
Taeniochromis holotaenia	24							
Tyrannochromis	30							

Dimidiochromis compressiceps (above) is known under the trade name of "Malawi Eye-Biter". The frequency with which this cichlid bites eyes is not higher than that of many other piscivores.

Left: *Buccochromis heterotaenia* is one of the biggest Malawi cichlids and may grow to about 40 cm.

Facing page: fry of *Nimbochromis polystigma* seeking shelter inside mom's mouth.

Behaviour in the aquarium

These large predators are problematic to house in an aquarium. They cannot be kept together with small Mbuna or *Aulonocara* or any other fish which might be regarded as a part of their menu. When a male of one of these predators is kept with smaller haplochromines, he invariably becomes the dominant fish in the aquarium. Therefore it is better to house these cichlids with species of similar size and temperament. Obviously we must avoid keeping together species that resemble each other and never keep more than one male of any single species in the same tank. Try to keep several species in an aquarium because this will spread the aggression of the individual males. In such cases two females, or even just one, can be housed with the male. When only one species is kept at least four females are required to keep problems at bay.

Aquarium

These predators need a very large aquarium. A community tank with only one species of these predators present should contain at

least 1000 litres. When several of these species are kept together the tank should also be 1000 litres minimum, not because of the fishes' aggression but in view of their large size. A special tank in which only one species is kept should contain about 750 litres. A hiding or nesting place should be available for each male. These can be made by piling rocks or pipes on top of each other leaving a cave large enough for a pair to spawn in.

Feeding

Most, if not all, of the species of this group are piscivorous, feeding mainly on other cichlids. Only *Rhamphochromis* feeds on non-cichlids (Usipa, *Engraulicypris sardella*, the lake sardine).

In captivity these piscivores can be fed with small fishes although it is advised to feed them with mussels, shrimp mix (page 35), and other large crustaceans. Feeding these piscivores with small live fishes may make them more aggressive towards smaller tank mates. Pieces of fish (e.g. cod or smelt), however, could be an alternative although shrimps and mussels are more nutritious.

Overfeeding, in particular with the wrong foods, may give a well-proportioned appearance but produces too much fatty tissue around the ovaries of the females. For this reason a fat female is not necessarily ready to spawn. The fishes may look full shortly after feeding but by the next day they should again appear slim.

Breeding

The most important factor in breeding these predators is getting them into good breeding condition. When fishes are overfed they show hardly any colour and show no interest in anything but food. A good way of inducing such fishes to breed is to stop feeding them for about a week. When males are colourful and actively defending a possible spawning site in the tank, spawning normally occurs within a few days. But if the females have ragged fins and don't seem to be ready, it is better to remove the male to another tank for a few weeks.

Mouthbrooding females should be caught at night and placed in a nursery tank by themselves. The clutch size of these predators may be as large as 250 eggs but varies frequently between 50 and 150 eggs.

Scale-eaters group

These two species have been exported sporadically for the ornamental fish trade. They cannot be kept in a community aquarium because of their feeding behaviour.

Behaviour in the wild

Corematodus taeniatus is a scale-eater which rips scales from the caudal peduncles of other cichlids. It mingles in with groups of sand-dwellers and continually attacks the other members of the school. *C. taeniatus* operates on its own. Breeding males are territorial and defend a nest on top of a rock. Most breeding males are found at small rocky outcrops bordering sandy biotopes.

Genyochromis mento is a Mbuna and occurs in many different biotopes. Its piscivorous behaviour is restricted to pieces of fins and scales of other cichlids. It attacks any cichlid which is not aware of the predator's intention. Territorial males who are in dispute with competitors over territorial boundaries are particularly vulnerable to *G. mento*'s attacks. *G. mento* is a very aggressive Mbuna, but males are not territorial.

Behaviour in the aquarium

It is impossible to keep *G. mento* in an aquarium with other fishes. It is also impossible for *G. mento* to be exported from Lake Malawi unnoticed because one such fin-biter causes a lot of damage to other fishes when they are kept together in the same aquarium.

C. taeniatus initially behaves in the aquarium as it does in the wild. However, after a while the other fishes in the aquarium learn how to evade the scale-eater's attack. After the community has established itself in the aquarium it is difficult to add new fishes to it because they are immediately attacked by *C.*

Scale-eaters group	max. size in cm	muddy bays	sandy shores	deep sand	rocks and sand	surge	rocks	open water
Corematodus taeniatus	20							
Genyochromis mento	12							

taeniatus. Only one male of this scale-eater can be housed in the same aquarium. The sex of an individual can be determined by checking the vent (see page 52).

Aquarium

G. mento can be maintained in a small aquarium of about 50 litres since it has to be kept by itself. *C. taeniatus* needs a larger aquarium with a length of at least 125 cm. It is recommended that plenty of shelter be provided for the other cichlids in the tank.

Feeding

The natural food of these two predators has been mentioned before. In captivity both species accept dry food and all kinds of frozen and live food.

Breeding

Neither of these species has been bred in captivity. In the lake *C. taeniatus* needs a very large territory which is defended against larger haplochromines. This may explain its pugnacious behaviour against conspecifics in the aquarium.

Victoria cichlids

by Ole Seehausen

Cichlids of Lake Victoria exhibit a wide array of forms, expressed in behaviour, ecology and morphology. There are no extreme types which are not connected by a number of intermediate species, making it extremely difficult for taxonomists to define and delimit groups. The consequence is that most researchers prefer to use the old generic name *Haplochromis* for almost all of the species, more than 95% of which are endemic to Lake Victoria. Attention was drawn to them recently because of the dramatic decline of populations following the explosive increase of an introduced predator (*Lates* sp.) in the eighties.

For many years the limited degree of interest shown by aquarists was in remarkable contrast to that of scientists. Several reasons are believed to be responsible: (1) Lake Victoria cichlids are very difficult to identify without taxonomic training. (2) No book author has yet made a serious attempt to provide aquarists with the reliable information that is needed to establish a broader interest. (3) The few paragraphs found in aquarium books were mostly copied from scientific literature and applied to misidentified fishes. (4) Impermissible generalisations were made from experience with one or two species. It is, for instance, wrong to state that aggressive behaviour is a general feature of Lake Victoria fishes. (5) Victoria cichlids often do not show their brilliant colours when kept under unfavourable conditions.

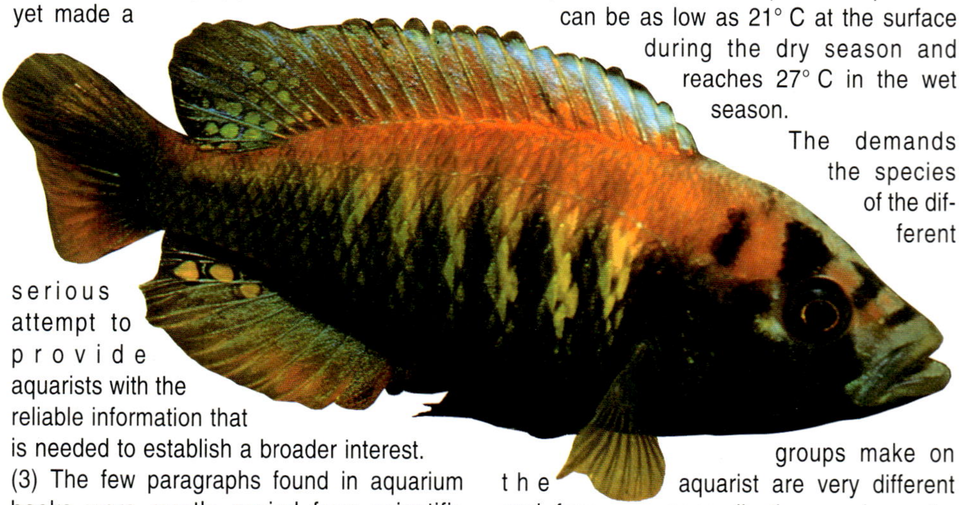

The more than 400 *Haplochromis* species are classified, on the basis of ecology and morphology, in 15 trophic (feeding) groups and sub-groups (Greenwood, 1974; Witte & Van Oijen, 1990). Only a very small selection can be presented here. These have been chosen mainly on the basis of two criteria: (1) species that exist (existed) in captivity; (2) species that are not kept in aquaria but are still found relatively frequently in the lake and belong to ecological groups which are present in aquaria.

The water in Lake Victoria is much less clear than that in Lakes Malawi and Tanganyika. We measured transparencies between less than 1 and 2.5 m in inshore areas. The pH is alkaline and ranges from 6.9 to 9.0 (Akiyama *et al.*, 1977), but the water is rather soft (between 2 and 8° DH). The temperature can be as low as 21° C at the surface during the dry season and reaches 27° C in the wet season.

The demands the species of the different groups make on the aquarist are very different and few generalisations can be made. These cichlids should ideally never be kept in pairs but in groups. It was believed until recently that all species are maternal mouthbrooders. Recently one case of biparental ovophilic mouthbrooding has been discovered (Seehausen, in prep.) and is described here. All the other species mentioned seem to be maternal mouthbrooders. Brooding females should be separated from the group. They can be kept in 50-litre nursery tanks, furnished with a heater, a sponge filter and a shelter (e.g. a flowerpot lying on its side).

Duration of incubation time (defined here as the time between spawning and first release of the fry) and post buccal care (defined here as time between first release and last guarding of the fry) differ remarkably between species and, where known, are given in the descriptions.

Regarding the use of the tables: names in quotation marks are so-called "cheironyms" which are used by the Haplochromis Ecology Survey Team (HEST) and the Lake Victoria Research Team. An asterisk after the name indicates a species that exists, or at least once existed, in aquaria. Maximum size data can never be more than an orientation help; it depends on many factors. Because it is impossible to constrict the natural habitat distribution of the species into a small number of habitat categories without losing important information, the reader should refer to the tables **and** to the text. "Deep water", for instance, can mean 2-5 m of depth in the case of some rock dwelling cichlids but more than 10 m in the case of open water species.

rock-dwelling algae scrapers

This group is widely distributed over the lake and its members resemble the Mbuna of Lake Malawi in morphological and ecological traits. Contrary to former belief, rock-dwelling scrapers of Lake Victoria exhibit high geographic variation and local endemism. Piebald or orange-blotched individuals (mostly females) are known in three of the species mentioned.

Behaviour in the wild

H. nigricans inhabits shallow waters over rocky substrates, preferably over horizontal rock surfaces. It is found from the surface to 2 m depth; in places with high water transparency it is found slightly deeper. Breeding males hold large territories; females and sexually inactive males graze in schools. *H.* sp. "Blue Scraper" is found in the same habitat but penetrates to greater depths. *H.* sp. "Giant Scraper" is concentrated in very shallow areas of less than 1 m depth. Details of *H.* sp. "Kruising" are unknown. This species has decreased in numbers and may be extinct. *H.* sp. "Velvet Black" is also found on rock surfaces but, in contrast to *H. nigricans*, in the interstices between the rocks as well. It has a wide depth distribution, variable between different populations, from the surface to a depth of 5 metres. *H.* sp. "Carp" lives predominantly in very shallow water but not the surf zone.

Facing page: a displaying male *Haplochromis nyererei*. Right: *Haplochromis nigricans* scrapes algae from the rocks and shows a similar behaviour to the Mbuna of Lake Malawi. Photo by Ole Seehausen.

***H. nigricans* group**	max. size in cm	muddy bays	sandy shores	deep, open water	open water	rocks surge zone	rocks, shallow water	rocks, deep water
*Haplochromis nigricans**	13							
H. sp. "Blue Scraper"*	14							
H. sp. "Giant Scraper"	18							
H. sp. "Kruising"	14							
H. sp. "Velvet Black"*	14							
H. sp. "Carp"*	18							

Behaviour in the aquarium

Males can become very aggressive when defending territories. They hold these territories permanently, even if no female is ripe for spawning. One should keep one male with at least four, better more, females. In tanks of more than 200 cm length it is possible to keep three or more (**not two!**) males. However, usually only one will hold territory. If two species of this group are to be kept together in a rocky aquarium, one needs a tank at least 200 cm long. In such cases one male per species may become territorial. These species can be kept together with other rock-dwelling species, i.e. insect pickers. They may also be housed with large snail-eaters such as *H. sauvagei* and *Astatoreochromis alluaudi.*

Aquarium

The aquarium must be at least 100 cm long and 50 cm deep. The natural habitat can be imitated with arrangements of big stones between which gaps and large holes should be present. The bottom between the stones and in the front third of the aquarium should be covered with sand.

Feeding

In their natural habitat these species remove filamentous algae from rock surfaces by pulling, pull-scraping, and scraping (Seehausen, 1993b). *H.* sp. "Blue Scraper" and *H.* sp. "Velvet Black" also take larger amounts of animal food (Bryozoa (moss animals) and insect larvae). In the aquarium all species take any type of food but a vegetarian component is probably important. Offering stones with a rich cover of filamentous green algae provides interesting opportunities to observe the natural feeding behaviour.

Breeding

The species of this group are maternal mouthbrooders with an incubation time of about 21 days and a post-buccal care period of up to three weeks. For breeding purposes it is necessary to keep the species by itself. The species of this group readily interbreed in aquaria and their offspring are fertile. It is wrong to assume that interbreeding happens only if the proper partners are not available. Even if the females always select the proper males, sneaking behaviour (the fertilisation of eggs by another, non-territorial male during spawning) by other males will frequently cause hybridisation. If high aggression levels prevent spawning, the fishes should be kept in an undecorated aquarium without stones and in groups of at least six individuals. Males do then not become territorial and are much less aggressive.

H. sp. "Flameback" group	max. size in cm	muddy bays	sandy shores	deep, open water	open water	rocks surge zone	rocks, shallow water	rocks, deep water
Haplochromis sp. "Flameback"*	10				■			
H. paropius	11			■				
H. sp. "Purple Head I"*	8	■						
H. cinctus-complex	11			■				
H. sp. "Morsei"	10			■				

H. sp. "Flameback" group

The species of this group of detritus and phytoplankton feeders belong to the offshore sub-littoral cichlid community. Detritivores/phytoplanktivores are little known among aquarists. The fish which is currently distributed among aquarists as *H.* sp. "Flameback" has been exported from the northern shore (Les Kaufman, pers. comm.). It resembles *H. paropius*; however it remains to be compared with the type material. The only other species of this group that is currently kept in aquaria has been named *H.* "purple head I" by HEST (Haplochromis Ecology Survey Team) but was first distributed in the U.S. as *H.* "all red". Recently the name of a third detritus feeder, *H. erythrocephalus*, appeared in the aquaristic literature, but this proved to be a misidentification.

Behaviour in the wild

H. sp. "Flameback" inhabits open water of unknown depth. *H.* sp. "Purple Head" occurs in depths of 2-10 metres over muddy bottoms in bays (Witte *et al.*, 1992). *H.* sp. "Morsei" is encountered over mud bottoms in open water, mainly at depths of more than 10 m. *H. paropius* is found at depths greater than 15 m over mud bottoms in open water (Greenwood & Gee, 1969). Species of the *H. cinctus*-complex live in open water deeper than 7 m over mud bottoms. The sublittoral detritus/phytoplankton eaters have declined considerably since the Nile perch upsurge. Many species have not been caught for several years (Witte *et al.*, 1992).

Behaviour in the aquarium

Detritus/phytoplankton feeders exhibit relatively low levels of aggression. They can be housed with zooplanktivores and small insectivores but not with larger species and particularly not with rock dwelling cichlids. The intraspecific aggression is, however, higher than in the open water zooplankton eaters. Because of this detritus eaters should not be kept in too small groups in small tanks.

Aquarium

The aquarium should have a minimum length of 80 cm. The aquarium requirements are similar to those of the zooplankton eaters (page 142). However, there is a need to offer hiding places among stones, wood, or vegetation because of a somewhat higher degree of aggression in breeding males. It is advisable to paint at least the back of the aquarium black and to use dark or even black sand. The fishes exhibit their attractive colours better in a black aquarium with strong lighting than in an aquarium with a light background and bottom but weaker light. Like the zooplankton eaters these species appear to be sensitive to nitrite.

Feeding

In Lake Victoria these species feed on bottom debris and phytoplankton (Witte & Van Oijen, 1990). Diatoms and blue-green algae make up the major part of the food and it is often difficult to tell whether the algae have been collected in the water column or from the bottom. It is likely that most species feed at both sites. Apart from algae, some insect larvae and zooplankton are often ingested.

In the aquarium the different mosquito larvae (black and white but no red larvae), brine shrimps, other zooplankton, shrimp mix, and flake food are readily accepted. It is recommended that vegetable flake food be offered. However, no data are available about the impact of purely animal-based foods on the condition of these vegetarians.

Above: *Haplochromis* sp. "Flameback" was exported from the northern shore of Lake Victoria.
Below: *Haplochromis pyrrhocephalus* is a fragile zooplankton feeder. Photo by Ole Seehausen.
Facing page: some biotopes of Lake Victoria resemble those of the rift lakes. Photo by Ole Seehausen.

Breeding

H. sp. "Flameback" is a maternal mouthbrooder. Breeding males are territorial and excavate shallow spawning pits. A sandy bottom is therefore advisable. Data about incubation and brood care duration are not available at the time of writing. All detritivores are likely to interbreed readily with small insect-eating species like *H. nubilus*, as well as with zooplanktivores and each other.

Zooplankton feeders	max. size in cm	muddy bays	sandy shores	deep, open water	open water	rocks surge zone	rocks, shallow water	rocks, deep water
*Haplochromis pyrrhocephalus**	9							
H. laparogramma	10							
*H. piceatus**	9							
H. sp. "Argens"*	10							
H. sp. "Double Stripe"*	12							

Zooplankton feeders

These are representatives of the offshore *Haplochromis* community. Before the Nile perch upsurge they were the most abundant group of haplochromines after the detritivores/phytoplanktivores (Witte & Van Oijen, 1990). A *H.* sp. "Double Stripe"- like fish has been exported to Sweden by Bo Selbrink as *H.* sp. aff. *longirostris.*

Behaviour in the wild

H. pyrrhocephalus is found in open water, mainly over mud bottoms. During the day it occurs at depths of 12-14 metres, during the night it inhabits the layers near the surface. *H. laparogramma* is found mostly below 20 m. *H. piceatus* lives at depths of 4-7 m over muddy bottoms in bays. *H.* sp. "Argens" inhabits the surface layers (upper 5 m) of the water column. *H.* sp. "Double Stripe" is encountered in open water over sand and rock bottoms (data from Goldschmidt *et al.*, 1990).

Most of the pelagic zooplanktivores have disappeared, only *H. pyrrhocephalus*, *H.*

laparogramma, and a rare species, *H.* sp. "Plumbus", are still caught.

Behaviour in the aquarium

All these species display very low levels of aggression. In an aquarium of 100 cm length a group of three males and five or more females can well be kept together. It is not uncommon for more than one male to show vivid breeding colours. Even brooding females are not much chased by the males provided that the group is not too small. Open water zooplanktivores require their own aquarium. They are dominated even by smaller insectivores as regards both feeding and display, and thus show hardly any colour when kept with other species.

Aquarium

The aquarium should be at least 80 cm long. The bottom should be of fine sand. Some large stones are particularly attractive to the fishes: they spawn near to them. The aquarium can be fully planted. It is advisable to paint at least the back glass black. In a light aquarium these species appear merely silvery and unattractive. Their beautiful colours are best displayed under a weak to moderate fluorescent light, perhaps with a violet component. *H. pyrrhocephalus* and *H. piceatus* often show particularly deep colours in old water, but at the same time they are sensitive to any increase in nitrite concentrations.

Feeding

In Lake Victoria these species prey upon copepods (e.g. *Cyclops*) and cladocerans (e.g. *Daphnia*) during the day. During the night they feed also on insect (chaoborid) larvae and pupae. Several species eat planktonic blue-green algae (*Melosira*) during algal blooms (Witte & Witte-Maas, 1987).

In the aquarium mosquito larvae (not red larvae), brine shrimps of all sizes, *Daphnia*, and *Cyclops* form a suitable diet. Flake food is taken as well, but, as usual, care must be taken not to feed flake which contains mammalian products.

Breeding

These species are maternal mouthbrooders with quite different incubation times: *H. pyrrhocephalus*: 13.5 days, *H. piceatus*: 15 days, *H.* sp. "Argens": more than 21 days. The post buccal care period is very short, lasting just two days. The clutch sizes are small with 12 to 20 comparatively large juveniles. In spite of the low level of aggression, mouthbrooding females have to be separated. The fry are otherwise eaten immediately upon release and the female has little chance of defending them. Species of this group readily interbreed if kept together.

Shallow water insectivores	max. size in cm	muddy bays	sandy shores	veg-etated fringe	open water	rocks surge zone	rocks, shallow water	rocks, deep water
Haplochromis sp. "Thick Skin"	8							
*H. brownae**	12							
H. sp. "Diversicolor"	8							
H. nubilus-group*	10.5							
H. theliodon	15							
H. riponianus-group	15							
H. cf. *chromogynos**	10+							

Shallow water insectivores

This group includes species whose names have been used in aquaristic literature for many superficially similar fishes that have been imported. In most cases the identifications were erroneous. Currently almost every dark blue or black *Haplochromis* is called *H. nubilus* in the trade. I know of at least four species sold under this name, some belonging to quite different groups including Lake Albert fishes. *H.* sp. "Thick Skin" is the name that was given by Witte and Witte-Maas to a fish with a peculiar morphology including a laterally compressed, tapering mouth, very long teeth in the outer row, and a dorsal fin with red spots which are also present in females. Ever since I tentatively identified one recently introduced population from Kavirondo Gulf as *H.* cf. "Thick Skin", the name has been indiscriminately used for many yellow fishes from different populations, some of which belong to different species. The fish that was actually named *H.* sp. "Thick Skin" is shown on page 144. It has never been imported.

Behaviour in the wild

H. sp. "Thick Skin" lives in shallow water down to a depth of 6 metres over sand bottoms. It is often found at shores exposed to wind and surf, and occurs together with the molluscivorous *H. xenognathus* and *H. plagiodon*. *H. brownae* occurs over sand bottoms at shorelines exposed to wind and surf. *H.* sp. "Diversicolor" inhabits shallow water over sand and mud bottoms. The species of the *H. nubilus*-complex prefer shallow water in rocky and vegetated habitats. They are also found in the rivers of the Lake Victoria basin. (This name is probably applied to more than one species.) *H.* cf. *theliodon* lives in bays over sand and mixed sand-mud bottoms. The species of the *H. riponianus*-group (probably more than one species is involved) are found at the edges of the vegetated zones and at the rock-reed interface. *H.* cf. *chromogynos* inhabits shallow water over rocks and sand (Greenwood, 1959a).

Behaviour in the aquarium

These species usually exhibit lower levels of aggression than most rock cichlids do, and territoriality is not pronounced. Aggression is, however, not restricted to the period immediately before spawning. In tanks longer than 100 cm several males of the same species can be kept together with a number of females, provided that the aquarium is properly furnished, and has sufficient shelter for subordinated individuals. Interstices between rocks form a fairly safe shelter for these species because dominant males are interested mainly in the open sandy areas and rarely follow competitors into the rockwork. This contrasts with the behaviour of some rock-dwelling species. All sand- and reed-bed-dwelling insect eaters can be housed with molluscivores. *H.* sp. “Thick Skin”, can also be housed with larger rock-dwelling cichlids if the aquarium is not too small. It is rarely attacked by species like *H. nigricans*, probably because of its very different coloration and small size. In contrast the blue and black species of the *H. nubilus* and *H. riponianus* group would be under steady pressure from the similarly coloured rock-dwelling cichlids.

Aquarium

For the smaller species the aquarium should have a minimum length of 80 cm. The bigger species demand a minimum tank length of 100 cm. The aquarium should be furnished with some large stones, pieces of wood, and/or plants. The bottom substrate should be of sand.

Feeding

In their natural habitat aquatic insect larvae form the major component of the diet of these species. *H.* sp. “Thick Skin”, *H. theliodon* and *H. riponianus* also prey upon snails. *H.* sp. "Thick Skin" has been observed pulling the soft parts out of the shell (Witte & Witte-Maas, pers. comm.), while the two bigger species crush the shells. However, their crushing ability is less than that of the specialised pharyngeal

The structure of the mouth of *Haplochromis* sp. "Thick Skin" (top) resembles that of *Mylochromis labidodon* of Lake Malawi, which is an insectivore searching for prey while turning over small stones.
Bottom: *Haplochromis* sp. "Black Nyererei" is a rock-dwelling insectivore. Photos by Ole Seehausen.
Facing page: This Victorian cichlid, *Haplochromis* sp. "Red Sided", was collected as fry from a female's mouth by Steve Somermeyer.

crushing molluscivores. In the aquarium these species take any type of food. Mosquito larvae (not red larvae) should form a major component of the diet, but minced mussels and/or prawns should be included for the bigger species.

Breeding

The species of this group are maternal mouthbrooders with an incubation time of between 18 days in *H. nubilus* and 21 days in *H. theliodon*. The post-buccal care period may vary considerably even within a single species: between 2 and 28 days in *H. nubilus* (pers. obs.). Otherwise what has been stated for epilithic algae scrapers (the *H. nigricans*-group) applies equally here. It is not recommended that different species be kept together in a breeding tank. The different species have a high potential for interbreeding.

Rock-dwelling insect pickers

A rather heterogenous species group which resembles the insectivorous Mbuna of Lake Malawi in morphological and ecological traits. Several of the species display a great geographical variation. The relationship between *H. nyererei* and *H.* sp. "Black Nyererei" is not yet known. Both forms occur sympatrically in many places.

Behaviour in the wild

The habitat of *H.* sp. "Black Nyererei" consists of holes and crevices between rocks in shallow water. The highest density occurs in water less than 1.5 m deep. However, at some islands the species has been caught at depths below two metres. Breeding males are territorial. Territories are more or less restricted to the rocky caves. *H.* sp. "Pseudonigricans" is also found in the rocky habitat but is less restricted to the interstices and is more

common in deeper water. *H.* sp. "Rock-Kribensis" is found on the surface of rocks. It apparently also occurs over sandy bottoms. *H. chilotes* shares the habitat of *H.* sp. "Black Nyererei" but penetrates to depths of at least 5 m. Before the Nile perch upsurge this species also occurred over sandy substrates (Greenwood, 1959a; Witte & Witte-Maas, pers. comm.). *H. nyererei* has the widest depth distribution of any species in this group: from the surface to below 5 metres. It is found mostly in the open water above the rocks, but also in interstices between them.

Behaviour in the aquarium

In general their behaviour resembles that described for the rock-dwelling algae scrapers (page 138). In many cases, however, the insect eaters are less aggressive and require smaller territories. In a suitably furnished aquarium of 100 x 50 cm three young males may become territorial. Suitably furnished means that the decor must reach to the surface. This can be achieved either with stones and thin slabs of slate, with (nibble-resistant) plants such as *Microsorium* and *Bolbitis*, or with bamboo (see page 11 how to cure wood). Old males, however, may become very aggressive. In order to promote vivid coloration in these fishes it is necessary to have a dark background and at least one of the ends of the tank should be covered (painted) as well (see page 13). These species can be housed together with other rock-dwelling species, i.e. algae scrapers, in large aquaria. Furthermore they can be kept with large molluscivores, e.g. *H. sauvagei* and *Astatoreochromis alluaudi.*

Aquarium

The aquarium should be the same as for the rock-dwelling algae scrapers (page 138). For *H.* sp. "Black Nyererei" and *H. chilotes* it is important to have an area of open sand without stones, because digging seems to be part of their natural foraging behaviour (Seehausen, 1993b). For this reason care must be taken to ensure the arrangement of the rocks is stable.

Feeding

In their natural habitat these species remove insect larvae from crevices between and under rocks by picking and digging. They feed also on Bryozoa (moss animals), less often also on blue-green algae which they scrape from the rocks. *H. nyererei* feeds predominantly on zooplankton but is able to utilise the other feeding techniques as well.

In the aquarium all species accept any type of food. It is advisable to include some larger crustaceans (e.g. *Gammarus*) in the diet, from time to time. The natural feeding behaviour can be observed when stones with Aufwuchs are placed in the tank.

Breeding

Refer to page 138, to what has been stated for rock-dwelling algae scrapers.

The incubation period of the larvae is about 21 days for *H.* sp. "Black Nyererei"; the fry are guarded by the female for about a week after they have been released for the first time. *H.* sp. "Rock Kribensis" has a shorter incubation period of about 18 days and no more than 2 days post buccal care.

Piscivores

The piscivores (fish eaters) used to be the most speciose trophic group in Lake Victoria with 49 described and more than 50 undescribed species (Witte & Van Oijen, 1990).

Rock-dwelling insectivores	max. size in cm	muddy bays	sandy shores	deep, open water	open water	rocks surge zone	rocks, shallow water	rocks, deep water
Haplochromis "Black Nyererei"*	14							
H. sp. "Pseudonigricans"*	11							
H. sp. "Rock-Kribensis"*	12							
*H. chilotes**	17							
*H. nyererei** (zooplanktivore)	12							
Shallow water piscivores								
H. sp. "Orange Rock Hunter"*	13+							
H. howesi	20							
*H. perrieri**	13							
H. guiarti	22							
H. sp. "Two Stripe"-group*	12+							
H. percoides	11.5							
H. harpakteridion	10							
H. cf. *pectoralis**	25							

Most species have completely disappeared since the Nile perch boom. A very low number of littoral (near the shore) species have still been seen in recent years. Similar declines have occurred in the paedophages (formerly more than 24 species), the only scale eater, and the shrimp-eaters (formerly more than 12 species). *H.* sp. "Orange Rock Hunter" was first collected in 1992 and differs from *H. howesi* mainly in coloration. Some of the piscivores deviate from all other Lake Victoria haplochromines by having female coloration which resembles that of males (Van Oijen, 1991). A species of the *H.* sp. "Two Stripe"-group has been exported to Sweden by Bo Selbrink as *H.* sp. aff. *longirostris.*

Behaviour in the wild

Haplochromis sp. "Orange Rock Hunter" and *H. howesi* inhabit the crevices and holes between the boulders of the rocky biotopes at a depth of 0.5 to 2.5 metres. *H. guiarti* lives in shallow (less than 7 metres) water over sand, shingle and rocks. *H. harpakteridion* prefers relatively exposed sandy shores near dense vegetation (Van Oijen, 1991). *H. percoides* and the species of the *H.* sp. "Two Stripe" group are found in shallow water over sand on exposed or partly exposed shores. *H. perrieri* and *H. pectoralis* inhabit a wide variety of predominantly near-shore biotopes and are occasionally found in rocky habitats (Witte *et al.*, 1992; Greenwood, 1967). All these species decreased drastically after the Nile perch boom.

Behaviour in the aquarium

H. sp. "Orange Rock Hunter" and *H. perrieri* show very low levels of aggression compared to most other haplochromines. Territoriality and aggressive behaviour are restricted to the days immediately before spawning. Both these species can be kept in a planted aquarium since they hardly dig at all. These species should be housed only with smaller and non-aggressive *Haplochromis*, i.e. with a group of zooplanktivores, provided that the size difference is not such that the latter will be regarded as prey.

Aquarium

The aquarium should be 100 cm long or longer, depending on the adult size of the species. Since many of the piscivorous species are rather solitary in their way of life, the aquarium should have a well structured decor with visual barriers like large stones or spots of dense vegetation. However, open areas are needed as well.

fry are offered. The species differ in their hunting techniques. *H. perrieri* has been described as a stalker of fish fry (Loiselle, 1991) while first observations indicate that *H.* sp. "Orange Rock Hunter" is more a pursuit hunter (pers. obs.).

Breeding

H. sp. "Orange Rock Hunter" is the first known haplochromine Great Lake cichlid in which males engage in mouth brooding (Seehausen, in prep.)! A male which was kept with two females spawned with both of them within 24 hours. After this all three individuals were brooding and all brooded their batch until the fry were released —a pair bond did not exist. The young were first released after 11 days. Post buccal care continued another 21 days. In *H. perrieri* only females brood and have an incubation period of 14 days followed by at least one week of post buccal care (Loiselle, 1991). In contrast to most other Lake Victoria haplochromines, brooding individuals of *H.* sp. "Orange Rock Hunter" continue feeding almost normally. Without opening the

Feeding

In the lake most of these species prey upon *Haplochromis* fry, but also on insect larvae. Large *H. howesi* prey predominantly on *Potamonautes* crabs which they catch among the rocks. Juveniles prey largely upon fish fry and *Caridina* shrimps (Van Oijen, 1992). The species which have been kept in aquaria are not very selective in their choice of food. They should be fed a protein-rich diet (such as raw fish) but avoid feeding them food in which mammalian products are included. Flake food is accepted but brine shrimps, *Mysis*, and mussels should be fed additionally. The natural hunting behaviour can be observed when fish mouth much they suck in flake food, particularly vigorously from the surface. During this the eggs or larvae are kept rather far back in the buccal cavity. This was observed in both sexes. The mouthbrooding parents become less vigorous in their feeding when the larvae become too big after about 10 days.

Oral shelling molluscivores

The molluscivores are a rather heterogeneous group as regards habitat. Only the oral shelling species are dealt with here. The second large group of molluscivores consists of the pharyngeal crushers (see page 151). They have the ability to crush even the more crush-resistant snails between their pharyngeal jaws.

Left: the author, Ole Seehausen, observed and photographed this mouthbrooding **male** *Haplochromis* sp. "Orange Rock Hunter". It is the first time that mouthbrooding behaviour has been observed in a male haplochromine.
Right: *Platytaeniodus degeni* is an oral shelling snail-eater.

Molluscivores	max. size in cm	muddy bays	sandy shores	deep water	vegetation fringe	surge	rocks, shallow water	rocks, deep water
*Platytaeniodus degeni**	11.5							
*Macropleurodus bicolor**	14							
*Hoplotilapia retrodens**	14							
*Haplochromis xenognathus**	11.5							
*H. sauvagei**	12							
*H. prodromus**?	14							
*H. plagiodon**	10.5							
H. sp. "Red Tail Sheller"*	10							
H. sp. "Bright Red Sheller"	10							
*H. ishmaeli**	14							
H. sp. "Stone"*	15							
*Astatoreochromis alluaudi**	15							

Behaviour in the wild

Platytaeniodus degeni, Macropleurodus bicolor, Hoplotilapia retrodens, and *Haplochromis sauvagei* inhabit shallow waters in relatively sheltered bays with mixed sand/mud bottoms. Before the Nile perch upsurge *P. degeni* occurred in depths down to 17 m (Greenwood, 1956); *M. bicolor* was also common at depths of more than 10 m. The other two species are restricted more to shallow water and often found near vegetation (*H. retrodens*) and/or rocks (*H. sauvagei*).

H. xenognathus, H. plagiodon, H. sp. "Bright Red Sheller" inhabit predominantly the wind and surf exposed shallow waters over sandy bottoms.

H. prodromus was found in deeper water (below 10 metres) over sand and mud. The species has decreased drastically and may be extinct. *H.* sp. "Red Tail Sheller" seems to be a littoral (near-shore) species but its actual habitat is unknown.

Behaviour in the aquarium

These species exhibit lower levels of aggression than do the rock-dwelling cichlids and their territoriality is not pronounced. The males defend territories only before spawning. In tanks larger than 100 cm length several males can be kept together with a number of females. In some species (e.g. *H. sauvagei*), however, only the dominant male may show breeding colours. The larger species (*M. bicolor* and *H. sauvagei*) can be housed with rock-dwelling algae scrapers if the tank size allows. All species can be housed with insectivorous rock cichlids and other insectivores such as *H. nubilus*.

Aquarium

The aquarium must be at least 100 cm long and 40 cm deep. The bottom should be covered with fine sand. Only in large aquaria can the natural habitat be imitated: a plain sand bottom that may have a few stones interspersed. In smaller aquaria opportunities to hide must be present (stones, wood, and/or vegetation).

Feeding

In their natural habitat these species prey upon large snails (*Bellamya*) which they wrench out of their shells (Witte & Van Oijen, 1990), as well as small bivalves and crustaceans which they crush between the pharyngeal jaws (Slootweg, 1987; Seehausen, 1993a). In captivity these species take any type of food. It is advisable to include molluscs in the diet. Deep frozen mussels are readily accepted. Even well-fed individuals often show a particular interest in living snails. The shelling technique can be observed if snails (e.g. *Planorbis*) of suitable size are offered. I never saw oral shelling cichlids preying upon *Melanoides* snails. These are a major prey of pharyngeal crushing molluscivorous haplochromines.

Breeding

The notes given for the rock cichlids (see page 138) apply also to oral shelling molluscivores. The incubation time for *H. sauvagei* is 21 days. It is followed by post buccal care of about one week. Interbreeding between species is very likely because of very similar male breeding coloration in several species. The fry of *P. degeni* will not accept fine flake food but have to be fed with *Artemia* nauplii, micro worms, or *Cyclops* during the first two weeks.

Pharyngeal crushing molluscivores

Members of this group are characterised by particularly heavy pharyngeal jaws furnished with stout molariform teeth. This "pharyngeal mill" serves to crush the shells of snails. Individuals that prey only upon soft food have less heavy jaws and finer teeth, resembling those of insectivorous haplochromines (Greenwood, 1965). At least nine species of pharyngeal crushing snail eaters are known. All but the three which inhabit shallow inshore habitats, have disappeared since the Nile perch boom. They lived predominantly over muddy bottoms in more than 5 m of depth (Witte *et al.*, 1992). *Astatoreochromis alluaudi* is not endemic to Lake Victoria and does not belong to its species flock but is considered a sister taxon of the Victoria and Malawi haplochromines (Meyer *et al.*, 1990).

Behaviour in the wild

H. ishmaeli inhabits shallow, near shore, waters over sand bottoms. *H.* sp. "Stone" lives between large boulders, in shallow water and down to depths of more than 5 m, apparently always in rather low population densities. *A. alluaudi* inhabits two types of inshore habitat: the fringes of papyrus stands or submerged vegetation, and rocky shores. It occurs from 1 to more than 5 m of depth.

Behaviour in the aquarium

It appears that these species exhibit intermediate levels of aggression. In many respects *H. ishmaeli* resembles the oral shellers (page 150). Very little is known about the behaviour of *H.* sp. "Stone". However, it appears that this species and *A. alluaudi* are more aggressive than the sand-dwelling snail eaters and less so than the rock-dwelling algae scrapers. *H. ishmaeli* can be housed together with oral-shelling snail eaters and insect eaters. The other two species can be housed together with rock-dwelling cichlids and large oral-shellers.

Aquarium

The aquarium must be at least 100 cm long and 40 cm deep. The aquarium should be appropriately furnished, particularly in the case of *H.* sp. "Stone" and *A. alluaudi.* Arrangements of large stones between which gaps and large holes are present will simulate the natural habitat of these species. A cover of floating plants such as *Eichhornia* or *Pistia* will reproduce the shady conditions of the habitat of those *A. alluaudi* populations that inhabit vegetated bays Rooted plants will be dug up frequently. The bottom should be covered with sand.

Feeding

In Lake Victoria these species prey largely upon snails (*Melanoides*) which they crush between their pharyngeal jaws. Aquatic insect larvae also form a component of their diet. In other lakes *A. alluaudi* feeds predominantly on insect larvae and plants (Greenwood, 1959). In the aquarium they can be fed in the same way as oral-shellers (see previous page). Their natural foraging behaviour can be observed when snails are offered, provided that these are not too big to fit between the pharyngeal jaws. If they are not overfed with other food, these cichlids will eat even hard shelled *Melanoides* snails.

Breeding

Refer to the section on breeding rock-dwelling algae scrapers (page 138). Data about incubation times are not available.

Other groups that are present in aquaria

Paedophages

H. barbarae (max. length 13 cm), which lived along sandy and rocky shores, seems to be extinct. It appears that a few piebald individuals were exported from Uganda to Sweden by Bo Selbrink in a consignment of *H.* sp. "Rock Kribensis" (Selbrink, 1986). The two species were believed to be one and the same, and *H. barbarae* seems to have now died out in captivity. It is an egg snatcher, stealing eggs of spawning haplochromines (Witte-Maas, 1981). *H. cronus* (max. length 17 cm) livds in shallow water along exposed shorelines (Greenwood, 1960). It has been imported by Selbrink under the name *H.* "cleaner"

Top: *Haplochromis ishmaeli* is a snail eater which crushes the shell with its pharyngeal mill. Photo by Ole Seehausen.
Two cichlid species from Lake Kivu have been introduced into the hobby by Steve Somermeyer: *Haplochromis* cf. *graueri* (centre) and *Haplochromis paucidens* (right). Latter species is known to be polymorphic; the photo shows a white-blotched female. These two species are best kept in groups.

and has apparently been kept in the U.S.A. under the name *H. brownae* (Loiselle & Kaufman, 1991). It can probably be maintained in the same way as the insectivores of the exposed sandy shores. In the lake it feeds on haplochromine fry (Greenwood, 1960). *H.* cf. *melanopterus* (max. length 13 cm) occurs at rocky islands and is the only paedophage that was still being caught in 1992. The habitat of *H.* sp. "Blue Paedophage" (max. length approximately 20 cm) is unknown. It has been exported from Uganda by Selbrink and was originally named *H.* "all yellow". It is a large species and, according to Loiselle & Kaufman (1991), preys upon cichlid buccal stage larvae or fry. All paedophages could be very interesting subjects for behavioural study in the aquarium. They exhibit different techniques of obtaining their prey. Some species attack brooding females by butting to force them to spit out eggs or fry or by mouth-engulfing to suck out the brood (Wilhelm, 1980). Most species seem to be extinct.

Pelagic phytoplankton eaters

A relatively small group of slender-bodied pelagic haplochromines which feed on phytoplankton in the surface layers of the open water. They have declined dramatically and are near extinction. All are undescribed. Only one, *H.* sp. "Citrus" (max. length 12 cm), may have found its way into aquaria but was not correctly identified. It is a slender lemon yellow fish with a thin black dorsolateral band and broad, irregularly shaped, black blotches on the flanks, arranged in an interrupted midlateral band. It was introduced to Sweden by Selbrink and wrongly identified as *H. obesus.* It would be wonderful if this species still exists in captivity. Its demands in the aquarium are likely to resemble those of the pelagic zooplankton feeders.

Plant eaters and scrapers

This group of mostly undescribed species inhabits shallow water, mainly near submerged vegetation. *H.* sp. "Red Back Scraper" (max. length 14 cm) and several other species also occur over rocks and scrape algae from both rocks and plants. Although these species are easy to collect, they are rarely seen in aquaria. Nevertheless they must be mentioned here because the names of two of them are familiar to aquarists: *H. obliquidens* and *H. lividus.* Both names have been incorrectly applied to several different species in the aquaristic literature, none of those which were examined had the diagnostic features of this group, but were instead insect eaters. Since several of these shallow water vegetarians still occur in the lake, it is possible that one or another of them will find their way into our aquaria or are already present there. Identification to species level is a major problem since most species are undescribed. For diagnostic features of the two groups refer to Witte & van Oijen (1990). These species can be kept in the same way as the larger insect eaters (page 146). They exhibit medium, in some cases rather high, levels of aggression and can be housed with the larger insect eaters and the less aggressive rock dwellers. The food should include a vegetable component.

Madagascan cichlids. *Paratilapia polleni.*

by Christian Simon

Because of its geographical separation and its geological evolution the island of Madagascar harbours a multitude of animals and plants, the majority of which are endemic. Among the animals the representatives of the family Cichlidae form an interesting group. On the one hand they are considered by several authors to belong among the most primitive species of the family (Stiassny & Gerstner, 1992; Stiassny, 1993). On the other hand these cichlids are in danger of becoming extinct within a few decades because of massive deforestation and the introduction of exotic species such as tilapias and snakeheads (Carlus, 1991). A remark by Dr. Melanie Stiassny (1993) perfectly describes the situation: "Which cichlids living today are the descendants of the early branches of the family tree? The answer is the cichlids of Madagascar —among the most endangered and least known of all."

During the last decade Madagascan cichlids made their debut in the aquaristic hobby, and one species in particular, *Paratilapia polleni* (called Marakely —"black fish"— by Malagasians), has become well-established among aquarists, at least in France. The aquaristic history of these cichlids is, without indulging in chauvinism, French. The first specimens exported from Madagascar were shown at the "Jardin des Plantes" in Paris at the end of the thirties (Catala, 1977). Much later, at the start of the eighties, the persistence of a handful French cichlid aquarists brought about the introduction of this species to the aquaristic world (Bardin, 1983). Some years later, Frédéric Defond in 1988 and Jean-Claude Nourissat in 1991, returned from Madagascar with several specimens of *P. polleni* (Carlus, 1991; Nourissat, 1992, 1993) most of which are still swimming happily in various large aquaria. The wild specimens brought back by F. Defond were spawned in October 1990 by Robert Beaujeu (Marseilles).

I have made a synthesis of the available literature, of the information I have received from my cichlidophile friends who specialise in Madagascan cichlids, and of my personal observations, and hope that this will provide sufficient information for aquarists who want to keep and breed Madagascan cichlids.

Distribution and habitat

In contrast to the other Madagascan cichlids —from the genera *Paretroplus, Oxylapia, Ptychochromis*, and *Ptychochromoides*— which have a restricted distribution on the island; *Paratilapia polleni* is encountered all over Madagascar. It is found in the highlands up to an altitude of about 1500 metres (Carlus, 1991) as well as on coastal plains, in particular those of the east coast (Nourissat, 1992, 1993). It inhabits lakes and swamps, but was never found in the rivers of the island (Nourissat, pers. comm.), although one author (Catala, 1977) reports its presence in warm soda springs in the south. *P. polleni*'s distribution encompasses the Mandritsara region in the north with its surrounding lakes, Fianarantsoa in the south-eastern part, and the lakes near the Pangalanes canal in the Ambila region which contain brackish water.

Such a wide distribution is not surprising if one knows the fishes' "plasticity in adaptation" to the different conditions found at the various places around Madagascar (Loiselle, 1993). *P. polleni* survives temperatures ranging between 15° C (Kiener, 1963) and 40° C (Catala, 1977) and tolerates a large variation in the physical and chemical composition of the water as well (Stiassny, 1993). In the north-western part of the island *P. polleni* inhabits soft water with a total hardness of about 3° but with a pH between 8 and 8.5 (Nourissat, 1993). On the other hand one may encounter this cichlid in very soft and acidic water as well (Defond in Carlus, 1991). And near the coast it can be found in brackish water (Nourissat, 1992). It is interesting to note that *P. polleni* is found mainly in biotopes which are not yet completely destroyed by deforestation (Stiassny, 1993). Bardin (1983) remarks that the Marakely is found predominantly in the black waters —the preferred habitat of many *Bedotia* species.

P. polleni is a bottom-oriented fish which spends most of its time among roots and branches. Its biotope consists of a sandy or rocky bottom with rocks, plants, roots, dead wood, and leaf litter.

The most striking difference between male and female is to be found in the maximum adult size which is about 30 cm for males and 22 cm for females (Stiassny & Gerstner, 1992). Males have better developed unpaired fins. Large males have a nuchal hump. There is no difference in coloration between the sexes. The intensity of the black colour is very much dependent on mood, age, and sexual maturity, and also on the presence of conspecifics and the conditions in which the fish is kept. Variations in coloration, in particular that of the female, are also noted during the breeding period. The colour of juveniles is totally different from that of adults. Juveniles are silvery-grey with a pattern of pearly spots and vertical bars which are only faintly visible. A blotch in the dorsal fin (tilapia-spot) is distinctly visible in juveniles only. It moves to the upper region of the body (pelmatochromis-spot) at about the same time that the adult black coloration appears, at a size of approximately 10 cm (Nourissat, pers. comm.). From my own observations (and those of Nourissat) it is apparent that juvenile coloration is retained much longer when a group of young fishes is kept together in the same aquarium. As soon as one individual is isolated it adopts the adult black coloration.

Two geographical variants are known: the northern variant which has large white-blue spots on the body (collected by F. Defond in 1988), and the south-eastern variant which is characterised by having tiny spots and which was collected in 1991 and 1992 by J-C Nourissat in the Fianarantsoa region, and by Reinthal and Stiassny in 1988 on the coast near Maralambo in the eastern part.

Behaviour in the wild

Underwater observations of the Marakely are few and far between. This results mainly from the nature of its preferred habitat among the roots and branches. The thesis of Raminosoa (1979) provides one of the best descriptions of the ecology of *P. polleni*. Adults are, in general, solitary and rarely venture out into open water. Pairs are found only during the breeding period, when one may also encounter *P. polleni* away from the protection of its natural environment. Whether or not there is a specific breeding season is difficult to assess. J-C Nourissat, who has visited Madagascar in both January and August and September, has observed only one pair guarding their fry. This was in January. Males appear to be weakly territorial but without becoming aggressive towards conspecifics or other species. *P. polleni* can be found together with other Madagascan cichlids as well as with tilapia! In fact it appears to be less affected by the introduction of tilapias than the other cichlids (Nourissat, pers. comm.).

Behaviour in the aquarium

The peaceful behaviour of *P. polleni* seen in the wild is exhibited in captivity as well. It should, however, be stressed that its peaceful behaviour is dependent on the amount of space each individua is given in the aquarium. If enough space is available *P. polleni* will not show any signs of aggression, either intra- or inter-specific. Only during breeding may other tank occupants be chased. Breeding in captivity seems to take place in summer (Stiassny, 1993; Nourissat, pers. comm.). In a sufficiently large aquarium several males and females can be kept together. They can be housed with other Madagascan cichlids such as *Paretroplus kieneri, P. petiti, P. dami,* or *Ptychochromis oligacanthus.*

Aquarium

An aquarium with a capacity of about 800 litres is recommended for a group of 6 to 8 individuals. It must be stressed that the peaceful behaviour of the Marakely rapidly turns into intra-specific aggression when sufficient space is not available. Two out of four individuals of about 10 cm which were placed in a 250-litre aquarium ended up "assassinated".

Photo above: In this muddy water in the northern part of Madagascar, near Mandritsara, Jean-Claude Nourissat collected *Paratilapia polleni.*
Photo facing page: The eggs of *P. polleni* stick together in long strings. Such heaps, which may contain more than 1000 eggs, can easily be moved by fanning of the female. Both photos by Jean-Claude Nourissat.
Below: *P. polleni.* A wild-caught male from northern Madagascar. This specimen was collected by Fréderic Defond and is still (August 1993) kept in a 300 litres aquarium. Photo by Robert Beaujeu.

that the Marakely is an inept piscivore (Loiselle, 1993), at least during the day. It seems to be more of a crepuscular predator. Stiassny (1993) indicates that the Marakely's diet consists principally of aquatic insects and their larvae, crustaceans and other invertebrates, and, occasionally, small fishes. Juveniles feed by preference on insect larvae and planktonic crustaceans (Loiselle, 1993).

Feeding *P. polleni* in the aquarium does not pose any particular problem because it has a voracious appetite and accepts almost anything. I have found, however, that it is only slightly interested in dry food, although this is accepted. Frozen or live crustaceans (such as *Mysis* and other shrimps) and also mussels are readily eaten.

Two males and three females placed in a 1000 litres aquarium never gave any problem (Beaujeu, pers. comm.). When a male and two females were placed in a 300 litres aquarium the male became very aggressive towards the females and finally killed one. But it was under these circumstances that Robert Beaujeu was able to experience, with great satisfaction, the breeding of about a thousand fry. Nevertheless it is recommended that the space given to the Marakely should be as large as possible.

The decor should consist of a bottom substrate of sand or fine gravel, some rocks and roots. Plants can be used too. The lack of a large aquarium may be compensated for by building many caves into which mainly the dominant individuals will retreat.

Feeding

The general appearance of the fish, together with the structure of the mouth, the dentition of the pharyngeal bones, and the short intestine, suggest a carnivorous feeding behaviour (Kiener, 1963). *P. polleni* is more of an insectivore than a piscivore (Nourissat, pers. comm.). Nevertheless Raminosoa (1979) indicates that large individuals are preferential piscivores; yet aquarium observations show

Breeding

The first spawnings in captivity were recorded in 1990: in July and August (Stiassny, 1992); October (Beaujeu, pers. comm.); October (Nourissat, pers. comm.). Since that time the pairs have continued reproducing and the offspring of the first few spawnings have also reproduced themselves.

In order to spawn *P. polleni* Robert Beaujeu placed one male and two females in a 300 litre aquarium. These fishes originated from the northern part of Madagascar (with large spots). Everything was done to induce them to spawn —the chemical composition of the water was altered, the decor of the aquarium, protein-rich food and vitamins were supplied, etc.—, but nothing seemed to work. In total desperation Robert decided to completely neglect the fishes except for an occasional feed or water change. After a few months one female died, probably due to the male's aggression. The other female remained hidden in one of the caves most of the time and showed herself only once or twice a week at feeding time. After about a year, without any apparent change in the artificial environment, the female was seen more often and was not chased by the male any longer. She was apparently gravid and started to excavate a small pit between a rock and a *Vallisneria* plant. The male remained at a distance most of the time but sometimes approached the female and swam around her. The pair would then assume a T-position for a few seconds after which they separated again. Robert did not have the chance to observe the actual spawning but one night noticed a "bunch" of eggs in the pit dug by the female lying on top of each other and held together by a gelatinous mass, but not fixed to a substrate. The egg-mass was more or less floating in the pit and between the roots of the *Vallisneria*. It contained about 1000 minuscule eggs. A large pair of *P. polleni* may produce about 3000 eggs (Nourissat, pers. comm.). On the third day after spawning the eggs hatched and the larvae were transferred to another pit by the female, who had to make several journeys to move them all. The tiny larvae (not much longer than 2 mm after the yolk had been absorbed) reached the free-swimming state in a remarkably short time. They accepted *Artemia* nauplii as soon as they became free-swimming and grew rapidly for the first few weeks. Half of the fry were taken from the breeding tank and raised separately in another aquarium. Robert made the unusual observation that the fry in the nursery tank grew much faster than those that remained with their parents.

During the guarding period the female played the major role in defending the fry while the male appeared to be totally neglecting them. This behaviour may have been caused by the fact that the breeding pair was not subject to disturbance by other fishes in the aquarium. I have observed that the male actively defends the fry when other (conspecific) fishes are present. Then the pair stay close together and position themselves over the cloud of fry. The other tank inhabitants are then chased into a corner of the tank. Other authors have also observed the active role of the male during the defence of fry (Stiassny & Gerstner, 1992). During the fry-guarding period the female has the same intense black coloration as the male or even more so. The coloration of the female is supposed to play an important role in communication with the fry (Stiassny, 1993).

The small fry of *P. polleni* grow rapidly and attain a size of several centimetres within a few months. The intra-specific aggression is weakly expressed. The guarding period lasts for at least a month.

Acknowledgements

I would like to address my gratitude to my friends Jean-Claude Nourissat, Robert Beaujeu, and Jean Carlus for their advice on the manuscript.

This chapter is dedicated to the memory of Frédéric Defond, known as Frédo, who disappeared in February 1989 in Madagascar. He was devoured by a crocodile while fishing for *Paratilapia polleni*.

Other African Cichlids

by Mary Bailey

Cichlids are found almost the entire length and breadth of the African continent, being absent only from the southern tip (too cold) and areas with no water —although they are in fact found in Saharan oases. They occupy a remarkable variety of habitats, and some are even stranger than the most bizarre Rift Valley species. Even the Lakes have failed to produce anything quite as odd as *Lamprologus lethops*, which is blind, depigmented, has a reduced swim bladder, and apparently lives in burrows under boulders at the bottom of rapids.

At present most of the available non-rift cichlids are from West Africa: from the rivers, streams, and pools of the coastal rain forest and the Congo basin. These river systems are also home to a group of cichlids which have evolved special features enabling them to inhabit stretches of rapids —the so-called "rapids cichlids".

Neither type of habitat lends itself to underwater study of cichlids. Those of the forest streams are found mainly in shallow water, where they find shelter in clumps of plants and holes in banks, and among roots and fallen branches. The rapids cichlids are able to live in their environment only because rapids contain areas of slack water, and because their reduced swim bladders provide minimal-buoyancy, enabling them to remain on the bottom.

The rain forests of West Africa are confined to a coastal strip a few hundred miles wide, their rivers draining the highlands immediately to the east; they are relatively short and lack the acidity created where water is in prolonged contact with decaying vegetation, as in the Rio Negro of South America. Water conditions are relatively soft with a pH range of 6.5-7.5, and a temperature range of 25-26° C, rising to 28° C in unshaded areas. The water is often slightly stained with organics, but usually clear. Seasonal flooding does occur, but is of very limited extent and duration, and the fishes remain in their normal habitat rather than moving into the inundated zone to breed. African forest cichlids tend to be solitary when not breeding.

The Congo system is far more extensive, but again conditions are fairly neutral and there is no prolonged or extensive inundation. Many of the river systems contain endemic cichlid species as well as others with a much wider distribution.

Western and central Africa also have their lakes. These are much smaller affairs than those to the East, but like them often have a high degree of endemism. Lake Barombi Mbo in Cameroun lies in the crater of an extinct volcano, and has a unique fish fauna. Other crater lakes likewise exhibit endemism, albeit to a lesser degree. South of the Congo another remarkable lake, Lake Fwa, possesses a number of endemic cichlid genera which may soon be available to the aquarist.

To the north-east of the rain forest lies an extensive area of savannah country, bordered to the north by the Sahara, and extending right across Africa to the Nile basin. This is the home of a few *Hemichromis* and haplochromines, but is largely the province of the tilapias. The range of these hardy cichlids extends northwards along the Nile and into the Middle East —they are better able to withstand the fluctuations in temperature and water levels (and thus chemistry/quality) found in these areas than are most of their cousins. A similar cichlid fauna is found to the south and east of the Congo basin, where the terrain is likewise open plains and hills instead of rain forest. Conditions are sometimes less hostile than in the northern savannahs, and there is a larger haplochromine component to the cichlid fauna. In general these extra-forest waters are reported as moderately hard with a pH of 7.0-7.5. Water temperature regularly attains 30° C or more.

Haplochromines

Astatotilapia burtoni (max. 12 cm); *Pseudocrenilabrus nicholsi* (max. 8 cm); *P. multicolor* (max. 8 cm); *P. philander* (max. 10 cm); *Orthochromis malagaraziensis* (max. 10 cm); *O. polyacanthus* (max. 15 cm); *O. torrenticola* (max. 12 cm).

This group includes small mouthbrooders of haplochromine ancestry.

Behaviour in the wild

Pseudocrenilabrus are found in small bodies of water (streams, pools, drainage channels, sink holes) and the shallow areas of some larger ones, and in swamps.

Astatotilapia have a similar range to that of *Pseudocrenilabrus* and are often found sympatrically with them, and with tilapiines.

The habitat of *A. burtoni* is rather sluggish or still waters, often with a low oxygen content and murky water. It is a generalised opportunistic feeder —i.e. it eats anything that happens to be available. It does not form a pair bond, nor, it appears, does it emulate the arena breeding of its lacustrine cousins. Males do sometimes build their nests —circular craters at the centre of their territories— fairly close together, but do not appear to actively compete with each other for passing females.

Orthochromis is a small genus of rheophilic cichlids. These fishes have a reduced swimbladder and it is assumed that the resulting lack of buoyancy allows them to move about on the bottom of areas of rapids without being swept away by the current, and to rest in the lee of rocks. *Orthochromis* are haplochromine mouthbrooders; there is no apparent sexual dimorphism.

Behaviour in the aquarium

Males are rather scrappy among themselves and occupy rather large territories (up to 90 cm across) for cichlids their size; they tend to pester females relentlessly, but are not a nuisance to heterospecifics. Substrate brooders are in general ignored. The spawning ritual follows the usual haplochromine pattern of circling and T-positioning, with a few eggs laid on each pass.

It is unwise to mix different species of the same genus; as they do not occur sympatrically there is a good possibility of hybridisation, especially as females are very similar.

Despite their flamboyant displays, these cichlids are easily dominated and should never be housed with boisterous mouthbrooders like Mbuna.

Left: this shaded stream in Malawi is inhabited by *Astatotilapia calliptera*.
Facing page: a male *Pseudocrenilabrus philander.*

Aquarium

Spacious accommodation is required to allow females some respite from the attentions of the male —a tank at least 90 x 30 x 30 cm is suggested, with a single male and 3-4 females. In a larger tank it is possible to keep two evenly matched males, and the resulting competition usually allows the females some peace and quiet.

The tank should be densely planted to provide shelter, and to allow females to escape the unwelcome attentions of the male. It is helpful to arrange the plants, and any other decor, to break up the line of sight along the tank, as "out of sight, out of mind" is generally applicable. Floating plants will provide cover near the surface in case females are harried at lower levels.

The water should be soft to moderately hard, neutral to slightly alkaline (depending on natural habitat, if known), with a temperature in the 24-26° C range. Water quality should be good —*Pseudocrenilabrus* are reported as being less tolerant of metabolic by-products than *Astatotilapia*. For *Orthochromis* a high oxygen content is desirable and a reasonable degree of turbulence permissible, but these fishes are more active if not subjected to a jacuzzi in miniature.

Feeding

Natural diet probably consists of aquatic invertebrates and any terrestrial insects which find themselves in the water. In captivity live or frozen foods are eagerly taken, as are chopped earthworms, prawns, and mussels, as well as flake and small pellets. Mammalian protein (and dried foods based on it) should be avoided.

Breeding

Male *Pseudocrenilabrus* and *Astatotilapia* are larger and far more colourful than females, which are drab olive. *Orthochromis* shows no clear sexual dimorphism, though to my eye some individuals (of *O.* cf *polyacanthus*) have bluer lips than others, and their dominant behaviour suggests these are males. The colour pattern of the anal fin may differentiate the sexes.

As long as the male is not allowed to harry the female excessively then she will fill with eggs without the need for any special feeding, and spawning will follow as soon as she is ripe. She should be removed to brood. In *Pseudocrenilabrus* brooding lasts for 12-14 days, during which the female does not feed. Brooding in *Astatotilapia* and *Orthochromis* lasts for about three weeks. Female and fry can be left together after first release for as long as she continues to brood them. She should be reintroduced to her normal quarters with care, to avoid too warm a welcome from the male (see page 17). The fry can take *Artemia* nauplii or microworms as first food. The brood of a 14 cm-large female *O.* cf. *polyacanthus* contained approximately 100 fry (Hooft, 1986).

Rheophilic cave brooders

Lamprologus congoensis (max. 11 cm); *Steatocranus casuarius* (max. 14 cm); *S. irvinei* (max. 16 cm); *S. tinanti* (max. 12 cm); *Teleogramma brichardi* (max. 12 cm).

Generally small, rheophilic cichlids found in areas of rapids.

Behaviour in the wild

All these cichlids have a reduced swim-bladder and it is believed that the resulting lack of buoyancy allows them to remain on the bottom, in areas of slack water in back eddies and in the lee of huge boulders, in the immense rapids systems which form their habitat. They also probably occupy cracks between boulders as hiding-places.

Aquarium observations of social and breeding behaviour suggest that they are highly sedentary, occupying rather small territories compared to other cichlids of similar size.

Captive *Teleogramma brichardi* have been observed to excavate holes under stones by burrowing headfirst.

Behaviour in the Aquarium

All species kept so far are substrate brooders, with rather to very large adhesive eggs laid in the shelter of caves, and correspondingly large fry. Obviously tiny fry would stand little chance of survival in strong currents. A variety of breeding patterns have been observed: *S. casuarius* forms relatively stable pairs with biparental brood care; *S. tinanti* is solitary except when breeding —again brood care is biparental. *T. brichardi* is said to be a harem brooder, but in my experience male and female associate only for the duration of the spawning —thereafter the male shows no interest in either female or spawn. The territory of the female is quite separate from that of the male.

Territoriality is directed largely against conspecifics, and the associated aggression can be very marked, sometimes lethal, in some species. I have found, however, that, at least in the case of some species, this is a function of *establishing* rather than maintaining territory. Peace reigns once the fishes have settled. So possibly all that is needed is a divider (see page 18) for the first few weeks!

Type of companion fishes depends on species. Aggression is mainly intraspecific and they can usually be mixed with other fishes without problems. I have kept *S. casuarius*, *S. tinanti*, and *T. brichardi* (1 pair of each) in a 120 x 40 x 40 cm aquarium, with great, and long-term, success. It is important to have some previous indication of general behaviour before attempting any mixture. *S. irvinei* is larger and proportionately more aggressive, and is better kept with tankmates of its own size.

Aquarium

It is inadvisable to use a tank measuring less than 90 x 40 x 40 cm for any of these cichlids, although once paired *S. casuarius* (and possibly some of the other semi-permanently bonding species) can be kept in a 60 cm aquarium. Although territories tend to be small, conspecifics should be able to distance themselves if necessary.

The water should be soft and neutral (the fishes have no objection to anything in the 6.5-7.5 range, and *S. casuarius* has been bred successfully at 15° DH and pH 8), of extremely good quality, and very well oxygenated. This last point should NOT be taken to imply a need for a high degree of turbulence; if one stops to think, one will realise that their "design" enables them to live under, rather than in, strong currents. My own experiments (with *T. brichardi*) involving an internal power filter with its outlet above the water, resulted in a favourite resting place immediately beneath the filter —in the area of minimum turbulence! When the filter was removed, and just undergravel used, the fishes became far more active and moved around the tank. Temperature should be 25-26 °C and lighting only moderate.

Obviously rocks should form the main part of the decor; although flowerpots are readily accepted as caves, many of these fishes like to "perch" some distance from the substrate. My *S. tinanti* used the roof of their cave, rather than the substrate, as a nursery.

Plants do not form part of the natural biotope, but are not molested if included in the aquarium.

Despite their bottom-dwelling propensities, some at least are accomplished jumpers, so a close fitting cover is advisable, and if a divider is used no gap should be left above it.

Feeding

Details of stomach contents are available for 3 species: *S. casuarius* algae; *S. glaber* diatoms and sand; *S. gibbiceps* snails (swallowed whole). This suggests that *S. casuarius* should be provided with vegetable matter in its diet, though in practice it is omnivorous in captivity and does not molest higher plants.

Apart from snails and algae, it is likely that insects and their larvae, other aquatic invertebrates, and shrimps are available food items in the wild. All of these are readily taken, as are earthworms.

Breeding

Males are normally appreciably larger, and, if a nuchal hump is present, it is much more prominent. Females of *S. tinanti* retain a dark spot in the dorsal into adulthood. Males of *S. irvinei* have iridescent bluish lips, absent in females. *Teleogramma* are easily sexed by the colourful belly of the female, and the different edging of the upper caudal, the latter visible even in part grown specimens.

One should never assume that a pair, even if kept together previously, will accept each other immediately in unknown territory. Once settled, individuals of opposite sex will normally live peacefully in the same tank, whether paired for breeding or living in their separate territories, as long as the decor remains undisturbed.

Where brood care is biparental a rather small territory seems to suffice; any actual intrusion is dealt with immediately, but there is no noticeable tendency to chase potential intruders simply because they are in sight. The fry are not led around the aquarium but remain in the breeding territory until large enough to disperse.

The fry can be fed on *Artemia* nauplii, microworms, crumbled flake, cod roe, and other small foods.

Forest stream cichlids

Anomalochromis thomasi (max. 8 cm); *Limbochromis* (max. 11 cm); *Nanochromis* (max. 9 cm); *Parananochromis* (max. 13 cm); *Pelvicachromis* (max. 12 cm); *Thysochromis* (max. 12 cm).

Dwarf cichlids, of tilapiine ancestry, mainly from forest streams in West Africa.

Behaviour in the wild

Nanochromis is found in relatively calm pools and backwaters among large rocks near the shore.

Pelvicachromis prefer small shallow waters with large clumps of plants, which provide it with shelter. Further hiding places, and spawning sites, are provided by holes in the banks as well as roots and fallen trees. The cichlids rarely stray far from cover of some kind. Females display to males as in captivity, and have been observed to compete for the attentions of a territory-holding male.

Limbochromis robertsi has been found in a rather stony habitat with overhanging vegetation but no aquatic plants. It is said to practise harem polygyny. There are no details of behaviour of *Parananochromis* in the wild, but those kept to date are monogamous cave brooders. *Thysochromis* combines open spawning with cave brooding, preferring a vertical or slanting substrate under an overhanging rock or root. *Anomalochromis thomasi* is monogamous and spawns on flat stones among plants.

Left: a pair of *Steatocranus tinanti*, a rapids cichlid. Facing page: *Nanochromis* sp. "Zaire". Photo by Roland Numrich.

Behaviour in the aquarium

Small though they are, *Nanochromis* tend to a high degree of aggression. Pairing is not permanent, and an apparently harmonious pair are likely to "divorce" after raising a brood. When ripe the female normally initiates courtship. Male territoriality may be extended towards both conspecific males and other West African dwarfs. Nevertheless this aggression can be managed fairly easily.

Insofar as they have been kept and bred, the remaining cichlids of this group are relatively peaceful. They can, however, become quite aggressive when guarding fry. All will dig to some extent prior to breeding, but not to the detriment of the appearance of the aquarium. Plants are not molested.

Aquarium

A single pair of any species requires an aquarium at least 60 x 30 x 30 cm, or a territory of approximately this size in a larger tank. The main key to management of aggression in *Nanochromis* is the provision of rather more living space than is normally allotted to such small cichlids; there must be room for the male to hold territory AND additional space for the female. The aquarium for *Nanochromis* should therefore measure at least 90 x 30 cm and a longer tank is preferable.

The water should be soft and slightly acid; any difficulty in triggering breeding should prompt lowering of the pH, but generally speaking 6.5 is suitable. Temperature 24-26° C. The water should be of excellent quality, and well oxygenated; as these fishes are chiefly bottom dwellers it is important to achieve thorough circulation —but without turbulence or strong currents.

A reasonably thick planting is suggested. Flowerpots are almost obligatory as refuges, being preferred to rocky caves whenever the fishes are given the choice. Well-cured coconut shells are a good alternative. Flat stones among the plants will provide *A. thomasi* with suitable spawning sites. The substrate should be sand or fine gravel, ideally not too light in colour. Lighting should be moderate, not bright.

It is not a good idea to house different variants of one species or different species of the same genus together.

Feeding

The natural diet probably consists of aquatic invertebrates, possibly with the addition of terrestrial insects. *Pelvicachromis* are bottom feeders and may consume detritus and algae. *Thysochromis* pick at stones and plants and may thus also eat algae.

All species relish *Cyclops, Daphnia*, chopped earthworms, mussel, and shrimp. They can also be given a good quality flake food containing no mammalian protein.

Breeding

Adult male *Nanochromis* are appreciably larger than females, and tend to have more heavily marked unpaired fins. Male and female are generally similar in coloration, but females of *N. transvestitus* are far more colourful than males. *Pelvicachromis* and *Parananochromis gabonicus* are easily sexed by the different shape of the pelvic fins —clubbed in females, pointed in males, detectable at a size of about 3 cm. *Pa. longirostris* males have longer and more strongly marked unpaired fins, and an extension in the upper caudal. *Pa. caudifasciatus* shows slight dichromatism in fin and body markings. Adult *Limbochromis* males have a strongly lyrate tail. *Anomalochromis* males are larger than females, have longer finnage, and less prominent spangling, giving them a paler appearance. *Thysochromis* males have long pointed unpaired fins with dark reticulations in their soft portions, while those of females are rounded.

When the female *Nanochromis* is actually near spawning she becomes so distended that she looks as if she has swallowed a marble and her ovipositor protrudes fully. When this point is reached spawning usually follows a

week or so later. If all goes well the female will now approach the male; the courtship may be tempestuous. Care of eggs is by the female, the male guarding the vicinity of the cave. Both parents tend the fry, but should be watched carefully for signs of renewed aggression by the male.

Breeding in the other species is normally achieved with minimal difficulty provided habitat and water chemistry are appropriate. Egg-eating can sometimes occur initially, but is not usually a long-term difficulty. A problem affecting some *Pelvicachromis* is lack of interest in breeding on the part of the male; this seems to affect only tank-bred males and to be a permanent problem. Such males should be replaced immediately.

The sex ratio of offspring can be manipulated by varying pH in *P. pulcher, P. taeniatus* "Nigeria", and *P. subocellatus* (and possibly other members of the genus). In the case of *P. pulcher* pH 6.5-6.8 produces approximately equal numbers of each sex; an increase in pH increases the numbers of females, and vice versa. The same principle applies to the other species but with slightly different "50:50" pH levels.

All species in this section have proved excellent parents practising biparental brood care. *Pelvicachromis* take their fry back into the cave at night, and it is important to turn the tank light off before the room light to simulate dusk and give them the opportunity to do so. Fry can take newly hatched *Artemia*, but microworm are more suitable for *Pelvicachromis*, which forage only on the bottom for their first few days; in practice they usually find enough to eat there anyway in an established tank.

Chromidotilapia

Chromidotilapia guntheri (max. 18 cm); *C. kingsleyae* (max. 20 cm); *C. batesii* (max. 12 cm); *C. finleyi* (max. 10 cm); *C. linkei* (max. 10 cm).

Small to medium sized mouthbrooders of tilapiine ancestry.

Behaviour in the wild

Few observations have been made. Fluviatile species appear to prefer to remain in the cover of branches, roots, and/or plants, or in hollows eroded in banks. Shallow, clear, slow-flowing waters, with gravelly substrates, are preferred.

Mouthbrooding is practised in all species where breeding behaviour has been observed. *C. guntheri* and *C. kingsleyae* are ovophilous paternal mouthbrooders, the female, however, sharing in brooding the fry after first release. *C. batesii* is a larvophilous maternal mouthbrooder. In the Moliwe form of *C. finleyi* eggs and fry are usually, but not always, brooded by the female alone; in the Campo race the eggs are periodically passed from partner to partner, with the female brooding initially. *C. linkei* is an ovophilous maternal mouthbrooder; males may collect eggs to protect them if the spawning is disturbed, subsequently repositioning them on the spawning site for the female to pick up and brood. These details are based on aquarium observations, and it is assumed that wild behaviour follows the same pattern.

Behaviour in the aquarium

These fishes tend to be rather shy, and are normally peaceful towards both conspecifics and other cichlids. Fighting may occur if more than one male is present at breeding time, unless the tank is very large. They are easily panicked and inclined to jump when frightened.

Aquarium

Size should be at least 75 cm x 30 cm (depth unimportant) for a pair of one of the smaller species (up to 12 cm total length), otherwise 90 cm x 40 cm or larger. Water chemistry appears to be unimportant in aquarium populations of *C. guntheri.* More recent imports are best kept in soft slightly acid conditions, the pH being lowered if spawning does not follow in due course or is unsuccessful. Good water quality is important. A low population level and dense planting, together with regular small water changes, should be used in conjunction with a low-turnover filter. Temperature 25-26° C.

A few flattish stones in sheltered spots towards the rear of the tank will serve as potential spawning sites. A surface layer of floating vegetation, or the leaves of long-leaved plants, will provide additional security and deter jumping, but even so a tight-fitting cover is advisable. The substrate should be as dark as possible, and the lighting muted if plant shade is not available.

Sensibly chosen companion fishes may help to obviate shyness. It is important that companion fishes are smaller than the *Chromidotilapias* and just as peaceful. *Pelvicachromis, Nanochromis* (and its allies), and *Anomalochromis* are ideal. If other bottom-dwelling cichlids are included then tank size must be increased to provide additional territory.

Feeding

The natural diet of insect larvae should be borne in mind, with live or frozen foods forming a substantial percentage of the food offered. Earthworms are enjoyed. Most foods are readily taken by settled individuals, but a diet of live food can be useful in winning their confidence initially.

Breeding

Only *C. guntheri* has been extensively bred and studied in captivity. Sexual dichromatism is apparent in all species kept. Adult females tend to have a rosy belly, more rounded in outline than that of the male; their dorsal fins show a metallic lustre absent in males.

In *C. guntheri* courtship is usually initiated by the female, who seeks out the male in his territory when she is ready to spawn. Her colours are intensified at this time, particularly on the belly. Initial courtship is often more akin to warfare, with frontal and lateral threat display; some fin and scale damage is probable, but unlikely to be serious.

In all the species bred so far the spawning site is usually a hard surface such as a stone, in a secluded corner, and this is cleaned before spawning begins. In *C. guntheri*, and probably in the other species as well, the eggs are laid and fertilised after the manner of substrate brooders, and picked up only after the entire clutch has been laid. They are slightly adhesive and stick to the substrate.

C. guntheri, once paired, are likely to remain together harmoniously for several years. The shared nature of brooding and post-release brood care make it imperative that pairs are not separated, i.e. the non-brooding partner should never be removed. In *C. guntheri* the female may try to initiate a further breeding session while the male is still paternally motivated; this may result in aggression towards her, which can be remedied by removal of the fry.

The fry are large enough to take *Artemia* nauplii and microworm as first foods. Food must be administered with the minimum of disturbance, as otherwise the male may take the fry into his mouth to protect them, preventing them from feeding!

Hemichromis

Hemichromis elongatus (max. 20 cm); *H. fasciatus* (max. 14 cm); *H. guttatus* (max. 11 cm); *H. lifalili* (max. 11 cm).

This section can be split into two groups: one containing medium to large predatory cichlids with rather drab coloration (*H. elongatus* and *H. fasciatus*), and the other with generally fairly small, red-coloured cichlids (e.g. *H. guttatus, H. lifalili*, and *H. letourneauxi*).

Behaviour in the wild

Little is known of the ecology of these species. They are known to be predators. Their intolerance of conspecifics in the aquarium suggests a solitary existence except at breeding time. Some species have been recorded as using plants, roots, and fallen trees as shelter. All are restricted to still or rather slow-moving waters. *H. paynei* is thought to spawn on plant leaves as it favours areas of dense vegetation where stones are uncommon. Those species which have been bred in captivity show a preference for a flat stone as a spawning substrate. As far as is known all species are substrate brooders which practice biparental brood care.

Behaviour in the aquarium

Despite its relatively small size *H. guttatus*

Top: *Chromidotilapia finleyi* from Nange. Photo by Roland Numrich.
Right: *Hemichromis* sp.
Facing page: *Tilapia buttekoferi*.

(usually mislabelled *H. bimaculatus*) is not a good community fish, although it is often sold as such. It will eat smaller fishes, and is territorial towards larger ones, even if they are considerably bigger than itself. Its hostility is particularly pronounced in the case of conspecifics, including potential breeding partners. *H. lifalili* can be housed with other soft water cichlids of similar size and habitat requirements, but ample allowance must be made for the territorial requirements of each species. It is unwise to attempt to keep more than a single pair of any *Hemichromis* in anything but the largest of tanks. Other companion fishes should be robust enough to withstand chasing at breeding time, and too large to be eaten.

Because of their size and piscivorous nature the species of the drab (*H. elongatus*) group are difficult fishes, quick to devour any smaller companions and to launch territorial attacks on larger ones. In consequence these species, unless kept as single specimen fishes, should be considered suitable for only the most experienced of cichlid aquarists.

Aquarium

A pair of *Hemichromis* require an aquarium at least 90 x 30 cm; for a pair of *H. elongatus* or *H. fasciatus* a 120 x 30 cm tank is necessary. The tank should be decorated with caves, bogwood, and groups of plants, and a few flat stones (for spawning sites) positioned between the clumps.

The water should ideally be soft and slightly or moderately acid; *Hemichromis* will tolerate hard alkaline water, but correct water chemistry is always preferable. Water quality should be excellent, but filter turnover rate slow so as to avoid excessive water movement. Temperature 25-26° C. Lighting should be muted if plant shade is not available.

Target fishes may be used to divert the aggression of the male away from the female.

Feeding

The diet should include a reasonable (25% or more) percentage of raw fish (dead or alive), together with pond foods (e.g. *Daphnia* and *Cyclops*), shrimp, mussel, and good quality flake.

Breeding

External sexual dimorphism is not apparent, so sexing by examination of the vent is necessary. Alternatively a more compatible pair can be obtained by growing on 5-6 juveniles until a pair forms, and then removing the remainder. If two mature fishes are to be introduced this should always involve initial use of a divider (see page 18). A brood may contain 200-300 fry, which are guarded by both parents, the female normally leading the school and the male defending the surrounding area. The fry can take *Artemia* nauplii as a first food.

Tilapias

Danakilia (max. 8.5 cm); *Oreochromis* (max. 45 cm); *O. mossambicus* (max. 35 cm); *Sarotherodon* (max. 30 cm); *Tilapia* (max. 30 cm); *T. buttekoferi* (max. 30 cm); *T. joka* (max. 15 cm); *T. mariae* (max. 30 cm).

Tilapiines are found throughout Africa and northward into the Middle East; there are also feral populations in other parts of the tropics. Some species are extensively farmed for food. They are not generally popular with aquarists because of their size, habits, and ability to produce large numbers of unsaleable fry. Some of the smaller species of *Tilapia* are, however, attractive cichlids worthy of greater attention, and the larger species are no more "antisocial" than many of their more popular cichlasomine cousins!

Behaviour in the wild

Habitats include lakes (including Rift Valley lakes), rivers, and lagoons (often brackish), generally in open country rather than forested areas. Some species are widespread, others endemic to small areas or single lakes. All are at least partially herbivorous. *T. buttekoferi* is a specialised snail-eater. Those species kept in captivity have demonstrated an ability to tolerate large variations in water chemistry and temperature, as well as poor water quality and low oxygen content. They are generally fishes of slow-moving or still waters.

Sarotherodon are monogamous ovophilous mouthbrooders, practising paternal or biparental incubation. Pairs separate from the shoal to spawn (sometimes a few days beforehand) but do not remain together afterwards. *Oreochromis* are arena-breeding maternal mouthbrooders, with both sexes polygamous. *Tilapia* are monogamous open-breeding substrate brooders. *Danakilia* are thought to be mouthbrooders on the basis of their large egg size (Trewavas, 1983), but no further details are known. The only known species has not been kept in captivity.

Behaviour in the aquarium

The large species are notorious for "landscaping" the substrate to their liking. Plants are likely to be eaten as well as dug up. The mouthbrooding species kept to date have proved to be remarkably peaceful for their size, but large *Tilapia* males (in particular *T. buttekoferi*) are highly territorial towards both conspecifics and other fishes. Precocious and prolific breeding is the norm.

Aquarium

Tank size will, of course, depend on the size and temperament of the particular species kept, but as a rule of thumb a 120 x 40 x 40 cm aquarium is the minimum for a pair of 25-30 cm fishes. A divider is virtually essential for an adult pair of *T. buttekoferi*. Decor can include anything except plants, or the tank can be left bare —these are not shy retiring cichlids.

Small *Tilapia* species (e.g. *T. joka*) can be kept with other small cichlids in planted aquaria; they are unlikely to harm plants if adequately fed.

If tank size permits *Oreochromis* and *Sarotherodon* can be kept in groups. It is unwise, however, to keep more than one adult male *Tilapia* per aquarium. Because of their tolerance regarding water chemistry all tilapiines are potential occupants of the mixed cichlid community, provided attention is paid to compatibility of size and temperament. Potential tankmates for the larger species may include *Etroplus suratensis*, medium to large South American cichlids, and Central American cichlasomines. The mouthbrooding species are more likely to be bullied than bullies.

I have never heard of anyone trying a community of mixed tilapiines, although this is probably feasible if care is taken in choice of species (similar size, dissimilar appearance). Some *Oreochromis* have been hybridised by fish-farmers, so in this genus at least there is danger of unwanted crosses.

Water chemistry and temperature should be to suit any tankmates; extreme acidity is probably best avoided in the long term. Water quality should be good despite tolerance of poor conditions in nature; their large appetites but (in most cases) preference for calm water indicate a need for efficient but not turbulent filtration.

Feeding

Tilapiines will eat anything offered and in quantity. Bearing in mind their natural habits, the diet should contain a high percentage of vegetable matter. Aquatic invertebrates also form part of their natural food. Mammalian products should be avoided.

Breeding

Oreochromis are sexually dimorphic —males are larger and more colourful. *O. macrochir* males have a genital tassel which serves the same purpose as egg-spots in haplochromines. *Sarotherodon* and *Tilapia* show no external sexual dimorphism. Sexing by examination of the vent may be tried, or several juveniles grown up together to obtain both sexes.

The mouthbrooding genera normally spawn in a pit; the substrate brooders will utilise a rock or excavate an area of the tank bottom. In nature *Sarotherodon* do not remain together after spawning; in the aquarium there may be insufficient space for them to separate but this does not seem to cause any problems. *Oreochromis* follow a pattern similar to haplochromines, with the male playing no part after spawning —but he is unlikely to harass the brooding female. Small *Tilapia* (and small adults of the larger species) will generally rear their fry without problem, but large males can be murderously territorial towards females and a divider may be necessary both before and after spawning. The use of target fishes (suitably protected by a divider) may permit more natural breeding, and in a very large cichlid community pairs may breed successfully, the male being kept busy defending the territory.

Broods are generally large (even in the mouthbrooders); unless there is a market for the fry they are best regarded as useful food for piscivores, and it is not uncommon for a pair of *O. mossambicus* to be kept simply as live food generators. If growing-on space is not a limiting factor large tilapiines are also excellent food for humans...!

Central American Cichlids

By Willem Heijns

The most important rule in keeping live fishes is to provide them with a suitable environment in which they will feel comfortable. The fishes will in turn reward their keeper with fascinating behaviour, splendid coloration, and good health. So what should an aquarist keeping Central American cichlids do to keep his or her fishes happy? The answer is relatively simple: provide them with an optimal environment, i.e. a sufficiently large aquarium with a "natural" decor, feed them natural foods, and supply them with water of the right quality.

First the water: many aquarists believe that cichlids from Central America should be kept in soft and acidic water. This is absolutely wrong! Most, if not all, waters in Central America have a pH which is above neutral —sometimes even close to pH 9!— and a hardness which is usually above 10 °DH —sometimes more than 100°! Soft and acidic tap water should therefore be made suitable for these cichlids by adding bicarbonate (see page 19). Water for Central American cichlids should have a pH above 7 and a hardness above 5 °DH.

In order to calculate the correct size of tank for a particular species we must take into consideration the following points: 1) the maximum size of the species; 2) its swimming behaviour; 3) the size of its breeding territory;

Right: *Paratheraps bifasciatus*, a vegetarian cichlid from the south of Mexico, defending its offspring.
Below: An aquarium for Central American cichlids. Photos by Willem Heijns

4) its aggression towards other species. I have developed a method of calculation whereby each of these factors is given a score so that I can deduce the correct minimum size of aquarium in which each species can be kept. I use a range of 1 to 5 for the swimming behaviour, breeding territory, and (anti-)social behaviour. A species with very calm swimming behaviour and a very small breeding territory, and which is very peaceful towards other cichlids, scores a 1 for all three categories. A cichlid which swims hyperactively all day long, needs a breeding territory larger than 5 metres in diameter, and which behaves aggressively towards all other fishes scores a 5 in these three categories. I add up these three scores and multiply the total by the species' maximum length. The result gives the minimum length of the aquarium. In the tables supplied with each group I have put the scores of the individual species.

When such a calculation is applied in practice you will find that cichlids kept in an aquarium with an appropriate length, live in harmony. One of the reasons is that the chase-distance is shorter than the total length of the aquarium. The chased individual is thus not forced to reverse its flight towards the aggressor. This notably improves the harmony in the community.

We must, of course, ensure that the aquarium is not overpopulated. It is difficult to give a practical rule, but to give some idea, a 200 cm-long aquarium could house a pair of each of four different species (8 individuals) as long as the length of the tank is sufficient for each of them (see page 63 for some further examples). The best way to find out about the compatibility of species is to watch their behaviour carefully.

The decor of the aquarium should contain ample hiding places such as piled up stones, hidden flowerpots, and/or heaped bog wood. The substrate should be coarse sand or fine gravel. Do not use coral sand or lava gravel.

In many publications it is recommended that Central American cichlids be kept in pairs. For this reason many aquarists often purchase their cichlids as "breeding pairs". However, we must realise that any male and female put together do not necessarily constitute a breeding pair. For this reason it is much better to begin with a group of 5 to 7 (juvenile) individuals and let the fishes pair off by themselves. After a pair has formed the other individuals can be removed from the tank. In this way the chances of the pair breeding successfully are as high as possible.

If only two individuals are available you may try and pair them by placing them in a **sufficiently large** aquarium with a clear divider. An alternative method is discussed on page 18. After a few weeks the divider may be taken out, but you need to observe the "pair" closely. In aquaria which are too small for the particular species things are bound to go wrong during the first few days; sometimes the fishes you are trying to pair are both of the same sex —Central American cichlids are difficult to sex— and this usually leads to catastrophic results if you don't separate them again. In my experience the biggest mistake one can make is to house cichlids in an aquarium which is too small for the species in question.

Archocentrus	max. size in cm	scores			leaf litter	shaded banks	rocks/ pebbles	mid-water	calm water	flowing water	small streams	large rivers
		S	T	A								
Archocentrus centrarchus	15	3	2	2								
A. nigrofasciatus	15	3	4	4								
A. sajica	10	3	3	4								
A. septemfasciatus	10	3	3	3								
A. spilurus	15	3	3	3								
A. spinosissimus	10	3	2	2								
Herotilapia multispinosa	15	3	2	2								
Neetroplus nematopus	15	4	3	4								
N. panamensis	12	3	3	2								

Scores (see p. 172): S= swimming behaviour; T= territorial behaviour; A= aggression towards other species.

Archocentrus group

This group can be divided into two sub-groups the species of which show different morphology and behaviour.

Behaviour in the wild

One sub-group includes *A. nigrofasciatus, A. spilurus, A. sajica*, *A. septemfasciatus, N. nematopus, and N. panamensis*. They differ from the other group —*A. centrarchus, A. spinosissimus*, and *Herotilapia multispinosa*— in having a terminal mouth and a breeding colour pattern with vertical bars (not always distinct), and by the fact that they are cave-brooders. The species of the other group are distinguished by having a lower jaw which is longer than the upper, a breeding coloration consisting of an almost entirely black pattern with a light coloured area above the eyes, and by the fact that they are open substrate brooders. The species of both groups are fairly small and can, for this reason, be kept in relatively small tanks.

Behaviour in the aquarium

The two groups show significant difference in behaviour. The species of the *A. centrarchus* group are relatively peaceful while those of the *A. nigrofasciatus* group may be rather aggressive towards other species. This is reflected in the size of territory needed by these cichlids. *H. multispinosa* is satisfied with a small territory while *A. nigrofasciatus* will try to occupy the entire aquarium in which it is kept. All other fishes, assuming *A. nigrofasciatus* can intimidate them, are chased from the territory. Suitable companions for this small cichlid are therefore larger species or those which are able to withstand its aggression. Species of the *Thorichthys* group are thus not suitable tankmates for *C. nigrofasciatus*.

Aquarium

The size of the aquarium depends on the temperament of the species: those of the *A. nigrofasciatus* group need a tank with a minimum length of about 90 cm (for *A. septemfasciatus*) to 170 cm (for *A. nigrofasciatus*) while a length of 70 to 100 cm is sufficient for species of the other group. The decor should include caves (flowerpots, bog wood, and/or rocks) for the cave brooders. Plants can be used if they are carefully anchored between small rocks.

Feeding

Species of the *C. centrarchus* group feed on vegetable matter although this seems to be restricted to algae and vegetable debris. Plants in the aquarium are usually left untouched. The species of the *C. nigrofasciatus* group feed on invertebrates and debris. All these species can be fed with *Mysis, Cyclops, Daphnia*, Shrimp-mix (page 35), and a good flake food (no mammalian fat). Red mosquito larvae, beef heart, and in particular *Tubifex* can be lethal when fed to any fish.

Breeding

The cave brooders need a dark site in which to deposit their eggs. It is usually the female who takes the initiative in spawning. She searches for a suitable cave and then tries to interest the male. Although sexual dimorphism is evident (females have a spot in the dorsal fin) brood care seems to be equally divided between both parents. Fry can be fed with *Artemia* nauplii as soon as they are free-swimming.

The species of the *A. centrarchus* group spawn on an open substrate. In contrast to all other Central American cichlids, the larvae are not kept in a small pit but are suspended on plants, roots, and, in captivity, the aquarium glass. It is the female's task to collect any larvae that "fall out of the nest" and spit them back into the brood. At night the larvae are suspended closer to the bottom than during the daytime.

Thorichthys group

The species of the genus *Thorichthys* are among the smaller Central American cichlids. This, in combination with their relatively peaceful behaviour, makes them ideal inhabitants for small aquaria.

Behaviour in the wild

In body shape *Thorichthys* resemble the sand-sifting species of the *Amphilophus* group. However, the *Thorichthys* species are not sifters but pick their prey —insect larvae, crustaceans, snails— from the substrate or from the sediment covering it.

Thorichthys species are common in the wild and, during the breeding period (from November to May) found mainly in pairs. Brooding pairs are found at a minimum distance of about 60 cm apart. Fry-guarding *Thorichthys* do not move their offspring through the habitat as many other Central American cichlids do.

All species except *T. callolepis* have a black opercular spot which imitates an eye. Intruders are intimidated by a frontal display of the fully-spread gill covers. The eye-spot makes the fish look like a much bigger opponent. Such behaviour may even be witnessed when we approach the aquarium too closely.

Behaviour in the aquarium

The territorial behaviour of *Thorichthys* species is very much ritualised. The pair bond persists even when breeding is not actively in progress. A pair defends a territory, which is usually no bigger than 30 cm in diameter, against all other intruders. The defence usually consists of frontal displays with gill covers spread and the gill membranes extended to the lowest possible position. Although territorial defence seems to form the main part of their daily routine they never harm small intruders. It is not advisable to keep *Thorichthys* together with *Archocentrus nigrofasciatus* or *A. sajica* or with Guapotes. It is possible to keep different *Thorichthys* species in the same aquarium but try to avoid housing similar-looking species together.

Aquarium

The aquarium should have a minimum length of about 120 cm. There should be some sort of shelter for subordinated individuals although aggression towards conspecifics is limited to chasing them from the territory. Most *Thorichthys* are cave brooders and need appropriate spawning sites which we can provide by using bog wood, flowerpots, and heaps of rocks. Plants are normally left alone but should be anchored properly to avoid uprooting during digging.

Feeding

Insects and their larvae are among the favourites of these species. Mosquito larvae are eagerly accepted but you should not feed them red mosquito larvae as these are sometimes collected in heavily polluted water. *Thorichthys* appear to be particularly vulnerable to poisoning resulting from contaminated red mosquito larvae. Krill, *Mysis*, shrimp-mix (page 35), and, every now and then, white worms, are much better foods.

Above: *Archocentrus sajica*; centre: *Archocentrus spinosissimus*; below: *Thorichthys pasionis*.
Facing page: contesting boundaries: *Thorichthys meeki* (left) and *T. aureus*.
Photos by Willem Heijns.

Thorichthys	max. size in cm	scores			leaf litter	shaded banks	rocks/ pebbles	mid-water	calm water	flowing water	small streams	large rivers
		S	T	A								
Thorichthys affinis	15	3	3	3								
T. aureus	13	3	3	3								
T. callolepis	12	3	3	2								
T. ellioti	15	3	3	2								
T. helleri	15	3	3	2								
T. meeki	15	2	3	3								
T. pasionis	15	2	3	3								
T. socolofi	13	3	3	2								

Scores (see p. 172): S= swimming behaviour; T= territorial behaviour;A= aggression towards other species.

Breeding

Most *Thorichthys* species are cave brooders, but not in the strict sense. The spawning site must be located in a somewhat sheltered spot but not necessarily covered, and must be provided by the keeper. A flat stone surrounded by some bigger rocks seems to attract *Thorichthys* pairs. Large flowerpots are accepted as well but are aesthetically unattractive unless they are hidden from view by rocks. Because open spawning sites are acceptable they can be arranged so as to provide a clear view for the onlooker. Once a pair has chosen a site they defend it with all their energy. Females are smaller than males and can further be recognised by having a sometimes faint, blue-black, spot in the dorsal fin. Sexing by examining the vents is difficult and is recommended only with adult specimens.

The eggs are deposited on a slab lying on the gravel, the underside of bog wood, or the inside of a flowerpot. Both male and female actively defend their offspring. The pair become hyperactive when the fry start to swim. Even large fishes are chased from the relatively small territory. The spawn size varies from 100 to 500 eggs. Proper culling should be the norm when raising cichlids (see page 54), but when large numbers are produced it is absolutely necessary. *T. meeki* has been mass-produced in breeders' tanks and has in consequence lost most of its splendid coloration. Fortunately wild caught individuals have been re-introduced into the hobby so that this beautiful species can now be enjoyed again in its full splendour.

Rheophilic group

This group (except for *Copora nicaraguensis*) consists of so-called rheophilic cichlids, i.e. cichlids living in fast flowing water. Because of this habitat preference and the fact that such water is normally found in rocky areas, which makes catching these cichlids very difficult, these species (except *C. nicaraguensis*) were not common in captivity until recently.

Behaviour in the wild

The species of this group have a slender to cylindrical body which makes them more stable in the moving water. Sub-adults are normally found in small groups when grazing on the rocky surfaces (*Paraneetroplus*) or feeding solitary on invertebrates from the substrate. Breeding pairs are commonly seen in the dry season —November to May— and both parents defend their offspring although the male appears to lose the incentive to do so when the slightest danger threatens. Some species

***Rheophilic*-group**	max. size in cm	scores			leaf litter	shaded banks	rocks/ pebbles	mid-water	calm water	flowing water	small streams	large rivers
		S	T	A								
Chuco godmani	25	3	3	2								
C. intermedius	25	4	3	3								
C. microphthalmus	25	4	3	3								
Copora nicaraguensis	20	3	3	2								
Tomocichla sieboldii	25	4	3	3								
To. tuba	30	4	3	3								
Paraneetroplus bulleri	30	4	3	3								
P. gibbiceps	25	4	3	3								
P. nebuliferus	25	4	3	3								
P. omonti	25	4	3	3								
Theraps coeruleus	12	4	3	3								
Th. irregularis	25	4	3	4								
Th. lentiginosus	25	4	3	3								

Scores (see p. 172): S= swimming behaviour; T= territorial behaviour;A= aggression towards other species.

repeatedly move their fry through the habitat (e.g. *P. bulleri*) while others keep their progeny within close range of the nest (e.g. *Th. coeruleus*).

Behaviour in the aquarium

Like many rheophilic species they are fast swimmers, and this fact may sometimes cause problems if too small a tank is utilised. The more dominant individuals will try to keep the others away from the food and the most desirable places in the aquarium. For this reason you should house these species in a large aquarium.

Some species show an interesting feeding behaviour. Probably because food is not easily obtained in fast flowing water *Th. lentiginosus* has developed a feeding technique which involves turning over small pebbles and rocks. Possibly edible particles that have accumulated under such objects are quickly snapped up as soon as they are exposed. Such behaviour has also been observed in the wild where it is mainly leaves which are turned over.

Aquarium

Using the formula described on page 172 you will find that most of these species need an aquarium longer than 200 cm. This is due mainly to their swimming behaviour, and for the same reason a lot of swimming space should be available in the tank. It is further recommended that a current is created by placing a power head at one end of the tank. A power filter can be used as well but in this case the outlet should be placed near the surface so that the flow can oxygenate the water. The decor should include large rocky caves as most of these species are cave brooders. The rocks should be placed close to the rear and end glasses so as to leave plenty of swimming space.

Feeding

The species of the rheophilic group include vegetarians and insectivores. They can best be fed with shrimp-mix (see page 35), krill, *Cyclops*, and occasionally white worms and earthworms. Worms should not be fed to *Paraneetroplus,* which are herbivores.

Breeding

With the exception of *C. nicaraguensis* breeding the cichlids of this group is not easy. A few species have been bred by several aquarists, but breeding reports of most others are scarce and some species have never been bred in captivity. Most rheophilic species are cave brooders and this is a prerequisite if you want to breed them. Little is known of the pair-bonding process. I found that after a few successful spawns a pair of *Th. lentiginosus* completely stopped breeding. Pairing in other species seems to be a very slow process which makes them the most difficult to breed Central American cichlids. Because of this they are rarely available in pet shops.

Detritus-feeders

This group includes species which find their food on or in the bottom. Their inclusion in this group is based purely on their common body shape and feeding behaviour. Several sub-groups are distinguished.

Above: a pair *Tomocichla sieboldii* guarding their fry. Photo by Ad Konings.
Right: a male *Theraps lentiginosus*. Photo by Willem Heijns.
Facing page: a male *Amphilophus longimanus* from Honduras. Photo by F. Ingemann Hansen.

Behaviour in the wild

A. longimanus, A. rostratus, and *A. robertsoni* are specialised in sifting the food from the substrate. They are sometimes referred to as Central American earth-eaters in analogy to the *Geophagus* and *Satanoperca* species of South America. Another sub-group consists of *A. citrinellus, A. labiatus, A. lyonsi,* and *A. zaliosus*. These appear to pick rather than sift their food from the substrate. Invertebrates form an important part of their diet. The species of this group are also known for their polymorphic coloration: individuals with an entirely orange coloration are known to occur, while the normal colour is grey to brown with dark vertical bars.

Nandopsis trimaculatus has been included

Detritis-feeders	max. size in cm	scores			leaf litter	shaded banks	rocks/ pebbles	mid-water	calm water	flowing water	small streams	large rivers
		S	T	A								
Amphilophus alfari	20	3	3	3								
A. altifrons	20	3	3	4								
A. calobrensis	25	3	3	4								
A. citrinellus	30	3	3	4								
A. diquis	20	3	3	4								
A. labiatus	25	3	3	5								
A. longimanus	20	3	3	2								
A. macracanthus	25	3	3	3								
A. nourissati	20	3	3	3								
A. robertsoni	20	3	3	4								
A. rostratus	25	3	3	4								
A. zaliosus	25	3	3	4								
Nandopsis trimaculatus	35	3	3	5								

Scores (see p. 172): S= swimming behaviour; T= territorial behaviour;A= aggression towards other species.

here because of its resemblance to several other members. It is, however, a piscivore.

Behaviour in the aquarium

The species of this group are not active swimmers but need a lot of space because of their intolerance of other tank inhabitants. The most peaceful among them is *A. longimanus* while *N. trimaculatus* is the most aggressive. More than one species from either sub-group should not be kept in the same aquarium, for instance, *A. citrinellus* should not be kept with *A. labiatus* or *A. robertsoni* with *A. rostratus*. They combine well with other *Amphilophus* species, species of the Guapote-group, the more aggressive species of the *Archocentrus*-group, and those of the Herbivore-group.

The feeding behaviour of the substrate sifters is remarkable: the head is plunged deep into the sand and the sand thus collected is sifted through the gills. Anything edible is retained and eaten. The depth to which the fish dives into the substrate is related to the length of the snout; the eyes never disappear under the sand, as otherwise it would lose visual contact with its environmenand be vulnerable to predation. *A. rostratus* has a very long snout —its name means "with a long snout"— and exhibits this digging behaviour all day long.

Aquarium

The minimum length of the aquarium depends on the temperament of the species housed in it. *A. longimanus* should be housed in a tank with a length of at least 160 cm while *N. trimaculatus* needs a tank with a length of 400 cm! Most of these species, however, can be kept in a 200 cm-long aquarium.

Because of the fishes' digging activity it is difficult to include plants, but with some patience it is possible. Some slabs of rock will provide potential spawning sites; all these species are open substrate brooders. The most important part of the decor is the substrate: coarse sand or very fine gravel is recommended. Coral sand and lava split have sharp edges and may cause gill irritation. This type of substrate can be lethal to substrate sifting cichlids.

Feeding

All species of this group are carnivores feeding predominantly on insect larvae and crustaceans. Because of their relatively large size they should be fed with krill, *Mysis*, shrimp-mix (page 35), and, occasionally, earthworms and white worms.

Breeding

All species are open substrate brooders. Pair formation is best achieved by letting a group of juveniles grow up together. Once two fishes have paired they commonly remain together permanently. The eggs, which may range in number from a few hundreds to almost a thousand per spawn, the larvae, and the fry are guarded by both parents. The fry can be fed on freshly hatched brine shrimp and microworms and are relatively easy to raise.

Herbivores

This group consists of vegetarians with a rather large maximum size.

Behaviour in the wild

Juveniles of these species are usually found in small groups or solitary. Adults live mainly in pairs, including outside the breeding season. Solitary adults, however, are not rare. Egg- or fry-guarding females are often encountered on their own because males are not the bravest of fish when it comes to guarding their offspring and have left the area before the observer arrives. The food consists of vegetable matter which most species find on the bottom or on the branches of trees that have fallen into the water. It includes algal tufts growing on leaf litter, fruit, and debris.

Behaviour in the aquarium

The species of this group can be very intolerant of conspecifics. This should be borne in mind when growing up a group of juveniles in the same aquarium. Adult individuals of the different species of this group are not easily housed together. Sometimes overpopulation reduces their intolerance towards each other but this should not be regarded as a suitable method for these cichlids. For this reason it is recommended that only one pair from this group be kept in an aquarium, or perhaps a combination of one *Herichthys* pair and one pair of *Paratheraps* or *Vieja*. Tank size, if calculated using the formula on page 172, should then be sufficient.

Aquarium

The size of the tank should be at least 200 cm for most species but some, such as *P. fenestratus* and *V. maculicauda*, need an

Herbivores	max. size in cm	scores			leaf litter	shaded banks	rocks/ pebbles	mid-water	calm water	flowing water	small streams	large rivers
		S	T	A								
Herichthys carpintis	25	2	3	3								
H. cyanoguttatus	25	2	3	3								
H. tamasopoensis	15	3	3	2								
Paratheraps bifasciatum	25	3	3	4								
P. breidohri	20	4	3	2								
P. fenestratum	30	4	3	3								
P. guttulatum	30	3	3	3								
P. hartwegi	25	3	3	4								
P. melanurus	20	3	3	3								
P. synspilum	35	3	3	2								
P. zonatum	20	3	3	3								
Vieja argentea	25	4	3	2								
V. heterospilus	25	3	3	2								
V. maculicauda	30	3	3	4								
V. regani	30	4	3	2								

Scores (see p. 172): S= swimming behaviour; T= territorial behaviour;A= aggression towards other species.

aquarium with a length of at least 300 cm. It is important to have ample shelter for subordinated individuals. Large (hidden) flowerpots or heaps of large rocks help to create such hide-outs. It is not advisable to have water plants in the tank as most likely they will be eaten by these herbivores.

Feeding

As mentioned earlier the natural food of these species is vegetable matter, and this should be included in the diet of captive specimens. An ideal food is shrimp-mix in which peas and *Spirulina* constitute a major part. It is readily accepted by all cichlids and easily prepared (see page 35).

Breeding

Breeding these species is simple when you have a harmonious pair; the most difficult part is obtaining such a pair. The best way is to grow up 5 to 7 juveniles in the same tank and let them pair off. However, once a pair has formed it does not mean that they will stay together for several spawns. It seems that the pair need to accept each other again prior to each spawning. The pair bond may break down during the raising of the fry or even at the egg-guarding stage. In other words these cichlids need vigilance and a large aquarium. In tanks smaller than the size advised it is better to take a part of the brood away from the parents if you want to be sure of raising some. Sudden changes in the male's temperament may result in complete loss of the brood and even severe damage to the female. The remedy is a large tank with other species to distract the pair.

Several of these species have a breeding period of about two years during which several broods are produced. After 4 to 5 spawns the pair does not seem to be productive any more although they may live for much longer. This may also lead to stress in the aquarium. The remedy is to save some of the offspring and grow them to adulthood.

Above: *Paratheraps synspilum* is a favourite cichlid among aquarists.
Right: *Vieja maculicauda* has a very large distribution in Central America mainly due to its tolerance to sea water. Photos by Willem Heijns

Spawn size is relatively large with more than 1000 eggs a possibility, although most broods range between 250 and 500 fry. Raising fry is easy if they are fed brine shrimp and/or microworms. They should be "weaned" onto dry food (when desired) from an early stage on as they seem to be slow to accept lifeless food. Shrimp-mix, however, is eaten by fry as well.

Left: *Nandopsis grammodes*.
Centre: a pair of *N. managuensis* (photos by Willem Heijns)
Bottom: a female *N. labridens* guarding fry at Media Luna, Mexico (photo Ad Konings).

Guapotes

The large species of this group are commonly known as "Guapotes". With the exception of *Petenia splendida* they are all currently placed in the genus *Nandopsis*

Behaviour in the wild

All these species are predators, but this does not automatically mean that they feed on fishes. Small species such as *N. bartoni* feed predominantly on small invertebrates. All are solitary hunters and are only rarely seen in small groups. *P. splendida* is a very large but rather placid predator with an extremely extensible mouth which it opens suddenly to suck in its prey. Other large predators, such as *N. dovii* and *N. managuensis*, cruise in mid-water searching for prey, usually

Guapotes	max. size in cm	scores			leaf litter	shaded banks	rocks/ pebbles	mid-water	calm water	flowing water	small streams	large rivers
		S	T	A								
Nandopsis bartoni	15	3	3	4								
N. dovii	70	3	3	4								
N. festae	40	3	3	4								
N. friedrichsthalii	25	3	3	2								
N. grammodes	25	3	3	4								
N. istlanus	20	3	3	3								
N. labridens	25	3	3	4								
N. loisellei	20	3	3	3								
N. managuensis	50	2	3	4								
N. motaguensis	30	2	3	3								
N. octofasciatus	20	3	3	3								
N. salvini	20	3	3	4								
N. tetracanthus	25	3	3	3								
N. umbriferus	60	3	3	4								
N. urophthalmus	20	3	3	3								
Petenia splendida	50	2	3	1								

Scores (see p. 172): S= swimming behaviour; T= territorial behaviour;A= aggression towards other species.

fish. The diet of the other species likewise includes fishes but they are also found feeding on aquatic insects or other invertebrates.

Behaviour in the aquarium

Solitary predators need a large feeding territory and are therefore rather intolerant of conspecifics or those species which they resemble in coloration. Unfortunately some of these species are normally kept in aquaria which are decidedly too small, and as a result harass other tank inhabitants. According to the formula on page 172, *N. dovii* requires a tank about 700 cm long! Of course, the formula gives only an indication of tank size but it must be obvious that such a species cannot be kept in a 200 cm-long aquarium. In order to avoid the demise of other tank inhabitants it is advisable not to keep this species together with others in tanks smaller than required. The same can be said about *N. managuensis*. Those species with a maximum size of 30 cm or less are good aquarium inhabitants and can be kept together with adults of the herbivore-group and with those of the detritus-feeders.

Aquarium

The minimum length of the aquarium should be around 200 cm for most of these predators. Shelter is needed for subordinated individuals and also when a group of juveniles is grown up together. Large rocks may create a simple but adequate cave for subordinated individuals. Plants are not recommended before a pair has formed and built a territory; once you know where digging activities are likely to be minimal you can try to include some plants.

Feeding

Large fishes need large food items. *Cyclops* and *Daphnia*, although eaten, do not satisfy a

Guapote's appetite. Krill, shrimp, prawns, and shrimp-mix are the recommended frozen foods. Live earthworms and, of course, feeder guppies are eagerly devoured. The very large Guapotes feed on live bait-fish and chunks of these can be fed to the smaller species as well.

Breeding

Breeding is not very difficult if you have a harmonious pair, which is best obtained by growing up 5 to 10 juveniles in the same tank. As soon as pair formation is observed the other individuals should be taken out. Once a pair are living in harmony they remain together almost forever. Aggression between the male and female of a established pair is rare and occurs only after all of their offspring have been removed. But even then major problems are rarely encountered and the pair soon start preparations for a new brood.

All species larger than 25 cm are open substrate brooders. Male and female have different tasks in defending their offspring: the female stays much closer to the eggs and fry than the male, who keeps fry-eating predators at bay. In the aquarium a slab, a piece of wood, or even the glass bottom is used as spawning site. Brood sizes vary from 200 (e.g. *N. bartoni*) to 3000 (e.g. *N. managuensis*). Because it is impossible to sell or give away so many juveniles of any of these species you should cull them vigorously (see page 54). Raising fry poses no real problems.

South American cichlids, large cichlids

by Mary Bailey

The lakes and rivers of South America do not form such conveniently discrete bodies as the East African Lakes; and although it is possible to split the tropical waters which hold cichlid populations into geographically separate units, there may be some overlap of species where these existed in more than one such area before current watersheds came into existence, or where the watershed ceases to exist during periods of inundation. For example a dwarf species, *Apistogramma trifasciata*, is, rather remarkably, found in two permanently separated major river basins. Sometimes, by contrast, these same watersheds may separate very similar, but clearly distinct, species. Recent researches, in particular those of Dr. Sven Kullander, indicate that similarly distinct species have arisen in the Amazon basin without there necessarily being any such barrier to intermingling beyond sheer distance and a sedentary temperament (e.g. *Mesonauta*) —yet at the same time *Apistogramma agassizii* has a continuous range, albeit with colour variations, equating to about half the length of the main watercourse. Some species have a very restricted distribution, while others are extremely widespread - and this is not always a function of size. In some cases we must await further research before we know how many species are actually contained in genera once thought monotypic, and we do not even know if our aquarium specimens will prove to be what we think they are, or some very similar, but undescribed, member of the same genus.

The most notable river basin of the South American continent is, of course, that of the Amazon, and this must be regarded as the major unit of cichlid-bearing waters. In addition there are the upper regions of the Rio Paraguay system (too cool for most cichlids at its mouth); the north-flowing Orinoco and the smaller rivers of the Guianas; the waters of the East coast of Brazil (most notable for *Geophagus brasiliensis*); and those of the North-West corner of the continent —both the relatively short rivers of the Pacific slopes of the Andes and those flowing northwards between the northern cordilleras to the Caribbean. This last area bears more resemblance to some Central American habitats than to the Amazon basin, and there is some overlap in the cichlid fauna, with Central American types (e.g. *Nandopsis festae*) occurring well down the Pacific coast, and the otherwise strictly South American genera *Aequidens* and *Geophagus* having a representative apiece in Panama. The lakes of the Andean *alto plano*, for example Lake Titicaca, are too cold (by virtue of their altitude) for cichlids, despite lying in tropical latitudes.

Within these tropical areas there are three main types of river: black water, clear water, and white water. Blackwater streams are those whose water is coloured to a rich peaty colour —sometimes compared to strong

The white sand contrasts vividly with the tea-coloured water of the Río Atabapo in Colombia.
Photo by Kaj Anderson.

tea— by organic material. The water is relatively clear despite its colour, as it carries very little suspended silt. The Rio Negro —the name means "Black River"— is probably the best known example, and after its waters join the main Amazon their colour can be seen for many miles downstream before becoming dispersed. Clear water streams are exactly that, clear uncoloured water; such rivers generally originate in areas of very old, hard, rocks (e.g. the Brazilian and Guianan shields) which do not erode easily, so that their waters are not burdened with inorganic debris. White water rivers, by contrast, originate in, or pass through, areas of young, softer, rocks (e.g. the Andes) and as a result carry a considerable load of inorganic matter which colours the water and greatly reduces visibility. In the main Amazon basin the water is generally soft and acid, but with geographical variation in degree dependent on the type(s) of rocks over which it flows and the organic content. Some of the headwaters, however, are slightly alkaline, as their waters have not yet been

acidified by prolonged contact with decaying organic material. The Paraguay basin and the Guianan rivers are also mainly soft and acid, but on average less extreme than those of the Amazon. The East coast and North-Western waters are more neutral.

The lowland rivers have extensive flood plains, largely covered in rain forest, and these are inundated for as much as half of the year during and following the rainy season. This flooded forest, known locally as *igapo*, provides a huge additional feeding and breeding ground for aquatic life. There are also lakes: areas of permanent open water on the floodplain, which become connected to the nearby river during the inundation period, when they are recognisable only as open areas in the flooded forest. Some were once parts of the nearby river, left behind when it changed its course (ox-bow lakes). Some may even be on huge islands of silt in the main streams. Towards the end of the dry season many become little better than mud-holes and fishes trapped in them are easy pickings for herons and other predatory birds. None of these Amazonian lakes is in any way an analogue of the large lakes of Central America and East Africa, although they are nevertheless favourite haunts of cichlids.

Cichlids are rarely found in the open waters of the large rivers, where they would be highly vulnerable to predation by not only larger fishes but also birds and caimans. The most notable exceptions are members of the *Cichla* genus, which are themselves large pursuit predators. Many cichlids instead inhabit streams and pools and lakes and, seasonally, the flooded forest. They tend to lurk in the tangle of roots along the margins of permanent waters (large and medium sized types), or in the leaf litter on the bottom (dwarfs). Rafts of vegetation are also colonised. Some species are adapted to life in areas of rapids (some *Crenicichla* and *Teleocichla*).

Tropical South America does not consist entirely of rain forest; there are regions of grassland, both of natural occurrence (*llanos*) and areas deforested early this century to make way for cattle. Many such areas are on the higher ground towards the eastern foothills of the Andes. These grassy areas are drained by streams and rivers and also contain small lakes and pools. These waters have their cichlid populations, mainly dwarfs; here they find cover not only from leaf litter (if any) but also among the stems of marginal vegetation, and sometimes among floating water plants. Some of these grassland areas are flooded during the rainy season, and are then colonised by aquatic life in the same way as the flooded forest. Cichlids have even been found in large "potholes" in the recently flooded roads!

Many habitats, especially those in the rain forest, are far from accessible (even if money is no object) for much of the year. Even when access is feasible visibility is often very poor, and underwater exploration of dense tangles of roots and branches is next to impossible. Small pools and streams are too shallow to permit diving. So observation and study is largely restricted to what can be learned from above the water's surface, and we cannot observe the cichlids "at home" in the way that we can their East African cousins. The information we do now have, however, is generally sufficient to allow us to provide reasonably appropriate conditions for South American cichlids in our aquaria.

Uaru

Large cichlids (maximum size 35 cm) found the length of the Amazon system and along some major tributaries.

Behaviour in the wild

Its preferred habitat is still or slow-moving water with tangles of roots and fallen trees. Stomach contents indicate a diet which includes invertebrates, but consists largely of vegetable material, including detritus and fruit.

In captivity, and therefore almost certainly in the wild, juveniles exhibit two different colour patterns before attaining adult coloration; the first of these is pinkish-beige mottled with darker markings and is retained until the fish measures 3-4 cm SL. This is followed by a grey-brown background with blue-grey irregular reticulation. At sizes between 7 and 11 cm adult coloration is assumed. It may be that the two different patterns indicate two different habitat types during the juvenile period.

Its sociable behaviour in captivity suggests that it is a shoaling fish.

Behaviour in the aquarium

A very peaceful fish towards both conspecifics and other species, even at breeding time —though when guarding eggs it has been known to nip the hand of the unwary aquarist! Fry and small juveniles, however, are sometimes cannibalistic and may also eagerly shred corpses of other fishes. All sizes are greedy feeders.

Specimens measuring more than about 8 cm *and* showing adult colour pattern often shed large amounts of mucus when moved; although this looks alarming the fishes usually recover quickly. Great care must be taken, however, when transporting *Uaru* of this size, as the discarded mucus can contaminate the water if the journey is of any length. They are best transported in buckets rather than bags, and a supply of clean tank water taken so that a complete change can be made if necessary.

Uaru are sociable fishes, and should **never** be kept as "singles", as a lone individual will almost invariably stop feeding, pine, and die. If an *Uaru* has to be isolated for any reason this should be within sight of conspecifics either behind a clear divider or, for hospitalisation, in an adjacent tank.

Aquarium

As mentioned above, the question of keeping just one specimen should never arise. A tank 120 x 45 x 45 cm is the minimum for a breeding pair with a standard length of 15-20 cm; larger adults require larger quarters. A group of 4-6 adults makes a splendid sight in a really large tank.

The decor should include large, properly cured, pieces of root and bogwood. Such items are sometimes varnished to prevent deterioration, but wood treated this way must **never be used** for *Uaru*. They enjoy nibbling any wood placed in their aquarium, and the ingestion of varnish is likely to prove fatal. Plants, even the tougher-leaved types, will be devoured within a few days, and should not be included. Nor should plastic plants, as *Uaru* seem not to recognise the distinction. Large rocks with a good-sized vertical or diagonal surface are required as spawning sites; heavy pieces of slate leaned against the tank glass are an alternative. Sharp edges to decor items should be avoided. And the cover glass should be heavy, as a "panicking" *Uaru* is quite capable of pushing it up and continuing out of the tank.

The substrate should, if possible, not be light and reflective, and the lighting should be subdued, so as to create the effect of a shady area near a bank.

The water should be soft and acid, with a temperature of 25-26° C for general maintenance. The heavy feeding required by small juveniles (see below) can cause problems, and it is best to change 25% of their tank water every other day.

Tank companions, if any, should be other medium to large, peaceful, fishes with similar water requirements. Among cichlids this includes *Heros, Mesonauta, Hoplarchus*, and *Hypselecara*.

Feeding

I have found that adult *Uaru* thrive, and breed, on a diet of earthworms, duckweed (*Lemna minor*) (and other unwanted plants), and pellets with a high vegetable content. They are also partial to lettuce, peas, shrimps, aquatic and other insects, and mussels. They should not be fed mammalian protein, and they will not eat fish.

Juveniles are omnivorous and will eat virtually anything offered, but again mammalian protein should be avoided. It is advisable to feed them heavily until they measure about 3 cm SL, as otherwise they are likely to eat bits of each other —fins normally regenerate, but eyes don't!

Breeding

Uaru, like most of their large South American cousins, show no external sexual dimorphism or dichromatism, and can be sexed only by direct examination of the vent (by an expert). Alternatively a group of 5-6 juveniles can be grown on together and allowed to pair naturally. The group can be kept together even when a pair has formed and spawned —although it may be necessary to use a clear divider to prevent the eggs being eaten by the non-breeders while the parents stand idly by!

Uaru are generally regarded as difficult to breed, but this has not been my experience. I am inclined to attribute my success, at least in part, to a low pH (5-5.5), soft water (<1° GH), and a (natural) temperature increase. This

Left: it is not rare among South American cichlids for two females to "pair up" and spawn. Here two female *Uaru amphiacanthoides* guarding eggs. Next page: *Hoplarchus psittacus* has been bred only rarely in captivity. Photos by Mary Bailey.

triggering by temperature probably reflects behaviour in the native biotope, where they are believed to be seasonal breeders.

The eggs are laid on a slanting or vertical surface; this may be the side of a large rock almost buried in the substrate, specially excavated for the purpose by the pair. I have never known them to

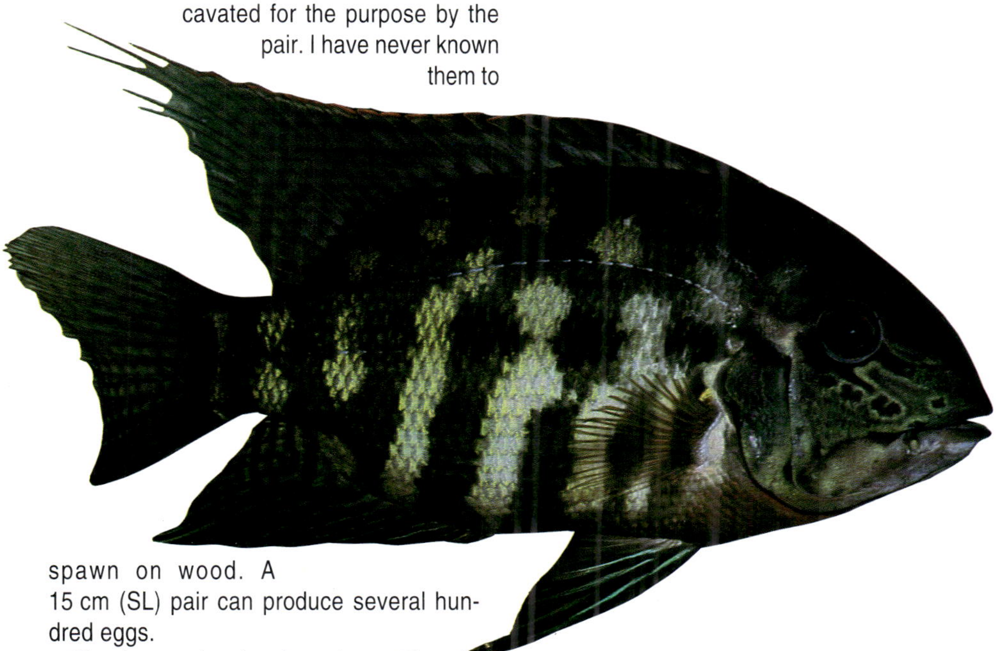

spawn on wood. A 15 cm (SL) pair can produce several hundred eggs.

The larvae hatch after about 72 hours and are then tended in a pit dug alongside the spawning site. Free-swimming fry can be fed on microworm and *Artemia* nauplii, but it is hard work keeping up with their appetites, and other small foods can be used.

Fry also "glance" on their parents, feeding on the mucus covering, which is increased at breeding time so that the adults take on a grey-blue cast. *Uaru* do not lead their fry around the tank. After 2-3 weeks the adults start to look rather frayed, often with actual holes eaten through the fins, and it is best to remove the fry. This is easily achieved; give the fry a small feed at a distance from the parents (who seem to reduce food intake during brood care, and often hardly feed at all), interpose a net between them and the adults, and they will swim into it on their way back to resume glancing.

Large "*Cichlasomas*"

Hoplarchus psittacus (max. 40 cm); *Mesonauta insignis* (previously known as *Cichlasoma festivum*) (max. 20 cm); *Hypselecara coryphaenoides* (max 25 cm); Heros severus (max. 30 cm).

Medium to large cichlids formerly included in *Cichlasoma* sensu Regan.

Behaviour in the Wild

Little is known of wild behaviour. Specimens have been caught in a variety of habitats (lakes, river margins, flooded forest), often among roots, fallen trees, and vegetation.

Stomach contents indicate a mixed diet, often varying with the season, of vegetable matter, invertebrates, detritus, and, rather surprisingly given their aquarium behaviour, fish. *Mesonauta* and *Heros* have been found in association with the island-like rafts of vegetation found in some mainstream rivers; *Mesonauta* appears to be a shoaling species except when breeding.

Behaviour in the aquarium

Peaceful inoffensive fishes, especially for their size. Territoriality may be a problem at breeding time, but serious damage to other fishes, even conspecifics, is unlikely as long as plenty of space is available. Plants may be nibbled, but not usually to any extent if other foods are available.

Hoplarchus has been bred only very rarely, and has utilised both horizontal and vertical substrates. The other three species are less bottom-oriented than many cichlids in their behaviour, and this is reflected in choice of spawning site. *Hypselecara* may use a horizontal or vertical surface in the open, or the underside of an overhang, the chosen substrate being well above the tank bottom. Fry are not brooded in pits, but in natural "troughs" in bogwood or rocks in whose absence they are simply deposited on any available flat surface. *Heros* prefers a vertical or diagonally sloping substrate, and either hangs the adhesive fry on a piece of wood or uses the same type of nursery "'trough" as *Hypselecara*. *Mesonauta* spawns on plant leaves, and has even more unusual brood care behaviour —the young are kept among plants, floating if available, and the fry swim around and above the parents rather than beneath them. This ties in with the vegetation raft habitat mentioned above.

Aquarium

Many general aquarists, and even some cichlidophiles, do not realise that *Hypselecara, Mesonauta*, and more particularly *Heros*, are ultimately large fishes, and fail to provide adequately large accommodation. A pair of young adults requires at least a 100 cm x 50 cm tank, and full-grown *Heros* need much larger quarters. Because of their ultimate size and "off-the-substrate" spawning preferences the tank should be at least 50 cm deep. *H. psittacus* is a very large fish when full-grown, and should be housed accordingly, 200 x 60 x 60 cm being the minimum size for a full-grown pair, and larger much better.

For all 4 species the tank should be decorated with properly cured roots and bogwood; pieces of slate leaned against the tank sides will provide alternative shelter/spawning sites. Plants are useful additional cover. In the case of *Mesonauta* plants are essential as spawning substrates and nurseries, and should include either floating plants or tall ones whose leaves float along the surface (e.g. *Cryptocoryne balansae*).

These fishes will reward minimal hardness and a pH of below 6 with better colour and deportment, and such conditions are still usually necessary for breeding. For wild specimens of these three genera, and for both wild and tank-reared *H. psittacus*, such conditions are mandatory for both maintenance and breeding, and if the pH can be lowered below 5.0 then so much the better. A temperature of 25-26 °C is suitable for general maintenance.

Lighting should be muted: this requirement can be met either by using a single tube, or by adequate surface vegetation providing shade beneath. Very light-coloured substrates should be avoided.

Given sufficient space these fishes do well in monospecific groups, or they can be mixed. They should **never** be housed with Central

American cichlids, which are temperamentally too intimidating as well as having quite different water requirements. They are best not mixed with *Astronotus*, which, although sympatric, is rougher in its behaviour. They can be mixed with *Uaru*, but this means sacrificing any desire for plant life. *Mesonauta* is peaceful enough to be housed with *Pterophyllum* and *Symphysodon*.

Feeding

Diet should be varied and contain plenty of vegetable material, avoiding mammalian proteins. *Hypselecara* (not mine!) fed long-term on a heavy diet of beef heart developed large whitish swellings around the vent which were diagnosed as hernias, caused by improper feeding. A change of diet to shrimp and vegetable matter effected an almost total cure, although none of the three females involved was subsequently observed to spawn.

Breeding

H. psittacus shows no external sexual differences, and needs to be sexed by venting (by an expert). *Heros* and *Mesonauta* males are generally larger and better coloured than females, and have longer fins, but these features are not evident until maturity. *Hypselecara* males are considerably larger than females, and have a remarkable upper head profile which rises almost vertically from the upper lip. This feature is not apparent in young males, but because of the ultimate size dimorphism these rapidly outgrow their female siblings.

Pairing may involve some superficial "violence", but injuries are rare. Once mated pairs usually remain together permanently in the aquarium. Breeding pairs are territorial but their space requirement is small for fishes their size, and as long as the aquarium is a sensible size other fishes, even conspecifics, are unlikely to be harried.

The frequent failure to breed *Heros, Hypselecara*, and *Mesonauta* almost certainly results from ignorance of their true habitat requirements. Given correct conditions and diet breeding should follow in due course. Young pairs may, however, take some time to settle down to proper brood care. The only solution is patience.

Hoplarchus is rarely kept and the sparsity of breeding reports probably reflects this as well as the space requirements of mature adults and their lack of external sexual dimorphism. A very low hardness and pH (<5) may be required to promote spawning. A technique sometimes used with *Symphysodon* —a drop in temperature (by water changing), followed by a gradual rise to 2 °C (or more) above normal (simulating the natural climatic prelude to the breeding season)— may trigger reluctant pairs.

Newly hatched *Artemia* and microworm are suitable first foods for fry of all 4 genera.

Oscars

Astronotus ocellatus (max. 30 cm).

Large cichlids, at least partially piscivorous. *A. ocellatus*, almost universally known as the "Oscar", exists in several aquarium varieties as well as the natural olive form with red-ringed ocelli and variable red body markings.

Behaviour in the wild

Astronotus is very widely distributed in tropical South American waters east of the Andes. As with many South American cichlids, not much is known of natural behaviour because of the difficulties involved in underwater investigation of the habitat. *Astronotus* prefers to live in tangles of roots and fallen trees in areas of minimal or zero current, e.g. backwaters and oxbow lakes. Stomach contents indicate a diet of vegetable matter, invertebrates, and fishes, including *Corydoras* species.

Behaviour in the aquarium

A. ocellatus is noted for its antisocial habits in captivity. It will move anything moveable, not just the substrate, but also decor and equipment if these are inadequately secured. Other fishes may be the subject of territorial attacks, or regarded as food items; even quite large fishes may be badly bitten by remarkably small *Astronotus*, and bite-sized ones are unlikely to survive long. Nevertheless *A. ocellatus* are just as well known for their tendency to "sulk", often for no obvious reason, and to the great concern of their owners. This is sometimes connected with dietary problems (see below).

The aquarium

A tank 120 x 45 x 45 cm is the minimum size for a pair, but a much larger aquarium is preferable. Unless undergravel filtration is employed a reasonably fine substrate is suggested, so that food particles —the species is a messy feeder— remain on the surface and can be siphoned off. Rocks should be too heavy to move and be based on the bottom so that they cannot be undermined. Equipment should be siliconed into place or protected behind special corner dividers, permanently fixed, and with perforations, or small gaps at top and bottom, to permit water circulation.

Filtration must be efficient and backed up by regular removal of uneaten food and water changes. Lighting should be muted. A water

Oscars —usually sold as juveniles— are beautiful cichlids. Juveniles (photo above) may grow to a 30 cm large predator in about two years (left; photo by Mary Bailey).

temperature of 25-26 °C is suitable for normal maintenance and breeding. Although *A. ocellatus* is often kept, and apparently thrives, in hard alkaline water its natural habitat should never be forgotten, and a pH of 6.5 or less is preferable.

Astronotus are often kept with Central American cichlids, despite the incompatibility of water requirements, and are often bullied by their rougher cousins. If they are kept with other large Amazonian cichlids then the bullying is usually by the *Astronotus*. As is so often the case with cichlids, it is a matter of the individual fishes involved. Many aquarists keep them by themselves, which I consider the ideal, or with a large *Plecostomus*.

Feeding

Despite their normally healthy and voracious appetites, *Astronotus* are prone to a variety of problems connected with diet, usually resulting from ignorance on the part of their owner.

The first of these is fussiness: refusal to eat foods other than the one(s) to which they have become accustomed. This is easily cured as long as the owner is more resolute than the fish. If the food is ignored then it is removed and the fish left hungry until the next day. This process of attrition may have to continue for weeks, but invariably succeeds as long as the owner is steadfast.

Far more serious are the results of feeding long-term on unsuitable foods, usually pellets. This can result in intestinal disorders, with the fish resting on the bottom, sometimes with, but usually without, abdominal swelling, and invariably refusing to feed.

A further problem is that these fishes are extremely messy feeders, which waste clouds of particles via the gills. This can largely be obviated by feeding them what they eat in nature —raw fish, crustaceans, insects, and greenstuff— rather than processed foods which disintegrate easily. Earthworms are much enjoyed once the fish conquers its usual initial fear of them!

Breeding

Despite detailed inspection by generations of fishkeepers, no one has yet managed to detect any external sexual dimorphism or dichromatism in *Astronotus*, so obtaining a pair is a matter of starting with a group, direct examination of the vent (by an expert), or luck.

The initial introduction of two unacquainted adults is best effected through a sheet of glass or perspex, and ideally both fishes should be strangers to the tank, so that no pre-existing territory is infringed. After a few days, if the pair have stopped (or almost stopped) trying to murder each other through the divider, this can be removed —but only under strict supervision. The courtship of a new pair is often extremely violent. Except when first introducing strangers the use of a divider should be the last resort. The aquarist must accept that some violence —and some damage— may be a necessary preamble to pairing. Once paired, however, they will usually live in perfect harmony, and subsequent spawnings take place with minimal courtship, if any.

Spawning usually takes place on a flat, precleaned, stone in the open, often only after a considerable amount of substrate shifting has taken place. Depending on the size and condition of the female 1000 or more eggs may be laid.

Astronotus are normally excellent parents. The fry can take newly-hatched *Artemia* as soon as they become free-swimming, and soon graduate to larger foods, including weaker siblings. Considerations of space mean that the aquarist should concentrate on rearing a smaller number of good quality juveniles.

Acaras

Aequidens sensu stricto (max. 20 cm); *Aequidens pulcher* group (max. 24 cm); *Bujurquina* (max. 12 cm); *Cichlasoma* (max. 20 cm). *Krobia* (max. 15 cm); *Tahuantinsuyoa macantzatza* (max. 13 cm)

The "Acaras" are a large group of fairly closely related cichlids distributed throughout tropical South America and extending into southern Central America. They are rather primitive and unspecialised (and hence adaptable and opportunistic) fishes, comparable to the African tilapiines. *Aequidens* sensu stricto and *Cichlasoma* overlap over much of their range, which includes the Amazon drainage as well as the head waters of the Paraguay and Orinoco. *Bujurquina* is sympatric with both genera but largely restricted to head waters. The *Aequidens pulcher* group is confined to the north west, including Pacific slope drainages, Panama, and Trinidad. *Krobia* is found in the north-flowing rivers of the Guianas; *T. macantzatza* in stony-bottomed streams in Peru.

Behaviour in the wild

Aequidens s.s., *Cichlasoma*, *Krobia*, and *Bujurquina* are found in soft, very acid to neutral water. Their biotope includes streams, lakes, pools, and inundated areas, and they are found over leaf-litter, roots, branches, and near marginal vegetation. Species of the *Ae. pulcher* group inhabit soft to medium hard water with a pH varying between neutral and alkaline. *Tahuantinsuyoa* appears to be found exclusively over stony substrates.

As far as is known Acaras are generalised opportunistic feeders, feeding largely on aquatic invertebrates. All are open-spawners. *Bujurquina* and *Tahuantinsuyoa* are monogamous larvophilous biparental mouthbrooders (in *Tahuantinsuyoa* brooding is more frequently by the female alone), the rest are monogamous substrate brooders, with the exception of *Ae. coeruleopunctatus* which sometimes breeds polygynously (a harem breeder).

Behaviour in the aquarium

In general these are remarkably peaceful cichlids for their size, with small territorial requirements for successful breeding. *Ae. rivulatus* (including "Gold Saum" and "Silver Saum"), however, is rather aggressive and territorial, more like a Central American cichlasomine in temperament.

Aquarium

Most can be maintained and bred in a 60 x 40 x 40 cm aquarium, but except in the case of the smallest species a 90 cm long tank is far better as it provides a more sensible amount of swimming space. Full-grown *Ae. rivulatus* may need to be separated by a divider (for at least some of the time) in a tank this size, and are better in a 120 cm tank or even larger.

The tank substrate should be fine gravel, and the decor rocks and bogwood. Although none of these species is naturally a cave dweller, they are more than happy to occupy flowerpots or rock-built caves. Plants can be included; they are unlikely to be eaten but may be dug up during pre-spawning pit-digging, unless protected with collars of pebbles. Flat stones should be provided as spawning sites.

Water chemistry is not critical for general maintenance, but the pH should be kept below 7.5 if possible. If any difficulty is encountered in breeding then an attempt should be made to simulate more closely the conditions of the natural habitat. In most cases this is likely to involve lowering the pH. Temperature is likewise not critical —24-25° C is adequate.

Water quality does not appear to be critical, but this should be regarded as offering a larger margin for error rather than an excuse for sloppy maintenance. Filter turbulence should be minimal, and lighting moderate unless shade is provided by floating or long leaved plants.

With the exception of *Ae. rivulatus* these cichlids should not be mixed with Central American cichlasomines. In suitably sized tanks (allow 60 cm of length per pair, reducing to 45 cm in tanks longer than 120 cm) they can be mixed with each other (it is sensible to avoid mixing very similar species), with other peaceful South American species (NOT *Astronotus*), or with tilapiines.

Feeding

All are eager unfussy feeders. Foods based on mammalian protein should be avoided, but otherwise any good quality prepared foods are suitable. In addition earthworms and pond foods (*Cyclops, Daphnia*, etc.) are much enjoyed and useful for bringing the fishes into breeding condition.

Breeding

Sexing is difficult, as there is little dimorphism or dichromatism. Males are generally larger with longer, more pointed, unpaired fins, but the distinction is not clear cut. Adult males of *Ae. rivulatus* often have a nuchal hump. Sexing by examination of the vent may be attempted (see page 52), or a group of 5-6 juveniles grown on to pair naturally. In the substrate-brooding species it is very common for two females to "pair" in the absence of a male.

Breeding is normally accomplished without any special attention; these are, however, seasonal breeders, and any reluctance to breed can generally be remedied by a large water change followed by a rise in temperature and a diet enriched with live foods. Failure of the eggs to hatch may be due to incorrect pH or, more usually, the absence of a male!

Pairing normally takes place with only minimal preliminary "hostilities" —if any. A small territory round the chosen spawning site is defended vigorously but other aquarium inhabitants are not harassed as long as they keep clear. Brood sizes vary from 100 to 300 eggs. The eggs hatch after 48-72 hours at 26° C. In *Bujurquina* the larvae are then brooded initially by the female, but later passed to and fro between the parents. The brooding parent spits them into a small pit from which the other collects them. Towards the end of the brooding period both parents may brood simultaneously. After release the fry are taken back into the mouth if danger threatens. In tahuantinsuyoa the female normally broods but may be relieved by the male. The other genera guard their larvae in nursery pits. Newly hatched *Artemia* are a suitable first food for both groups.

Egg/fry cannibalism is uncommon; adults which show any repeated tendency towards this behaviour should not be used as breeding stock.

Large predators and planktivores

Cichla ocellaris (max. 90 cm); *Caquetaia spectabilis* (max. 20 cm); *Acaronia* (max. 25 cm); *Chaetobranchopsis* (max. 30 cm); *Chaetobranchus* (max. 30 cm).

A group of large, often predatory cichlids, rarely kept because of their adult size or lack of availability. They are grouped together here for convenience rather than because of any relationship. They are suitable only for very large aquaria and experienced aquarists.

Behaviour in the wild

Cichla are large pursuit piscivores. They are prized as food fishes and have been introduced to other tropical waters as both food and game fishes, to the considerable detriment of native fish faunas. *Cichla* inhabits black as well as white water rivers with a chemistry varying from soft and very acid to slightly alkaline. They are usually found in the deeper parts of slowly moving water, but not normally in mainstream currents. *Caquetaia* are lurking predators, feeding on shrimps and insects as well as small fishes. They are found in soft and very acid to neutral water. They lurk in marginal vegetation and

Facing page, top: A mouthbrooding *Bujurquina mariae*. Photo by F. Ingemann Hansen. Centre: a fry-guarding female *Aequidens metae*.
Bottom: a female *Cichlasoma portalegrense* guarding her eggs.

Right: the mouth of *Caquetaia spectabilis* is very protrusible.

among roots and branches in slow moving streams, pools, and lakes. *Acaronia* have a similar diet, and a preference for lurking among marginal and aquatic plants. They have been recorded as inhabiting forest pools in which many smaller fishes are stranded at the end of the inundation. This provides them with a captive food supply until the next rainy period. Temperatures in these pools may rise to 30° C and they sometimes become choked with vegetation.

Chaetobranchopsis and *Chaetobranchus* are thought to be plankton feeders on the basis of their mouth structure and dentition.

Like many large predators the piscivorous species live solitary except when breeding. Where breeding behaviour has been recorded these cichlids have proved to be open spawning monogamous substrate brooders; the breeding behaviour of the two plankton-feeding genera is totally unknown.

Behaviour in the aquarium

The piscivorous species are, not surprisingly, likely to pursue their natural habits if housed with suitable sized prey. *Cichla* and *Acaronia* are remarkably peaceful for their size —the latter is, in effect, simply a piscivorous Acara. Reports on *Caquetaia* vary from non-aggressive to impossible to keep with each other or other fishes! In general they are aggressive towards conspecifics but tolerate other species. *Chaetobranchus flavescens* is a peaceful cichlid. No details are available for its congeners or for *Chaetobranchopsis*. The available data relate (except in the case of *Caquetaia* and *Acaronia nassa*) to non-breeding individuals —aggression may, of course, increase dramatically at spawning time.

Aquarium

Cichla require a very large aquarium, not just because of their eventual size but because they are active swimmers —a minimum length of 180 cm is suggested for all but small individuals. The other species can be housed in tanks measuring 120 x 45 x 45 cm or larger. The substrate should be fine gravel, and the decor large stones and pieces of bogwood. Plants can be included (and should be for *Acaronia*), but should be secured against digging with collars of large pebbles. The lighting should be moderate; the large eyes of *Acaronia* suggest dim conditions in nature and this preference should be respected in captivity —low illumination or shade from floating or long-leaved plants.

Water chemistry appears not to be critical for successful maintenance, and is certainly not critical for breeding *Cichla*, which has established feral populations in waters of varying chemistry, including brackish. *Caquetaia* has been bred in neutral to slightly alkaline water, but the other species may require an acid pH for successful breeding. Wild caught fishes are best offered natural conditions initially. A temperature of 25-26° C is suitable for general maintenance. Water circulation should not be turbulent.

I have seen *Cichla ocellaris* housed successfully with *Astronotus*, *Osphronemus*, and large catfishes in a 240 x 90 x 90 cm tank, and this may be feasible in smaller quarters. It is advisable to house *Caquetaia* with other cichlids with a similar size and temperament. In a suitably large tank they can be kept with *Astronotus, Hoplarchus*, and other large Amazonians.

The other three genera are better not housed with Central American cichlids; besides large Amazonians large tilapiines are potential tankmates. Our experience of these fishes is so small that no hard and fast rules can be given. Unless the aquarist is experienced in dealing with large cichlids, and tank space is available for emergency re-housing, it is better to avoid experiment and stick to single-species set-ups —with a divider handy!

Feeding

Raw fish should form a major part of the diet of the piscivores. Live fish may be necessary until wild-caught individuals are accustomed to aquarium routine. Shrimps, prawns, and earthworms are other suitable foods. The plankton-feeders, by contrast, require large amounts of small food particles. In the first instance they should be tried on *Cyclops* and other small pond foods. Once they are feeding prepared foods can be offered. They should NEVER be given large chunks of food as they are not designed to process these, despite having large mouths. Feeding large fishes with small foods may lead to an increased risk of pollution from uneaten particles, so special attention should be paid to maintenance unless using live foods.

Breeding

There is no obvious external sexual dimorphism. Sexing is probably possible by examination of the vent (by an expert). Wild-caught individuals are often juveniles, so if they are available in numbers a group can be grown on together to pair naturally.

If spawning does not occur in sufficiently large individuals, then a large water change followed by an increase in temperature and food supply may act as a trigger. If male *Caquetaia* prove excessively aggressive towards females then target fishes (protected by a divider) may help, otherwise a divider may be needed to separate the pair before and after spawning.

Although *Cichla ocellaris* has been maintained in the aquarium since the 1930s there are no records of spawning, perhaps because the individuals kept have not been large enough. *Caquetaia* spawn readily; their eggs (100 to 300 per spawn) are rather small and hatch after 48-60 hours at 25-26° C, with the fry becoming free-swimming about 4 days later. The parents share all the brood-care duties, i.e. the male tends the fry and the female defends the territory, as well as vice versa. In *Acaronia nassa* the female initiates courtship, and a very high temperature (35° C has been used successfully) may be required to trigger this activity. The fry take 71-96 hours to hatch at 30° C, i.e. far longer than usual. This high temperature requirement probably reflects the preferred habitat (see above). Although these cichlids are undoubtedly equipped to deal with high temperatures and low oxygen levels, increased aeration is a sensible precaution.

There are no records of spawning in *Chaetobranchus* and *Chaetobranchopsis*.

Eartheaters (geophagines)

This group consists of the genera *Geophagus, Satanoperca, Gymnogeophagus, Biotodoma,* and *Retroculus*, and is usually also taken to include *Acarichthys* and *Guianacara*. *Guianacara geayi* was formerly included in *Aequidens* and later in *Acarichthys*. *Satanoperca* contains species formerly contained in *Geophagus.*

Eartheaters sift substrate through their gills to extract food, and have a general requirement for a substrate of very fine, non-sharp, sand which will not damage delicate gill filaments. Undergravel filters are thus inappropriate. They practice a variety of breeding strategies.

The geophagines can be divided into five different groups:

Red-Hump *Geophagus* group: *G. steindachneri, G. pellegrini, G. crassilabris* (all 20 cm max.).

Large Eartheaters group: *G. brasiliensis* (max. 30 cm); *G. surinamensis* (max. 25 cm); *Satanoperca jurupari* (max. 25 cm).

Smaller geophagines group: *Gymnogeophagus* (max. 16 cm); *Biotodoma* (max. 15 cm).

Cave brooding geophagines: *Acarichthys heckelii* (max. 20 cm); *Guianacara geayi* (max. 15 cm).

Rheophilic geophagines: *Retroculus lapidifer* (max. 24 cm).

Behaviour in the wild

Cichlids of the Red-Hump group are found in north-flowing drainages between the northwestern Andean cordilleras and in Panama. Their native waters are moderately hard and alkaline streams, often fairly fast flowing with pebbly as well as sandy substrates. They are advanced arena-breeding polygamous maternal mouthbrooders, with males holding adjacent territories and competing for females.

The large eartheaters occur in the Amazon basin and in north-flowing Guianan drainages. Slow-moving or still waters with a thick bottom layer of sediment, leaf litter, and other detritus are preferred. Specific details of the habitat of *G. brasiliensis* (found in Brazil and Uruguay) are unknown. It does not fit into any group in terms of appearance or habits, and is included here because of its size.

Satanoperca and some *Geophagus* are pair-forming mouthbrooders, whose courtship resembles that of their substrate-spawning cousins. The eggs are laid and fertilised and then collected up; maternal, paternal, and biparental brooding are practised, depending on species. Non-brooding males guard both territory and female. The remaining species of this group are monogamous open-brooding substrate spawners; *G. surinamensis*, depending on population, is a substrate-brooder OR larvophilous mouthbrooder!

Gymnogeophagus replace other geophagines (except *G. brasiliensis*) in the southern part of the overall range. The natural habitat is small clear or white water forest streams and pools with soft, slightly acid water. They prefer calm areas near to the bank. *Biotodoma* are found in similar habitats in the Amazon and Orinoco basins. They are stone or pit-spawning open-brooders.

With the exception of *Gg. rhabdotus* (a substrate brooder) *Gymnogeophagus* are larvophilous maternal mouthbrooders: the eggs are laid on a flat stone or in a small pit in the open, covered with a layer of sand, and guarded by the female. When they hatch they are uncovered and collected into the female's mouth. The male guards the territory and the female.

Guianacara form monogamous pairs but older stronger males may have harems if spare females are available.

A. heckelii dig long, sometimes multiple-entranced, breeding tunnels in the bottom. Females fight among themselves for unoccupied holes, and then display to passing males. Once pairing has occurred the male takes over territorial defence. Harems have been reported. *A. heckelii* usually accepts flowerpots as tunnel-substitutes.

Retroculus are found in fast-flowing water with rocky substrates or sandy bottoms with scattered rocks. They have a partially reduced swim-bladder and appear to spend much of their time resting on the bottom. *R. lapidifer* collects small stones in its large mouth and builds a nest from these. It is not known whether *Retroculus* are substrate brooders or mouthbrooders. The former is more likely.

Behaviour in the aquarium

Males of the Red-Hump group are scrappy among themselves, but a single male is more likely to harass females. They are not unduly aggressive towards other fishes.

G. brasiliensis is rather aggressive. The other geophagines are generally peaceful. Some breeding males (e.g. *A. heckelii*), however, can be rather territorial.

Left: A male *Geophagus steindachneri*.
Below: a pair *Satanoperca leucosticta*.
Photos by Ingemann Hansen.
Facing page: a male *Biotodoma wavrini*.

will breed, but do not develop a hump; likewise the hump disappears if a male is removed from a group. The species are closely related and should not be mixed for fear of hybrids.

G. brasiliensis should never be housed with its quieter relatives, but the remaining species may be mixed with other Amazonians of comparable size and temperament.

The water should be fairly hard with pH 7-7.5, well-oxygenated but not turbulent for the Red-Hump geophagines. The other species require soft and fairly acid (pH 6-6.8) water. The filtration must be effective without causing turbulence —although *Retroculus* is a rapids cichlid extreme turbulence should probably be avoided.

Temperature 25-26° C, lighting moderate.

The aquarium

A minimum tank size of 90 x 40 x 40 cm is suggested for a male and 2-4 females of the Red-Hump group (150 x 50 x 50 for a group of both sexes) or for *Guianacara*; the large eartheaters, *A. heckelii*, and *Retroculus* should be housed in a 120 x 50 x 50 cm or larger tank. A pair of the small *Gymnogeophagus* and *Biotodoma* can be housed in a 75 x 40 x 40 cm tank, but a harem of 2-3 females needs a larger (120 cm long) aquarium.

The substrate should be fine sand, with scattered flat stones in the case of the open-spawners, or with plenty of bogwood, and ceramic pipes or flowerpots as caves, for the cave brooders. *Retroculus* needs small round pebbles for nest-building. It is unkind to attempt to inhibit the foraging behaviour of the eartheaters by having a very coarse substrate or by use of a gravel tidy.

A belt of plants (potted or bordered with large pebbles to deter uprooting) along the back and ends will provide shelter. Clumps of plants in the centre help separate female territories if a harem is kept.

The Red-Hump geophagines are best kept in single species tanks with several males. Not only will this make life easier for females, but males, in the presence of competitors, develop a remarkable red hump. Single males

Feeding

Aquatic invertebrates and crustaceans (live or frozen); good quality flake or small pellets (without mammalian protein). Small or chopped earthworms are much enjoyed.

Breeding

Males of the Red-Hump group are brighter than females at sizes of 8-10 cm and have a red-brown crown or hump; they are ultimately appreciable larger than females. Spawning procedure is remarkably similar to that in African haplochromines. The female does not have a buccopharyngeal pouch, but uses her mouth and gill cavity, spreading her gills to enlarge the volume —the close-packed gill rakers, designed to sift food, prevent the eggs from falling out backwards. Brooding females are usually safe in plant cover but should be isolated if harassed. The fry are released after

16-21 days, and guarded for a further 1-3 weeks.

Adult males of *G. brasiliensis* are larger than females and have longer unpaired fins and a nuchal hump. They prefer a spawning site close to shelter or between rocks. Deformed fry are sometimes a problem (perhaps due to inbreeding, as this species has been in captivity for many years) and meticulous culling is vital.

The other species of *Geophagus* and those of *Satanoperca* show no obvious sexual dimorphism, so sexing must be by examination of the vent (see page 52) or a pair obtained from a group of juveniles (or adults if the tank is large enough). If breeding does not follow automatically from correct maintenance then a drop in pH and an increase in food (especially earthworms) and temperature is usually effective. They are true open-spawners —and as the mouthbrooders are pair-forming (primitive mouthbrooding behaviour) there is no need for concern about post-spawning harassment of brooding females.

Males of mouthbrooding *Gymnogeophagus* are larger and more colourful than females and tend to have a nuchal hump. *Gg. rhabdotus* do not show any difference in coloration prior to spawning, but males are larger and have more pointed unpaired fins. If maintenance is correct no special trigger is needed for spawning. The eggs hatch after a maximum of two days and the larvae are brooded for about a week.

Biotodoma shows no sexual dichromatism, but adult males are larger and have longer unpaired fins, sometimes with significant elongation of upper and caudal rays. The fry of these pit brooding cichlids are initially too small to take *Artemia* nauplii, but in a well-established aquarium will find sufficient micro-organisms to feed on during their first few days.

Neither *Acarichthys* nor *Guianacara* is strongly dimorphic. Males have more developed finnage and are noticeably larger. Initial courtship may be a trifle stormy, but injury is unlikely. The eggs are laid on the side or ceiling of a cave, and tended by the female. *A. heckelii* is often reluctant to breed; a lower pH may help, as may experimentation with pipes buried in the substrate. Given a choice, caves with narrow entrances are preferred. The fry sometimes do not emerge until two weeks after spawning.

Apart from the nest-building mentioned above, nothing is known of the breeding procedure in *Retroculus*.

Unless otherwise stated fry of all groups can take *Artemia* nauplii as a first food. Brood sizes vary from 40 (Red-Hump geophagines) to about 600 in *Geophagus surinamensis*.

Dwarf cichlids

by Kaj Andersen

Apistogramma-group

Apistogramma currently includes about 90 species, which rarely exceed 10 cm total length. They are distributed throughout the Amazon basin, the upper drainages of the Paraguay and Orinoco, and the north-flowing rivers of the Guianas. Because of their size, habitat, and secretive habits, it is likely that many more species remain undiscovered. *Apistogrammoides* (max. size 6 cm) is a monotypic genus found near Pucallpa in Peru. It differs slightly from *Apistogramma* morphologically, but is similar in habitat, behaviour, and requirements.

Behaviour in the wild

Apistogramma are found in small streams —a few metres wide and 10-20 cm deep— and permanent pools in rain forest and savannah. They are even found in potholes in roads at the end of the rainy season, but it is to be assumed that populations left stranded in such temporary waters do not survive. In some pools population density can be astonishingly high, numbering thousands. Some of these waters almost dry up during the dry season, and it seems that only juveniles survive. The substrate is fine sand or gravel overlain with layers of leaf litter and sediment. *Apistogrammas* often hide and breed under dead leaves, and find additional shelter among marginal plants, roots and branches, and sometimes stones, where they are relatively safe from their main enemies —dwarf *Crenicichlas* and juveniles of larger predatory fishes, as well as birds. They are not normally found in large rivers where suitable cover is rare and the current stronger —they prefer still or slow-moving waters. Water chemistry varies from very soft and acid to slightly hard and alkaline; temperature may rise above 30° C during the dry season. They are found in black, white, and clear water.

Behaviour in the aquarium

Apistogramma tend to be shy unless provided with dense cover and "dither fishes" (e.g. small tetras) to give them confidence —it is thought that in nature they hide when the tetras disperse at the approach of danger, and the absence of such fishes in captivity is taken as a cue to remain hidden!

Many species are harem brooders (polygynists) —*A. nijsseni* is a notable exception— with males holding a "super-territory" up to 120 cm in diameter (length, in the aquarium) in which 2-6 females hold their own territories, about 25 cm in diameter and centred on a "cave" (flowerpots or suitably cured coconut shells are preferred). The territorial male defends his territory and "wives", while the latter maintain strict boundaries between their own patches. "Sneak males", with the size and appearance of females, may also hold female-type territories under the protection of the dominant male, and fertilise clutches while the latter is busy seeing off intruders. It is thought that these territorial and breeding patterns mirror wild behaviour.

Some species (e.g. *A. cacatuoides*) are rather short-lived, females in particular living just long enough to raise a brood (sometimes two), i.e. 9-12 months. Others (e.g. *A. nijsseni, A. agassizii*) may live for several years.

The aquarium

Aquarium size should be such as to accommodate the territorial requirements of its occupants, though a single pair can be bred in a tank as small as 40 x 30 x 20 cm deep, as long as they have previously become acquainted in a larger aquarium. A 120 x 45 cm (depth is not critical) aquarium will house a

single 5-6 female harem, or two 2-3 female ones. It is better not to keep more than one male of a species per tank as weaker ones may be killed by the strongest.

The substrate should be sand or gravel fine enough for the female to dig (an important part of breeding behaviour; coarse gravel often results in no breeding) and, if possible, dark-coloured. Caves should be spaced so that they lie at the centres of potential female territories (a group of caves will be seized by a single female); breeding success is more likely with a low "ceiling" and small entrance. Plants in the immediate vicinity provide

Facing page, top: *Apistogramma agassizii* is one of the most popular dwarf cichlids, but needs soft acidic water to prosper.
bottom: a male *Apistogramma bitaeniata*.
This page, top: a male *A. borellii* of a strain called "Opal".
centre: a male *Apistogramma nijsseni*. This species tends to be less polygynous than most other *Apistogramma*.
bottom: a fighting male *A. cacatuoides* of a strain called "Doppel-Rot".
Photos by Ad Konings.

nurseries for fry, and caves thus equipped are chosen in preference to those without. Bogwood or stones can be used to hide flowerpots for aesthetic reasons. Lighting should be moderate or shade provided by floating plants.

Water chemistry requirements vary from species to species —a few (e.g. *cacatuoides, borellii, steindachneri*) can be kept and bred in moderately hard water with a slightly alkaline pH (but, at least in the case of *cacatuoides*, this may result in a predominance of male fry). In general, however, very soft, slightly to extremely (pH < 5) acid water is necessary. The needs of individual species should be researched. A temperature of 26° C is adequate for maintenance and breeding —higher temperatures are unnecessary and life-threatening. Water quality **must** be excellent, but dead leaves, mulm, and algae should be allowed to remain (within reason) to generate micro-organisms for fry to eat. Low-turnover undergravel filtration is ideal for the suggested low population and planted set-up. Currents should be avoided —power filters and powerheads are totally unsuitable.

As well as "dither fishes", tankmates may include other soft water dwarfs if the territorial requirements of all species are respected. They can also be kept and bred successfully with *Pterophyllum* (see p. 217) and *Symphysodon* (p. 219). Catfishes, even *Corydoras*, should **never** be included in *Apistogramma* tanks; they will eat eggs and fry, and the cichlids themselves are competent scavengers.

Feeding

The natural diet includes insects (aquatic and terrestrial) and their larvae, crustaceans, and other invertebrates. In captivity they are best fed live pond foods (not red mosquito larvae), small *Artemia*, and white, grindal, and micro worms. If they have not been "spoiled" by a long-term diet of live food they will readily take frozen foods, cod roe, finely chopped mussel flesh, and flake. A short-term generous diet of live food may help trigger breeding, especially in wild-caught fishes.

Breeding

All known species are sexually dichromatic and/or dimorphic. Females are generally yellow with black markings, and have rounded unpaired fins; males tend to blue-green with more elaborate finnage, sometimes with spots,stripes, or other markings. They are also (ultimately) much larger and sometimes have much bigger mouths. Most can be sexed at 2.5 cm upwards.

Ideally buy juveniles or young adults; in some species fully adult fishes may be near the end of their lifespan. If possible buy from a breeder who does not hatch artificially (see below): If attention is paid to the details given above, breeding should follow without further stimulus once a female is ripe. A water change, followed by a decrease in pH (via peat filtration —peat contains hormones which help stimulate breeding) and rise in temperature, may help in the event of reluctance to spawn.

The male often courts his females continuously; caves with a small entrance permit them to avoid harassment (the larger male cannot get in!), though some females are quite capable of driving him away. When the female is almost ready to spawn she digs a small pit in her cave, using the "spoil" to make the entrance even smaller. Soon afterwards she welcomes the attentions of the male, who courts her with vigorous beats of his tail. She lays her eggs on the ceiling of the cave, while the male remains outside, using further tail-beats to drive his sperm into the cave —better fertilisation occurs if the ceiling is low. Afterwards the female may block the entrance further so that she is trapped inside; when the fry are free-swimming she digs her way out and leads them around her territory. At this stage she will usually not tolerate the presence of the male —if she cannot keep him away he should be removed or he may harm her/eat the fry. In harems females will steal fry from each other at the least opportunity!

A female *Apistogramma* often eats her clutch. If this occurs at the egg stage it may indicate she was hatched artificially and did not learn brood care from her mother (for which reason artificial hatching should be a last resort to establish rare new species, not the matter of course practised by unscrupulous commercial breeders). She may eat her fry if they are too few for there to be a probability of any surviving (in the natural habitat). With only a very short life-span in which to perpetuate her genes she stands a better chance of so doing by "recycling the protein" and trying again, usually after 10-14 days. The longer the fry survive the less likely she is to eat them, even if many are lost, because she has "invested" more time and energy in them than when they were newly hatched. Females signal to their fry using their black markings, in particular the pelvic fins; when danger threatens fry are "told" to rest on the bottom beneath her. I have seen a female *A. trifasciata* eat several fry which ignored her command —but only those few; presumably because disobedient fry are unlikely to survive and not worth tending.

Artemia nauplii can be offered when the fry emerge, but sometimes this food is too large (e.g. in *A. nijsseni*); in an established tank, however, fry will usually find sufficient micro-organisms (particularly if algae and mulm have been allowed to remain) to feed on, so infusorian cultures are unnecessary.

Butterfly cichlids

Microgeophagus ramirezi (max. 7 cm); *M. altispinosa* (max. 15 cm).

M. ramirezi is one of the most popular cichlids for the general community, but in practice requires high quality, soft, acid water to prosper. Aquarium populations are nowadays poorly coloured compared with their wild cousins. *M. altispinosa* ("Bolivian Ram") is far less sensitive and less well known.

Behaviour in the wild

M. altispinosa inhabits calm waters in small streams and at the fringes of larger ones; the substrate consists of mulm, leaves, and tangles of wood. *M. ramirezi* is likewise found in small streams but also occurs in open pools and shallow lagoons where water temperature may rise to 35° C and where sunlight penetrates to the bottom uninterrupted by suspended sediment or vegetation.

The hardness of the water in the natural range of *M. altispinosa* is about 4° DH with a neutral to slightly alkaline pH (7-7.6). *M. ramirezi* is found in water with more extreme values: pH 4.5 and a hardness below 1° DH.

Both species are monogamous open substrate brooders, using stones, roots and branches, or marginal vegetation as spawning sites.

Behaviour in the aquarium

Both species can be kept in a community of small South American species. Both are very peaceful and are easily stressed by the presence of larger or more boisterous fishes. An alternative is to keep these cichlids in a tank by themselves.

Left: A female *Microgeophagus ramirezi* guarding her offspring. The "Ram" can be bred successfully only in soft and acidic water.
Right: *Dicrossus filamentosus*, the checkerboard cichlid, is a very peaceful cichlid best kept in the company of other dwarf cichlids or by itself in a special tank. Photos by Ad Konings.

Aquarium

A tank for *M. altispinosa* should measure 75 x 40 cm, for *M. ramirezi* a 60 x 40 cm aquarium is sufficient. Depth is unimportant in both cases. The rear and ends of the tank should be thickly planted; the centre should have clumps of plants between and behind which small (8 cm diameter) stones can be placed as spawning sites. Some individuals are cave-spawners so a few flowerpots, in similar positions, will not come amiss. Lighting should be muted or shade provided by floating or long-leaved plants.

Small tetras ("dither fishes") and other small peaceful dwarfs are suitable tankmates as long as sufficient territory is available.

The substrate should be fine gravel (2 mm) or coarse sand as these cichlids pass it through their gills in a similar way to other larger earth-eaters such as *Geophagus* and *Satanoperca*.

Temperature should be around 25-26° C (higher temperatures are likely to cause stress). The pH should be close to the values found in the wild (given above). The hardness should be kept above 3° DH (see page 22) unless the tank is under-populated. Water quality should be excellent, with minimal nitrate content. Filtration as for the *Apistogramma*-group.

Feeding

Refer to page 210 and what has been said for *Apistogramma.*

Breeding

Males of *M. ramirezi* are slightly larger than females, and have larger pelvic fins, anterior dorsal spines, and dorsal membranes. Females tend to have a more colourful belly region, even when not breeding. *M. altispinosa* shows similar slight dimorphism.

As mentioned before both species are normally open substrate brooders. The eggs are deposited on a horizontal surface or plant leaf. Spawning is initiated by the female who leads the male to the previously cleaned, chosen site. Ripe females have a red to magenta coloured belly which is displayed to the male. A normal spawn contains about 200 eggs, which will hatch only if the pH is correct. Depending on water temperature the eggs hatch in two to three days and the larvae are then moved to a pit which the pair have dug before. Both parents guard the eggs and fry. Approximately three days after hatching the larvae become free-swimming fry and can be fed with newly hatched *Artemia* nauplii or micro worms. They can stay with their parents until they are about 10 mm long.

M. ramirezi has been bred in captivity many times and it is therefore common to find aberrant individuals among the offspring, the result of inbreeding. Wild caught individuals are available and you should replace one of the parents if the number of runts or "oddities" per brood exceeds 5%.

Checkerboard cichlids

Dicrossus filamentosus (max. 9 cm); *D. maculatus* (max. 9 cm); *Crenicara punctulata* (max. 12 cm).

The checkerboard cichlids are small cichlids with a very mild temperament.

Behaviour in the wild

D. filamentosus inhabits small streams with slowly flowing water in the upper Orinoco drainage. It is found in large numbers swimming in and out of small nooks in the substrate, which is about 50 cm deep and consists of leaf-litter, vegetable debris, and tangles of wood. In this habitat aquatic plants are rare and found only near the banks. *D. maculatus* and *C. punctulata* are thought to occupy similar habitats in the Amazon basin, with a further population of the latter reported from Guiana. The pH varies between 4.5 and 5 and the hardness is usually lower than 1° DH.

Dicrossus and *Crenicara* are open substrate brooders. The ventral fins of female *D. filamentosus* are clear (white) in virgins and turn red shortly before spawning.

Behaviour in the aquarium

All three species are very peaceful and are good companions for *Apistogramma* and other dwarf cichlids. Several males can be kept together in the same tank.

Aquarium

The aquarium should have a capacity of 150 litres and a length of at least 80 cm, and be furnished with an undergravel filter. The substrate should be dark, but do not use lava split as it has sharp edges and may cause gill irritation. The back and sides of the tank should be densely planted with clumps of plants and flat stones (spawning sites) in the central area, as for *Microgeophagus*. Bogwood and flower-pots are optional.

The presence of "dither fishes" will make these cichlids more confident and outgoing. This is particularly important in the case of *C. punctulata*, which is very timid. For the same reason lighting should be muted or shade provided by plants.

The water should have a hardness of about 3° DH, a pH between 4 and 5, and a temperature of about 27° C. Water quality should be excellent, without nitrates. Slow-turnover air-driven undergravel filtration is ideal. Currents and turbulence should be avoided, and power filters are quite unsuitable.

Feeding

In the wild these cichlids feed on tiny food particles of a mainly invertebrate nature. In captivity they need live food to bring them into breeding condition. Brine shrimp, white, grindal, and micro worms, *Cyclops*, and small *Daphnia* are eagerly accepted as are white and black mosquito larvae. Dry and frozen foods are taken readily provided the fishes are accustomed to them at an early age.

Breeding

In *D. filamentosus* the male grows much larger than the female, and has a large lyrate tail and colourful highlights on his flanks. The female has a rounded caudal fin and shows no colour on the flanks apart from the pattern of black blotches. *D. maculatus* exhibits similar dimorphism, except that the tail in males is pointed. Males of *C. punctulata* have elongated unpaired fins, and are larger and more colourful than females. Females, however, have reddish pelvic fins and the lateral blotches are usually bolder.

Dicrossus are best bred in harems, more than one per tank being possible if space permits (the tank size given earlier is suitable for one harem). Spawning is initiated by the female who leads the male to a previously cleaned spawning site. 100 to 150 ivory-coloured eggs are laid. The female positions herself close to the eggs while the male defends the area around the spawning site. If there are no "dither" ("target") fishes present it may be better to remove the male from the tank and leave the care of the offspring to the female. Males sometimes feed on fry when they start to move around the tank. After the eggs hatch, 2 to 3 days after spawning, the larvae are moved frequently to sites (roots or leaves) high up in the aquarium. Six to seven days after spawning the larvae become free-swimming fry and are led through the aquarium by the female. It is important to have newly hatched *Artemia* ready to feed the fry on the first day. About 10 days later they can eat *Cyclops* and tiny *Daphnia*.

C. punctulata is easy to breed. Both parents choose a spawning site, though the female tends to initiate courtship. Brood size is about 150, and the incubation period as for *Dicrossus*. Hatches are often poor —a lower pH would probably remedy this problem. The fry can be fed *Artemia* nauplii as a first food.

It has been reported that if there is no male in a group of *C. punctulata* a female will change sex into a fully functional male. If this male is removed another will develop. BUT, this discovery was made before the existence of "sneak males" in *Apistogramma* came to light, so the sex-changed males may be simply subordinates which become dominant when opportunity arises.

Taeniacara candidi

Taeniacara candidi (max. 7 cm).

Taeniacara is one of the smallest cichlids from South America. It is best kept in a single species tank.

Behaviour in the wild

These tiny cichlids are found in the same types of habitat as *Apistogramma*. Practically nothing is known of their behaviour in nature.

Behaviour in the aquarium

Taeniacara males (and to a lesser extent, females) are extremely intolerant of the presence of conspecifics, and the dominant male will often exterminate all opposition. Even when just a "pair" is left it is not uncommon for the male to hunt out and kill the female.

Aquarium

In general the tank should be set up as for *Apistogramma*, but with modifications. It should be large relative to fish size: 120 cm x 40 cm is not too large for a pair and their offspring. Depth is not important. The tank should be extremely densely planted; tangles of Java Moss are useful in addition to leaf-bearing plants. Given that males may become murderous long before they are fully grown, caves should have tiny entrances in the hope that females will be able to get inside, but their persecutors not. "Target" fishes in the form of tetras, danios, small livebearers, etc. may help divert the male.

Water quality is supremely important —the tiniest traces of metabolic wastes may weaken the fishes and allow bacterial infections to take their toll. Not only ammonia and nitrite but also nitrate should be kept to zero; tap water should be tested prior to water changes and any nitrate removed.

Feeding

These cichlids feed on the smallest of aquatic invertebrates and in captivity prefer live food. Frozen food is sometimes accepted A varied diet is important. Live *Artemia* white, grindal, and micro worms, and, of course, live *Cyclops* and *Daphnia* are a good substitute for the natural diet. Dry food is eaten only if the fishes are accustomed to it from an early age.

Breeding

Males are larger and have more splendid finnage than females. They are also easily identified by their temperament, even at an early age. Ideally start with a single male and as many females as possible, or as many fry as can reasonably be obtained. IF a pair forms then breeding should follow without further trauma as long as conditions and diet are right. Harem polygyny has been reported, but not observed by three successful breeders (Mary Bailey, pers. comm.). The spawning site is the ceiling of the female's chosen cave.

Once a pair have settled they may or may not live in harmony for some time; it is not unknown to find the female dead without warning. One breeder achieved success by leaving fry in the breeding tank until they measured about 2 cm, by which time a further brood had been hatched and was free-swimming. At sizes of more than 2 cm juveniles may be regarded as competition by the male. Fry feed initially on micro-organisms in the well-planted and established tank —the breeder may be unaware that spawning has taken place until they appear from the undergrowth, by which time they are usually large enough to take *Artemia* nauplii or larger foods.

The aquarium

A 60 x 30 x 30 cm aquarium is adequate for a pair. The water should be soft and acid (pH 6.5), with a temperature of about 26° C. Filtration is unnecessary if the tank is well-planted. The substrate should be fine, preferably dark, gravel and the decor consist of thick clumps of plants. *Nannacara* need caves in the form of rocks, flowerpots, or cured coconut shells. Lighting should be moderate unless plants provide plenty of shade. These cichlids can be housed with other soft acid water dwarfs as long as sufficient territorial space is available for all.

Dwarf Acaras

Cleithracara maronii (max. 10 cm); *Laetacara dorsigerus* (max. 8 cm); *L. curviceps* (max. 8 cm); *L. flavilabris* (max. 11 cm); *Nannacara anomala* (max. 8 cm); *N. aureocephala* (max. 11 cm).

Dwarf cichlids related to *Aequidens* rather than to *Apistogramma* or *Microgeophagus.*

Behaviour in the wild

These cichlids are found in still or slow-moving waters, sometimes in marshy areas, with tangles of roots, branches, and marginal plants. The water is soft and acid. *Nannacara* are cave-brooders, normally monogamous though occasionally polygynous. *Laetacara* and *Cleithracara* are pair-forming open-spawners which use a stone, pit, or leaf as substrate.

Behaviour in the aquarium

Nannacara can be scrappy among themselves, but are normally peaceful towards other species. *Laetacara* are peaceful; if water quality is less than perfect they are exceptionally prone to Hexamitiasis (see page 55) and skin parasites. *C. maronii* is completely inoffensive, even when breeding —it is easily intimidated by larger or more boisterous fishes and this should be avoided.

Feeding

Pond foods (live or frozen) are ideal, supplemented with good quality flake.

Breeding

Nannacara males are considerably larger than females, and are differently coloured and patterned. *N. anomala* is easy to breed (even in hard alkaline water) but *N. aureocephala* may require a pH less than 6 to promote successful breeding. *Cleithracara* males have elongated soft dorsal and anal fin-rays, while in females the fin is pointed but not prolonged. This species is unlikely to breed if in any way intimidated by tankmates. *Laetacara* males are larger than females and have longer unpaired fins. It may be necessary to raise the temperature to 27 or 28° C or lower the pH to trigger breeding. The fry of all species can take *Artemia* nauplii as a first food.

Angelfishes

by Mary Bailey and Kaj Andersen

Angelfishes

Pterophyllum scalare (max. 15 cm); *Pt. altum* (max. 18 cm, up to 33 cm deep).

Pterophyllum are thought to be most closely related to *Symphysodon*. In terms of form and finnage they are probably the most bizarre cichlids of all, and certainly the most commonly kept —there can be few general community tanks without at least one Angel. *Pt. scalare* has been in captivity for more than half a century, and the occurrence of "sports" has led to the development of numerous colour varieties as well as types with "veil" finnage. *Pt. altum* is a more recent introduction.

Many Angels sold as altum are very similar to scalare, and are of questionable identity. True *altum* are quite distinct: they have a "nick" in the upper head profile *and* the dorsal and anal fins are much longer in proportion to body size than in comparable scalare.

Behaviour in the wild

Habitat and habits are very similar to those of Discus (p. 219). Angels normally live in shoals (25-30 individuals), with pairs separating off to breed, returning to the shoal with their part grown brood. Breeding is seasonal, coinciding with the inundation when more living/breeding space and an increased food supply is available. The chosen spawning site is off the bottom —a root, branch, or (inundated terrestrial) plant leaf.

The range of *Pt. scalare* encompasses much of the Amazon drainage, where it is found in a variety (chemistry and colour) of types of water. *Pt. altum* is confined to the upper parts of the Orinoco and Rio Negro systems, and is essentially a blackwater species.

The small mouth is extensible, and is used to prey on insects and their larvae, as well as small fishes, in the middle and upper layers of the water. They are said to hunt along the underside of rafts of floating vegetation.

Behaviour in the aquarium

Angels are peaceful fishes, among themselves and towards heterospecifics. They are, however, partially piscivorous and not averse

Facing page: a female *Laetacara flavilabris* guarding her offspring. Photo by Ingemann Hansen.
Right: *Pterophyllum altum* needs a deep tank and soft acidic water.

to the odd neon tetra. They are slow graceful swimmers and it essential that they are not kept with boisterous tankmates. The flowing finnage can be an irresistible temptation even to species which are not normally fin-nippers. Angels do not dig or otherwise harm plants.

The aquarium

A pair of *scalare* can be kept in a 60 x 40 x 40 cm aquarium, but it is far more satisfying to keep a shoal of 5 or 6 in a 120 cm tank. Full-grown specimens really require a depth of 50 cm, and 60 cm or more should be regarded as mandatory for large *altum*.

Aquarium-bred *scalare* will thrive in almost any water chemistry, but soft and slightly acid is preferable. Wild *scalare* (sometimes available) may require more acid conditions and these are essential for *altum*. A temperature of about 26° C is adequate. Lighting should be moderate, or shade provided by floating plants, which are in any case desirable given the native biotope.

The decor should consist of bogwood and some long-leaved plants —although submerse aquatic plants are scarce in the natural habitat, there is plenty of "underwater vegetation" in the flooded forest where these fishes spend much of their time. It is important to leave plenty of swimming space. There should be no filter turbulence.

Suitable tankmates are dwarf cichlids, small tetras (too large to be swallowed), small catfishes, and Discus.

Feeding

"Tame" Angels will pick food from the bottom, but by nature they feed in open water and from the surface. They are thus one of very few cichlids ideally designed to take floating flake! Ideal foods are those which swim —*Daphnia, Cyclops*, mosquito larvae (not red), surplus fish fry. They will chase small worms (earth, white, grindal) down to the bottom, but it is better to use a worm feeder or to hand feed with individual worms. Do not feed any of your fishes *Tubifex*! Prepared foods are taken, but it is important to make sure that any sinking food is eaten, especially if no other fishes are present.

Breeding

This is where most problems are encountered. Firstly Angels are quite unsexable until they breed. Then males develop a small scaly hump, more pronounced when competing males are present. The best method of obtaining a pair is to maintain a small shoal.

The second huge problem is that man has succeeded, by dint of generations of unselective captive breeding (often using artificial hatching), in creating a race of *scalare* which has little idea of proper breeding procedure. A pair tank-bred *scalare* that rear their own fry is a rarity. **It is vital** that the same mistakes are not made with wild *scalare* and *altum*; we must avoid artificial hatching and select for proper parental care.

Spawning is initiated by the female. The eggs are laid on a vertical surface —a root or a leaf. Broods vary from 100 to 350 eggs. If no male is present females may "pair", as in some other South American cichlids (see page 192). If fry are "achieved" then commonly heavy losses are reported by inexperienced breeders. These may be caused by using inbred stock, but usually seem to result from starvation. Fry need *Artemia* nauplii and micro worms from the first moment they are free-swimming. Do not feed them liquid food or infusorians.

No details are available on the captive breeding of *Pt. altum*.

Discus

by Dirk Ottlik

Discus

Symphysodon (max. 20 cm).

To my mind the Discus (*Symphysodon*) is by far the most charming cichlid, and one which has appeal for aquarists all over the world despite conflicting reports on its maintenance and breeding requirements. Hobbyists and professional breeders alike have contributed to the mystique which surrounds this cichlid in a way not seen in any other well-known or popular aquarium fish. Contrary to popular opinion the maintenance of Discus is not an enigmatic secret known to just a few; it is simply a case of taking into consideration a few basic principles which can be deduced from the natural environment.

Behaviour in the wild

Symphysodon inhabit the slow-flowing, soft acid waters of the Amazon drainage. They are shoaling fishes and are frequently found in small groups among the tangles of roots and branches of fallen trees. They occur in all kinds of water —black, white, and clear— but always in slow-flowing or even still water.

Their natural food consists of insects and their larvae, crustaceans and other invertebrate prey.

Behaviour in the aquarium

Simulation of the natural habitat —decor as well as chemistry— is the best approach to keeping Discus healthy. It is advisable to keep at least 5 or more adult or 8 or more juvenile Discus in the same tank. Adult Discus are very peaceful among themselves and tolerant of other species as well. Juveniles will sometimes chivvy the smallest of their group until it stops feeding and dies, and then pick the next smallest, and so on —sometimes until only one is left. This is most common in small groups with no companion fishes to distract them. It must be stressed that boisterous and/or piscivorous species should not be kept with Discus. Good companion fishes are catfishes of the family Loricariidae, but one should stick to the smaller species. Dwarf cichlids can also be kept with Discus and are recommended to enliven the bottom area of the tank. Small and gentle tetras, which are too large to be swallowed, can be added as well. Try to avoid species which may dominate Discus. A Discus aquarium should never have a crowded appearance.

Aquarium

A Discus aquarium should have a capacity of at least 200 litres, but larger is better. A depth of 45 cm or more is desirable for adults. Smaller tanks may be used for breeding or for growing on juveniles.

The water chemistry should be similar to that found in the wild, i.e. the pH should be between 5.8 and 6.8 and the temperature between 28° and 30° C (temperatures in the rainy season are known to be lower —25-26° C; when not breeding Discus it is better to maintain them at about 26° C which is much less stressful). Refer to page 22 for how to lower the pH. The hardness and conductivity (a measure of the amount of dissolved minerals) are of minor importance. It is advisable to keep Discus in water with a hardness between 3° and 15° DH. When preparing soft water one should be careful not to lower the carbonate hardness below 3° DH because at such low levels the nitrification process is impaired and you may rapidly experience high nitrate and nitrite values which are very detrimental to the fishes' health (see also pages 21-22).

The lighting should be subdued. Open swimming space as well as cover should be available —roots or bogwood suspended from the top or flat stones leaned against the rear glass. These deep-bodied fishes should be able to station themselves under cover. The substrate should be dark and not too coarse; sand or gravel with a maximum diameter of about 3 mm is appropriate.

Plants are absent from the natural biotope but some may be used in the aquarium. Not all plants can tolerate the high temperatures required for breeding, but *Echinodorus* species may be included in the decor.

Feeding

Most Discus die because they are fed the wrong food! Because of their popularity and their high prices, numerous special Discus foods and preparations are produced. Most, however, contain beef heart, milk products, or other products from warm blooded animals. As has been stressed throughout this book: **do not feed beef heart or other products from warm blooded animals to your fishes!** They simply cannot process the fats from these products, which instead accumulate in their livers. Before you buy any prepared food carefully examine the ingredients list on the packet (see page 34).

One of the best prepared foods one can give to Discus is the shrimp-mix described on page 35. Frozen white and black mosquito larvae (no red larvae!), *Cyclops, Daphnia*, and *Artemia* are also recommended. Earthworms are relished by Discus. Flake and pellets are usually accepted as food but are not sufficient to bring these fishes into breeding condition.

Breeding

The first problem one encounters when starting with Discus is where to buy good stock. Discus are tremendously popular and

Right: Discus (*Symphysodon aequifasciata* is shown here) are extremely popular and many different strains have been developed by professional breeders. One should, however, not forget that these fishes come from slow-flowing waters and should be kept in acid, but not necessarily soft, water. The most common problem in keeping these charming cichlids is their loss of appetite, due mainly to the feeding of beef heart or other products from warm blooded animals or stress resulting from incorrect environment.
Facing page: Rio Amazonas near Leticia, a natural habitat of Discus. Photo by Frank Warzel.

they have been bred and inbred for 30 to 40 generations. Although they are available in almost any pet shop one should restrict oneself to buying Discus in specialist shops or directly from breeders. Discus, and in particular wild-caught Discus, in the dealer's tanks should react alertly to their environment. Fishes skulking in a corner of a bare tank, or showing dark coloration, should be left in the shop. It is advised that, when you want to start with Discus, you obtain tank-raised individuals. It is important to bear in mind that all individuals of one brood should be of approximately the same size. Uneven growth is a sign of inadequate maintenance and/or inadequate culling. Buying your fishes from a breeder gives you the opportunity to observe the other broods, the parents of the fishes you want to buy, and the general quality of aquarium maintenance.

After you have obtained the fishes it is a good idea to keep them in quarantine for at least one month (see page 59), even when they are tank-raised. In fully furnished tanks newly introduced Discus hide behind the decor, making it difficult to feed them and monitor their health. In a bare quarantine tank —no substrate or shelter— healthy Discus quickly recognise their owner and lose their initial shyness.

Distinguishing between the sexes is difficult and possible only by examining the vents (by an expert). Usually pairs form from the group in the community aquarium and spawning may occur here as well. The eggs are laid on a slanting or vertical surface —bogwood, slate, plant leaves, or a specially designed clay cone. Broods vary from 200 to 400 eggs which are guarded by both parents. Fry need to feed on the mucus secretions of their parents' skin. Only after a few weeks can they be fed additionally (twice a day) with brine shrimp nauplii and microworms.

The *Crenicichla* group

by Frank Warzel

Large *Crenicichla*

Large *Crenicichla* species are predatory cichlids which are best kept in pairs or together with other large and robust cichlids.

Behaviour in the wild

The food spectrum of these *Crenicichla* is much more diversified than has been assumed previously. It ranges from insects and their larvae, crustaceans, and snails to fish. Some species have developed a remarkable specialisation in respect of their feeding behaviour. *C. cyclostoma* appears to feed solely on caddis fly larvae, whereas *C. jurubi*, a species from the Rio Uruguay, is specialised on small snails and crustaceans. Most species of this group, however, feed on tetras or small cichlids whenever they can catch them by stalking. *C. cametana, C. jegui, C. percna*, and *C.* sp. "Xingú I" are predatory species feeding almost exclusively on fish. The different hunting techniques employed by these piscivores are related to the preferred habitats of the particular species. An excellent swimmer, such as *C.* sp. "Xingú I", chases its prey in mid-water, whereas an ambush hunter, such as *C. cametana*, hides under stones and rocky ledges waiting for prey to swim by. *C. jegui* and *C. percna* are bottom-oriented ambush hunters which may rely on their cryptic coloration when approaching their prey.

These large *Crenicichla* live a mostly solitary life. Juveniles of at least some large species (such as *C. marmorata* and *C.* sp. "Xingú I") are normally found in large groups still guarded by their parents.

Behaviour in the aquarium

When more two or more species of *Crenicichla* are to be kept in the same aquarium they should be of approximately the same size. The juveniles and young adult individuals of species which have longitudinal stripes on the flanks can be kept together but subadults of most other *Crenicichla* can be very pugnacious towards each other. In order to prevent losses such species should be reared separately or in sparsely decorated but densely populated aquaria. By contrast sexually mature individuals are usually unproblematical when kept as a pair. The combination of several *Crenicichla* species in the same aquarium is possible. In such cases one should house together species in which the basic coloration is as different as possible. This is, however, a general rule; individual differences may call for a re-arrangement of the aquarium population.

Because of their predominantly piscivorous appetite small cichlids (smaller than half the size of the largest *Crenicichla*) should not be kept in the same aquarium.

Aquarium

The space the different species need depends on their temperament and adult size. Placid species like *C. geayi* or *C. semifasciata* and also the smaller species such as *C. cyclostoma* are satisfactorily kept in tanks with a capacity of about 250 litres. Other species need much larger aquaria just because of their large adult size. *C. jegui*, which is mostly seen hiding beneath stones, needs a large open area on the bottom of the tank.

Strong movement of the water appears to be beneficial to the well-being of *Crenicichla* and seems to improve their motivation to breed as well.

Feeding

Although most *Crenicichla* are piscivores you do not need to feed them with live fishes. All species which have been kept in aquaria

Large *Crenicichla*	max. size in cm	leaf litter	shaded banks	rocks/ pebbles	mid-water	calm water	flowing water	small streams	large rivers
C. cametana	30			■			■		■
C. cyclostoma	16			■			■		■
C. geayi	20		■			■		■	
C. jegui	30			■			■		■
C. lepidota	25		■			■	▒	■	▒
C. marmorata	40		■		▒	■			■
C. percna	35			■		▒	■		■
C. saxatilis	25		■	▒		■	▒	■	▒
C. semifasciata	25		■			■		■	▒
C. sp. "Xingú I"	40			▒	■		■		■

have accepted frozen foods. Besides frozen fish (whole or minced), shrimps or shrimp mix is eagerly taken as well. Smaller sized foods like black and white mosquito larvae, *Mysis* or other crustaceans are a good alternative. *Crenicichla* hunts in mid-water but also on the bottom. Flake food or pelleted food is not recommended.

Breeding

All known large *Crenicichla* are monogamous, and pairs, at least in captivity, stay together even when no eggs or offspring are being defended. It is sometimes possible, in particular after a major water change (more than 50%), that marital strife may result in a less favourable situation for the female which is normally smaller and dominated by the male. One should have the means available to separate the pair while leaving them in the same aquarium. In the case of a quarrel the male can be put for a few days inside a perforated container (see page 18).

The eggs are almost always fixed to the ceiling of a cave, which is near the bottom and enlarged by the excavating activities of the female. In particular species of the *Batrachops*-group (*Batrachops* was formerly regarded as a separate genus, but is now included in *Crenicichla*, where it forms a discrete group), such as *C. geayi, C. semifasciata, C. cametana*, etc., need a thick layer of substrate in which they can excavate their nests. These species, together with species of the *C. saxatilis*-group (such as *C. lepidota*), belong to those *Crenicichla* which are relatively easy to breed.

The pH of the water should be below 7 in order to prevent the deterioration of the eggs. Moreover males can become rather destructive when the eggs do not develop into larvae.

The differences between the sexes in adult *Crenicichla* is relatively simple to determine. Females are normally fuller and appear to have a deeper body than males. A more pronounced difference exists in the breeding coloration of the individual species. Females of the *Batrachops*-group have a red or orange-red band in the dorsal fin whereas in females of the *C. saxatilis*-group this fin shows conspicuous markings or round blotches. Females of the very large species show a light-coloured or sometimes white outer edge to the dorsal fin.

The breeding in captivity of the other large *Crenicichla* has been only partly successful. As far as I know only *C. marmorata* has been bred successfully. The differences in water

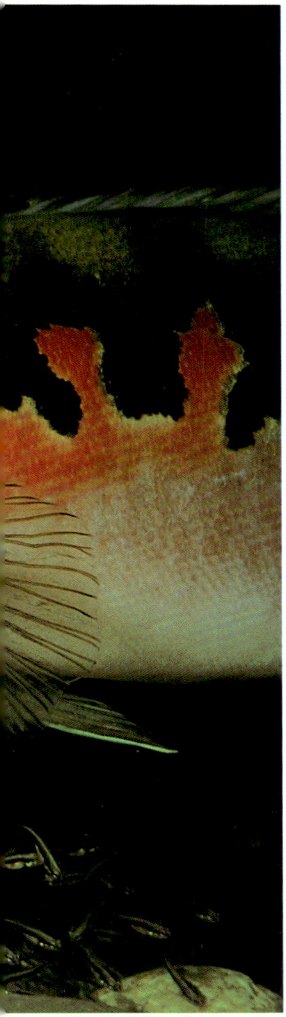

Large photo left: A female *C. marmorata* guarding her two-day old offspring. Inset: Juveniles at an age of approximately 10 weeks. *Crenicichla* juveniles with such horizontal markings can be kept in groups without problems.
Bottom left: A pair *C. geayi* guarding their free-swimming fry.
Top: A sub-adult male *C. lepidota*
Centre: A female *C. semifasciata* in breeding dress.
Bottom: A pair *C. percna* (male below). Photos by Frank Warzel.

chemistry values and food (on one occasion the pair was fed live fish exclusively) may be important factors in the harmonisation of a pair. The water should be soft and have a pH below 7. Spawns of my *C. marmorata* only developed when the pH during spawning was below 6. At a pH of 5.3 (and conductivity of 260 µS/cm at 28 °C) about 95% of the eggs hatched. Under these conditions it takes about 10 days before the larvae become free-swimming fry.

Many species in the group of large *Crenicichla* have never been bred in captivity; some highly specialised species, such as *C. jegui*, have not yet even been paired.

The spawn size of the large *Crenicichla* ranges from 200 to 400 eggs.

Dwarf *Crenicichla*

The dwarf *Crenicichla* are a heterogeneous group consisting at present of 11 species. The aquarium requirements of some of these cichlids are rather different from that of the others.

Behaviour in the wild

The *Crenicichla* species listed in this section show a wide variation in their habitat preferences even though they are all closely related. They can be divided into two categories. One group, with *C. heckeli, C. urosema, and C. compressiceps,* represents those species which prefer the fast flowing waters. The other group consists of non-specialised species and includes *C. notophthalmus* and *C. regani*. Juveniles and sub-adult individuals live solitary, adults are sometimes found in pairs. Breeding territories are defended by both male and female as long as no fry are present, but when offspring are there this task is completely taken over by the male. *C. notophthalmus* and *C. regani* show relatively slow swimming behaviour and are often found hiding under leaf litter, roots, or dead wood. They avoid sites with increased water flow.

The rheophilic species *C. compressiceps, C. heckeli*, and *C. urosema* are active swimmers and appear to have much larger feeding territories than the species of the non-specialised group. They are strongly bottom-oriented and are usually found near rocks or among the rubble of the bottom. In this respect *C. heckeli* is the most specialised of this group. In the wild almost all *C. heckeli* observed are considerably smaller than the maximum size of 7 cm.

Behaviour in the aquarium

It is possible to house different dwarf

Crenicichla species in the same aquarium. Such a tank should contain ample shelter and the *Crenicichla* species should be approximately the same size in order to prevent interspecific aggression. All *Crenicichla* are strongly territorial and mercilessly chase subordinated individuals. This is especially true of the rheophilic species which, for this reason, are not recommended to aquarists starting with this kind of cichlid. But *C. notophthalmus* and *C. regani* likewise show no hesitation in defending their territorial possessions against conspecific competitors. The latter two species need soft and acidic water, a point which should be taken into consideration when keeping them with other cichlids. After a pair of these species has established a bond and taken possession of a territory they hardly ever venture into other parts of the aquarium.

Aquarium

As for most strongly territorial species the longer the aquarium the better. A well-harmonised pair need an aquarium with a capacity of about 100 litres. In order to imitate the natural environment, in particular that of the rheophilic species, the aquarium should be decorated with rocks and the substrate should be sand or fine gravel. Heaps of rocks form the centres of the territories. Open sandy areas are usually accepted as the borders. If subordinated individuals need additional shelter then the aquarium can be planted.

Feeding

C. compressiceps, *C. heckeli*, and *C. urosema* are predatory species. In the wild they feed on small crustaceans and insect larvae which are found mainly in the nooks and crannies of the rocks. *C. notophthalmus* and *C. regani* are at least partially piscivorous. They feed on small fishes as well as on invertebrates. Their mouths, however, are relatively small in comparison with those of other *Crenicichla*.

The feeding of dwarf *Crenicichla* in captivity should not be a problem. They accept all kinds of frozen foods which are not too big for their mouths. *Mysis, Cyclops, Daphnia*, shrimp mix (page 35), mosquito larvae (avoid feeding red larvae), and *Artemia*. The most gluttonous species of the group is *C. compressiceps* which may even fill its stomach with tiny *Artemia* nauplii. Dry food is not recommended.

Breeding

It is not necessary to try and match a pair or to wait until a pair has formed from a group of these cichlids. Fully mature females are normally in breeding condition and, in particular in the case of those species which have spots in the dorsal fin, become very attractive to mature males. In such cases the male, which usually is the larger of the two, should be introduced to the female after she has adjusted herself to the aquarium, and not the other way around.

The sex of mature dwarf *Crenicichla* is simple to determine. Female *C. compressiceps* lack the vertical stripes in the tail while females of the other species are characterised by the conspicuous markings in the dorsal fin. Only *C. urosema* seems to lack such sexual differences, at least in the case of the variant from the Rio Tapajos.

All *Crenicichla* are cave brooders and it is therefore recommended that they be provided with suitable spawning sites. Coconut shells (must be properly cured; see page 10) cut in half form excellent spawning caves especially when the entrance is large enough to allow entry by the female but is too small for the male. The female is able to fan the male's milt into the cave so that it is not necessary for the male to enter. When such spawning caves

Dwarf *Crenicichla*	max. size in cm	leaf litter	shaded banks	rocks/ pebbles	mid-water	calm water	flowing water	small streams	large rivers
C. compressiceps	8								
C. heckeli	7								
C. notophthalmus	12								
C. regani	14								
C. urosema	10								
C. sp. cf. *regani*	9								

Facing page, centre: At least six different *Crenicichla* species are found in the Río Inirida; here near Puerto Inirida.
Photo left: A female *C. regani* (Tocantins) guarding her three-days old fry.
Top: A male *C. compressiceps* defending his territory.
Centre: A female *C. notophthalmus*.
Bottom: A male *C. notophthalmus*. Photos by Frank Warzel.

are not provided the female may choose to spawn in narrow sites under bogwood. The rheophilic *Crenicichla*, however, prefer to spawn under stones, in particular large flat stones, under which the female excavates the nest.

Water chemistry requirements depend on the species. At pH 7 the eggs of *C. compressiceps* may hatch normally, while spawns of *C. notophthalmus, C. regani*, and *C.* sp. aff. *regani* will not. The pH for these species should be below 6, for *C. notophthalmus* even below 5. With an increase of the pH above the recommended value the number of eggs that deteriorate increases as well. The spawns of the rheophilic species range between 30 and 60 eggs whereas those of the other species, which do not live in fast flowing water, contain between 80 and 200.

Teleocichla	max. size in cm	leaf litter	shaded banks	rocks/ pebbles	mid-water	calm water	flowing water	small streams	large rivers
T. cinderella	14			■			■		■
T. gephyrogramma	7			■			■		■
T. monogramma	9			■			■		■
T. proselytus	10			■		▒	■		■
T. prionogenys	9			■			■		■
T. sp. "Xingú I"	10			■			■		■
T. sp. "Xingú II"	16			■			■		■

Teleocichla

This group contains small, rheophilic cichlids which are very elongated and have a predominantly bottom-oriented behaviour.

Behaviour in the wild

All species known live in the clear waters of mainly large rivers which have their origin either in the central highlands of Brazil or in the eastern Guyana mountain range. The main characteristics of these rivers are a sandy or rocky bottom and large rock-formations with cascades and rapids. Despite the fact that *Teleocichla* species are well-adapted to life in fast flowing water, they seem to avoid rivulets feeding the main river. On the other hand I was able to find them in places where one would not expect such highly specialised cichlids. We found *T. proselytus* in the Tapajos drainage system, not only in the rocky rapids, but also over sand in shallow water near sandy beaches.

Irrespective of the ecological circumstances, adaptation to a bottom-oriented existence is clearly shown by all *Teleocichla*. Besides a reduced swim-bladder all *Teleocichla* possess long strong pelvic fins which are used as supports when they rest on the bottom. Because of their length the head is raised well above the substrate. Some species are able to hold the pectoral fins in a position such that the fish is pressed against the bottom, thus relieving it from the need for continuous movement against the flow.

Feeding behaviour has not yet been observed in the wild, but the laterally compressed and pointed mouth, the lower jaw of which is longer than the upper, is characteristic of predators which pick their prey from the substrate. In this case the food of *Teleocichla* may consist of small crustaceans, insect larvae, and tiny snails.

Teleocichla appear to live in small groups although individualistic behaviour within such groups suggests that they consist of territorial and solitary individuals. Only one species, *T.* sp. "Xingú I", was observed displaying schooling behaviour.

Behaviour in the aquarium

Observations in the natural environment are confirmed by behaviour in the aquarium: *Teleocichla* are solitary and show an inclination to chase other, predominantly conspecific, cichlids. Fortunately their aggression is restricted to short chases after which the dominated individual is left alone. Adult females, however, are able to dominate larger males. The degree of aggression depends on the species and on the population density in the aquarium. *T. gephyrogramma* and *T. monogramma* are strongly territorial species and should be maintained as pairs in the aquarium. *T. proselytus* or *T.* sp. "Xingú I", however, can be kept in small groups. Only species which are not in direct competition in claiming territories can be housed with *Teleocichla*.

Aquarium

Small to medium-sized aquaria with a capacity of at least 150 litres are recommended. They should have as large as possible a bottom area. The height of the tank is of minor importance. The sandy bottom should include small stones, pebbles, and coarse gravel in order to imitate the rock-strewn substrates of the natural habitat. Solitary rocks on the sandy substrate are normally accepted as territorial boundaries. A strong current produced by a power filter (power head) is recommended but not essential.

Feeding

Teleocichla is specialised to feed on small food particles and should therefore be fed with small items. Frozen or live *Cyclops, Daphnia, Bosmina, Artemia*, or mosquito larvae (no red larvae) are recommended. Tiny, live *Artemia* nauplii are eagerly accepted and may keep them busy feeding for the rest of the day. The food is normally picked from the bottom. Dry food is not accepted.

Breeding

Teleocichla species are rarely imported, thus information about their breeding requirements is restricted to the few successful spawnings achieved so far. In one case a *T. proselytus* male was kept together with three females (and no other fishes) in a breeding aquarium which measured 100 x 60 x 40 cm. The bottom substrate consisted of a 5 cm-deep layer of a mixture of sand and pebbles on top of which lay several flat stones and pebbles of various sizes. The water was filtered over sponge (see page 27) at a turnover rate of about 800 l/hr. The water quality was adjusted to match the natural values of about 150 µS/cm, pH 6.3, and a temperature of 28° C. Each female —all three females were the same size— occupied a territory in the centre of which she had excavated a nest under a stone. The male spawned with all three females with a period of 2-3 weeks between spawnings. A strong pair bond, such as is normally seen in *Crenicichla*, their closest relatives, was not observed. A difference was observed in the number, size, and incubation period of the eggs as well. It took about two weeks before the *Teleocichla* fry emerged from the brooding cave. This is about six days longer than is the case in dwarf *Crenicichla*. The free-swimming *T. proselytus* fry had a length of about 9 mm and showed much more independent behaviour than fry of dwarf *Crenicichla*.

The first spawns contained about 30 fry whereas later spawns from the same females numbered between 5 and 10 fry. The fry were easily raised with *Artemia* nauplii. After about three to four weeks, sometimes later, the female starts to chase the fry from the brooding site and prepare herself for the next spawning.

Large photo left: A female *T. proselytus* (TL 5 cm) guarding her fry two days after they began to swim free. The female was collected in the Rio Tapajos, about 30 km south of Alter do Chão.
Photo bottom previous page: A male *T. proselytus* with a length of about 7 cm from Cachoeira Barburé near Pimentel, Rio Tapajos, Brazil.
Top: An adult female *T. cinderella* (TL 8 cm) from Rio Araguaia, Brazil
Centre above: A juvenile *T. cinderella* from Rio Araguaia.
All photos by Frank Warzel.

Asian cichlids

by Mary Bailey

Etroplus	total length in cm.	biotope
Etroplus maculatus	10	Brackish lagoons and estuaries, sometimes in fresh water lakes
E. suratensis	45	Estuaries and brackish coastal lagoons

Etroplus are the only truly Asian cichlids (a few tilapiines have, however, infiltrated the Middle East from Africa), being found in the coastal regions of Sri Lanka and Southern India. The genus is morphologically quite distinct from other cichlids, and probably became geographically separated from the rest of the family at an early date. The two species are sympatric and are often referred to as Chromides. *E. suratensis* is much prized as a food fish in its natural range.

Behaviour in the wild

Etroplus are common in their habitat, which they share with other non-cichlid estuarine species as well as (mainly juvenile) marine fishes. The waters they inhabit are richly vegetated with *Halophila ovata* and other species of "sea-grass", which play an important role in their ecology. When breeding *E. suratensis* clears this vegetation from its selected site, then digs a pit up to 120 cm in diameter and usually 5-10 cm deep. The eggs are sometimes laid on an adjacent substrate (plant leaves, a rock, or a mangrove root/branch), sometimes on the nodular roots of the sea-grass protruding from the sides of the pit. Although territories are isolated multiparental care of fry has been observed, with up to 6 adults merging their broods and guarding them, the largest pair taking the lead and the other adults acting as outriders.

E. maculatus holds a much smaller territory (45 cm diameter) in slightly shallower water (typically no deeper than 50 cm, and often only a few centimetres deep) and is so numerous that large areas of the vegetated bottom are occupied by adjacent territories. It digs a much smaller nest than its congener, and spawns on overhanging leaves, often a mere 3 mm wide. This requires considerable accuracy in egg-deposition —the more so as the leaves move with the current— which is achieved by lowering the pelvic fins until these contact the leaf, guiding the female along its length.

E. suratensis breeds during the dry season when the water is at its clearest (during the monsoons it is turbid with silt) and most saline (30 ppt). *E. maculatus* breeds non-seasonally; it continues parental care until its offspring are themselves almost mature, and this restricts the number of broods per year. Seasonal variation in conditions may be considerable: temperature 27-33 °C; pH 8.5-9.0; salinity 5-30 ppt (the second figure in each case being for the dry season).

Sea-grass is also important as shelter for the relatively small *E. maculatus* and for juveniles of *E. suratensis*, shoals of which have been seen to "vanish" as a result of each individual positioning itself head-up alongside a separate plant leaf. In adults of both species coloration is cryptic —the stripes of *E. suratensis* allow it to hide among plants, while *E. maculatus* is well-camouflaged against the sand when it ventures out from shelter.

E. suratensis is herbivorous, feeding largely on algae. *E. maculatus* is an opportunistic carnivore with a variety of food resources. Apart from aquatic organisms it will prey on the eggs and fry of other *Etroplus* of either species, and it maintains a symbiotic cleaner-fish relationship with *E. suratensis*, removing fungus and parasites. The habit of *E.*

suratensis spawning on grass roots, which are set with egg-like parasitic galls, appears to provide an effective camouflage against predation by bands of non-breeding *E. maculatus*. In addition both adults continuously guard the nest, presumably for the same reason, while in *E. maculatus* the parents take turns to guard or forage; the closeness of their vigorously defended territories probably affords extra protection against marauders.

Juveniles of both species "glance", i.e. feed on the parental mucus covering. It is thought that this contacting not only provides food in the early stages, but latterly reinforces the bond between parents and young, perhaps preventing parental cannibalism in *E. maculatus*. The long period of brood care in this species is probably necessary to ensure genetic continuance given the high risk of conspecific predation. *E. suratensis* fry are likewise tended until they are too large to be eaten by *E. maculatus*.

Behaviour in the aquarium

In captivity *E. maculatus* can be scrappy towards conspecifics, but generally ignores other fishes, including cichlids. It is territorial when breeding, which it does readily and frequently —up to 12 broods per year may be produced if the fry are removed at an early stage, as may be necessary due to considerations of space. More than one pair can be kept per tank if there is sufficient space. It will thrive in fresh water as well as brackish as long as hardness and pH are relatively high.

E. suratensis is often kept as juveniles of up to 6-8 cm, but is rarely grown to adulthood and bred; apparently through failure to provide correct water conditions and/or diet or sufficiently large accommodation. Without a degree of salinity it will rapidly ail and die. It is rather peaceful for a fish of its size. It can be kept with its smaller congener or with other salt-tolerant species (among cichlids this means some tilapiines; those Central American cichlasomines which sometimes occur in brackish conditions are probably too aggressive).

Both species have a tendency to dig multiple pits when breeding in captivity, whereas in the wild a single pit per pair is the norm. Otherwise, where conditions allow, captive behaviour resembles that in the wild state.

Aquarium

E. maculatus can be kept as single pair in a small aquarium; as part of a cichlid or non-cichlid community; in a monospecific group; or with *E. suratensis* in a large tank. The territorial requirement of approximately 45 cm diameter per pair should be borne in mind; in effect as long as this amount is allowed per pair in terms of tank length the tank width is immaterial.

E. suratensis requires a large tank for even a single adult pair —at least 120 x 60 x 60 cm. A degree of salinity is essential (at least 2 gm sea salt per litre (10 gm/gallon UK; 8 gm/gallon US)), as is a high degree of oxygenation.

The substrate should ideally be of fine gravel or coarse sand, but its composition does not appear to be critical. Cover for *E. maculatus* should be provided by plants (especially those with long strap-like leaves, e.g. *Vallisneria*), If saline conditions are to be used then the plants should be acclimatised gradually before fishes are added. Plastic plants should be used for *E. suratensis* (which is liable to eat real ones) with additional cover provided by well-cured bogwood and roots. *E. maculatus*, like many cichlids, has proved more than happy to occupy flowerpots! Isolated rocks and stones may be included in the decor. A temperature range of 26-27 °C will suit both species for normal maintenance. *E. suratensis* does not thrive at lower temperatures.

Feeding

E. suratensis should be fed on vegetable matter or vegetarian dried foods.

E. maculatus can be fed aquatic *Daphnia* and *Cyclops*, unwanted fry or minced fish, shrimp (including *Artemia*), and dried foods (with no mammalian protein). In tune with its natural habits, cod (or other fish) eggs are relished.

Only small quantities of food are required each day by adult fishes, although neither species appears prone to the problems of obesity seen in some other cichlids.

Breeding

Normal maintenance conditions will usually suffice for breeding, but an increase in temperature and salinity may act as a trigger for reluctant pairs.

E. suratensis needs to measure about 15 cm before it is large enough to breed; it is a slow-growing species and takes upwards of 18 months to attain sexual maturity. It shows no external sexual differences (except that males are larger) and must be sexed by examination of the vent (which should be undertaken only by an expert in this technique). Alternatively a group may be grown on together and allowed to pair. It prefers vertical spawning sites. Spawns may number upwards of 500 eggs.

E. maculatus is mature at sizes of 4 cm or so (attained at an age of 4-6 months). Males are larger and females have white markings on the upper and lower edges of the caudal, most marked when actually breeding. 100 or more eggs may be laid during a spawning, and any available surface used as the substrate. Where several adults are present re-pairing with different individuals may occur between spawnings, and in the absence of a male females may "pair".

Both species court (frontal and lateral display, nipping, jaw-locking) for several days before spawning. The eggs hatch after 72 hours at 26-27° C and are free swimming after a further 5 days. Fry should be left with the parents for as long as space allows, as their growth rate appears to benefit from their feeding on parental mucus. The first few broods are sometimes subject to die-off, and this may be due to failure of young adults to produce sufficient mucus.

Right: In their natural habitat *Etroplus maculatus* (smaller fish at the bottom) maintains a symbiotic cleaner-fish relationship with *E. suratensis* (larger fishes). However, it also feeds on the eggs and fry of the larger herbivore.

References

AKIYAMA, T., KAJUMULO, A. & OLSEN, S. (1977). *Bull. Fresh. Fish. Res. Lab.* 27; pp 49-60.

AMLACHER, E. (1970) *Textbook of Fish Diseases.* TFH Publications. pp 183-185.

BARDIN, T. (1983) A la recherche des cichlidés endémiques de Madagascar. *Rev. fr. Cichlid* (French Cichl. Assn.) 29; pp 21-34.

CARLUS, J. (1991) *Paratilapia polleni. Rev. fr. Cichlid* (French Cichl. Assn.) 113; pp 24-28.

CATALA, R. (1977) Poissons d'eau douce de Madagscar. *Rev. fr. Aquariol.* 1; pp 27-32.

FERGUSON, H.W., ROSENDAL, S. & GROOM, S. (1985) *Vet. Rec.* 116: pp 687-89.

GOLDSCHMIDT, T., WITTE, F. & De Visser, J. (1990) *Oikos,* 58; pp 343-355.

GREENWOOD, P.H. (1959a) *Bull. Br. Mus. nat. Hist. (Zool.)* 5 (7); pp 179-218.

GREENWOOD, P.H. (1960) *Bull. Br. Mus. nat. Hist. (Zool.)* 6(4); pp 227-281.

GREENWOOD, P.H. (1965) *Proc. Linn. Soc. Lond.* 176; pp 1-10.

GREENWOOD, P.H. (1967) *Bull. Br. Mus. nat. Hist. (Zool.)* 15(2); pp 29-119.

GREENWOOD, P.H. (1974) *Bull. Br. Mus. nat. Hist. (Zool.)* Suppl. 6.

GREENWOOD, P.H. & GEE, J.M. (1969) *Bull. Br. Mus. nat. Hist. (Zool.)* 18 (1); pp 1-65.

HERRMANN, H.-J. (1987) *Die Buntbarsche der Alten Welt; Tanganjikasee.* Hobbing Verlag, Essen, Germany.

HOOFT, J. 't (1986) Het reophiele geslacht *Orthochromis. NVC-periodiek* (Dutch Cichlid Assn.) 12(5).

KIENER, A. (1963) *Publ. Centre Techn. Forest. Trop.* 24; pp 1-224.

KONINGS, A. (1990) *Cichlids and all the other fishes of Lake Malawi.* TFH Publ. Neptune, USA.

KONINGS, A. & DIECKHOFF, H.W. (1992) *Tanganyika secrets.* Cichlid Press, St. Leon-Rot. Germany.

KUWAMURA, T. (1986) *Physiol. Ecol. Japan,* 23, pp 31-43.

LIEBERS, V. (1991) Allergien durch Fischfutter. *DCG-Info* (German Cichl. Assn.) 22 (6); pp 141-142.

LINKE, H. & STAECK, W. (1981) *Afrikanische Cichliden I. Buntbarsche aus Westafrika.* Tetra Verlag, Melle, Germany.

LINKE, H. & STAECK, W. (1984) *Amerikanische Cichliden I.* and *II.* Tetra Verlag, Melle, Germany.

LOISELLE, P.V. (1991) Spawning *Haplochromis (Prognathochromis) perrieri* (Pellegrin, 1909). *Buntb. Bull.* (Am. Cichl. Assn.) #142; pp 29-34.

LOISELLE, P.V. (1993) *Paratilapia polleni,* a threatened cichlid from Madagascar, Part 1. *Cichlid News,* 04/93; pp 11-16.

LOISELLE, P.V. & KAUFMAN, L. (1991) The status of the Lake Victoria *Haplochromis* species currently maintained by aquarists. *Buntb. Bull.* (Am. Cichl. Assn.) #142; pp 19-28.

MEYER, A., KOCHER, T.D., BASASIBWAKI, P. & WILSON, A.C. (1990) *Nature* 347; pp 550-553.

MINDEN, U. (1990) (Re-)Integration einzelner Cichliden in bereits bestehende Aquariengemeinschaften. *DCG-Info* (German Cichl. Assn.) Vol. 21 (7); pp 160-164.

NOURISSAT, J.-C. (1992) Madagascar. *Rev. fr. Cichl.* (French Cichl. Assn.), 118; pp 8-29.

NOURISSAT, J.-C. (1992) Madagascar 1992. *Rev. fr. Cichl.* (French Cichl. Assn.), 129; pp 8-36.

OCHUMBA, P.B.O. (1990) *Hydrobiologia* Vol. 208; pp 93-99.

OIJEN, M.J.P. van (1991) *Zool. Verh. Leiden.* 272; pp 1-95.

OIJEN, M.J.P. van (1992) *Zool. Med. Leiden* Vol. 66 (40); pp 561-579.

RAMINOSOA, N.R. (1979) Contribution à l'étude écologique et biologique du *Paratilapia polleni,* dans le marais de Manganosy. Thèse, Univ. de Madagascar, Tananarive.

REICHENBACH-KLINKE H.-H. (date unknown) *Fish Pathology* . TFH Publications. pp 147-149.

SEEGERS, L. (1992) Neu aus Tansania: Malagarasi-Grundelbuntbarsche. *Aq. Heute,* vol. 10 (3); pp 112-117.

SEEHAUSEN, O. (1993) Victorian cichlids. Part 2: The oral shelling/crushing molluscivores. *The Cichlids Yearbook,* Vol. 3.; pp 50-55.

SEEHAUSEN, O. (1993) Foraging and spatial behaviour of rock dwelling cichlids in Lake Victoria in the light of competition, community structure and speciation. MSc. thesis, Universities of Hannover & Leiden.

SELBRINK, B. (1986) Viktoriasjöns Ciklider, del 9: *Astatotilapia barbarae. Akvariet* (Sweden) 60 (4); pp 177-178.

SLOOTWEG, R. (1987) *Oecologia* 74; pp 193-202.

STIASSNY, M.L.J. (1993) Cichlids are different! *Trop. Fish Hobb.* 03/93; pp 84-98.

STIASSNY M.L.J. & GERSTNER, C.L. (1992) *Env. Biol. Fish.* 34; pp 219-233.

SZWECHLOWICZ, J. (1991) A *Julidochromis* breeding tank. *The Cichlids Yearbook,* Vol. 1; pp 92-93.

TIJSSELING, G (1992) Breeding *Tropheus* the natural way. *The Cichlids Yearbook,* vol. 2, p 85.

TREWAVAS, E. (1983) *Tilapiine fishes of the genera Sarotherodon, Oreochromis and Danakilia.* Brit. Mus. (Nat. Hist.), London, UK.

WARD, J.A. & WYMAN, R.L. (1975) *Oceans,* January: pp 42-47.

WARD, J.A. & WYMAN, R.L. (1977) *Env. Fish. Biol.* 2(2): pp 137-145.

WILHELM, W. (1980) *Behaviour* 74 (3-4); pp 310-323.

WITTE, F., GOLDSCHMIDT, T., WANINK, J., Van OIJEN, M., GOUDSWAARD, K., WITTE-MAAS, E., & BOUTON, N. (1992) *Env. Biol. Fish.* 34; pp 1-28.

WITTE, F. & OIJEN, M.J.P. van (1990) *Zool. Verh.* Leiden 262; pp 1-47.

WITTE-MAAS, E.L.M. (1981) *Neth. J. Zool.* 31 (4); pp 786-789.

Index

About the authors

Kaj Anderson (Dronninglund, Denmark). More than 25 years experience with cichlids. Specialised in the smaller South American cichlids. Member of the Danish Cichlid Association since 1973. Expeditions to Colombia, Ecuador, and Venezuela. International speaker on South American cichlids.

Mary Bailey (Crediton, UK). More than 21 years experience with cichlids. Cichlid consultant for "Practical Fish Keeping" since 1985. On committee of the British Cichlid Association (Technical Editor and Treasurer) since 1982. Studied English language and literature. Now freelance writer, translator, and proof-reader.

Kjell Fohrman (Gothenburg, Sweden). More than 15 years experience with cichlids. Organiser of cichlid meetings in Scandinavia. President of the Gothenburg Chapter. Speaker on African cichlids, filtration, water, and food. Wholesaler of cichlids and tropical fishkeeping products (for example the backgrounds on page 13).

Lasse Forsberg (Aneboda, Sweden). More than 20 years experience with cichlids. President of the Scandinavian Cichlid Association and editor of its magazine "Ciklidbladet" (1983-1988). Studied science of fishes and fisheries at the University of Gothenburg. Profession: all aspects of fishes and fisheries from fishfarming to environmental issues.

Charley Grimes (Indianapolis, USA). More than 32 years experience with cichlids. Much in demand as a speaker on cichlids, killifish, and livebearers. Most popular lecture: live foods.

Willem Heijns (Stiphout, Netherlands). More than 18 years experience with cichlids. Editor of "Cichlidae", the magazine of the Dutch and Belgium Cichlid Association, for more than 11 years. Specialised in Central American cichlids.

Ad Konings (St. Leon-Rot, Germany). More than 20 years experience with cichlids. Author and co-author of more than 10 books on cichlids. Specialised in underwater observation and photography of cichlids. Studied biology at University of Amsterdam. Research at Erasmus University Rotterdam on DNA cloning of human genes. Has made more than 15 expeditions to Africa and Central America. Publisher of cichlid-related books and videos (Cichlid Press).

Gary Kratochvil (San Antonio, USA). More than 21 years experience with cichlids. Specialised in breeding rift lake cichlids. Life member of the American Cichlid Association. Has collected cichlids in Malawi and Mexico. Currently cichlid breeder.

Dirk Ottlik (Oberhausen, Germany). More than 25 years experience with cichlids, 18 of them with (wild-caught) discus. Has made collecting expeditions to Zaïre and Peru. Currently cichlid breeder and wholesaler.

Ole Seehausen (Hannover, Germany). More than 15 years experience with cichlids. Specialised in Lake Victoria cichlids. Research on rock-dwelling cichlids of Lake Victoria (with the Haplochromis Ecology Survey Team (Leiden, Netherlands and Mwanza, Tanzania)). Studied biology at the Universities of Hannover and Leiden. Currently in Tanzania studying for a Ph. D.

Christian Simon (Allauch, France). More than 12 years experience with cichlid. Specialised in African cichlids. Studied biology, physiology, and biochemistry at the University of Aix-Marseilles III. Ph. D. research on animal and human (neuro)physiology at the "Centre National de la Recherche Scientifique" (Marseilles). Currently translator of cichlid-related publications and scientific director of "Africa Import-Export" (Marseilles & Paris).

Frank Warzel (Mainz, Germany). More then 20 years experience with cichlids. Specialised in pike cichlids (*Crenicichla*) for more than 6 years. Has made several collecting expeditions to South America.